JEWISH

PRIDE

BEN M. FREEMAN

JEWISH

PRIDE

Rebuilding a People

First published in 2021 by No Pasaran Media

ISBN 9781913532130

Also available as an ebook
ISBN 9781913532147

Typeset by seagulls.net
Cover design by Emma Ewbank
Project management by whitefox
Printed and bound by Clays

Photography credits:
Amy Albertson, Just a Guy, Tel Aviv www.hagaigalili.net
Ashager Araro, Just a Guy, Tel Aviv www.hagaigalili.net
Ben Freeman, Gary Swart, Hong Kong @the_refined_fellow
Elisheva Rishon, Lindsey Byrnes, Los Angeles @lindseybyrnes
Eliyahu Lann, Five Castles Portraits, Melbourne www.fivecastles.com.au
Hen Mazzig, Marc Jorden @marcjorden
Isaac de Castro, Veronika Varga, California @veronikavarga
Rachel Riley, Sarah Cook, UK www.sarahcookcommercial.co.uk

To my mother, Sarah, and my father, Malcolm,
for instilling in me Jewish Pride.

CONTENTS

I would like to thank the following people for inspiring me, supporting me and guiding me throughout the process of writing this book. I couldn't have done it without them:

Gary Swart
Jessica Cohen
Eve Barlow
Joanna Mok
David Hirsh
Elizabeth LaCouture
Jason Petrulis
Winston Pickett
Tracey Allen
No Pasaran Media

PROLOGUE

'The non-Jewish world hates Jews,' is something my late father used to tell me.

We would often argue about this over Shabbat dinner, and I would always retort: 'No, Dad, things have changed!' I knew antisemitism had not disappeared, of course, but I grew up at the tail-end of the post-Holocaust period when overt antisemitism was still taboo and this shaped my thinking. Since his passing, three years ago, I have reflected on our conversations and with the return of overt antisemitism, my perspective has changed.

When my father spoke of the 'non-Jewish world', he did not mean individual non-Jewish people. He knew that many non-Jewish people did not hate Jews, and many actively support us. But this is not about individuals; this is about something much bigger than all of us. This is about the ideology, social norms and traditions that make up non-Jewish society – and they are soaked with the poison of antisemitism.

Every morning I wake up and see multiple news stories about antisemitism and every morning my heart aches. Sometimes this hatred is expressed through acts of physical violence as we saw in the mass shooting in the Tree of Life Synagogue in Pittsburgh in 2018, or when Rabbi Yaakov Schlesinger was stabbed on the streets of London in June 2020. Sometimes it looks like the participants in a Parisian 'anti-racism' march in 2020 shouting '*sale Juif*' ('dirty Jews'). Sometimes it comes in the form of a microaggression where your non-Jewish colleague tells you that the Jews should have learned from the Holocaust. Or sometimes it is shown when a Jew with internalised antisemitism demonises the State of Israel.

For millennia, Jewish people have been abused and murdered by the non-Jewish world. We are also always expected to acquiesce to their demands. We have to be more Christian, less Jewish, more universal, less specific, more modern and less traditional. We are told – and we tell ourselves – that we have a moral responsibility to stand up for other communities, but, most importantly, that we must never, ever stand up for ourselves. We change our names and our physical appearances and are even afraid to tell people that we are Jewish. Despite these attempts to fit in with the non-Jewish world, we are still 'othered' and we are still punished for being Jewish.

This collective trauma is a form of gaslighting on a global scale. We are constantly manipulated and denigrated by the very people whose acceptance we try so hard to earn. We want to be a part of wider society, but our admittance is often laced with conditions that are impossible to meet – and this has a real and lasting impact on how we as Jews feel about our Jewishness. Simply put, it makes us feel ashamed.

Jewish people have been forced time and time again to warp and change who we are to fit in. Despite this, we are still rejected. We have seen our identity and culture appropriated by the non-Jewish world, which then uses it against us. We are told that Zionism, the Jewish movement of self-determination in our indigenous homeland, is akin to Nazism – and that we are perpetrating the same crimes against the Palestinians that the Nazis committed against us. This is gaslighting, and, as such, only serves to wound us.

Yet despite what the non-Jewish world often tells us, we have a choice. We can reject who we are or we can reject the non-Jewish world's idea of who we are. In order to heal our collective self-esteem, we *must* have Jewish Pride. That is not to say that we should isolate and ghettoise ourselves. Rather we should interact with wider society – but we must do so proudly.

We must never warp or change our identities to fit in. We do not need to make ourselves 'acceptable', because we are acceptable, just as we are. Yet we cannot force the non-Jewish world to see that. This is *their* journey. *Our* journey is one of Jewish Pride.

We must redefine ourselves through our historical cultures and our cultures today – and continue celebrating our resilience. Our people have survived multiple genocides and we have outlived those that attempted to destroy us. We must celebrate the incredible diversity in our community, heal where we need healing – and, above all, know that, despite our differences, we are one people.

This is a call for Jewish Pride.

The only people who get to define Jewish identity are Jewish people. Yet, understanding one's self, and feeling proud of who we are as a collective, is not something that will happen overnight, particularly if we have been exposed to the repeated traumas of shame. This is a journey and it involves work but it is one that we must begin anew.

Our journey is not about fighting antisemitism. It is about rejecting the shame of antisemitism. Rejecting the non-Jewish world's inaccurate definitions of what it means to be a Jew. It is an exploration of Jewish identity, based on Jewish values, Jewish ideas and Jewish experiences.

I love being Jewish.

I want all our people to embrace and love our Jewishness – and reject the shame of antisemitism.

This is Jewish Pride.

INTRODUCTION

My name is Ben Maxwell Freeman.

I am an author and educator. I was born in Glasgow, Scotland. I am 34 years old and I am a proud Jewish gay man.

The concept of pride has been incredibly important to me as a gay person. It helped me reject the shame of homophobia and accept who I am. What I have been exploring is how I, an LGBTQ+ Jew, can harness the concept of pride to empower and inspire my Jewish community in the way it has done for my LGBTQ+ community.

Being a member of two minority groups has forced me to think very deeply about my identity, about the essence of who I am. With reference to my sexuality, while I came out at the age of 19, my journey towards being comfortable with myself was challenging and wrought with difficulty. Like many LGBTQ+ people, I suffered from severe mental health issues which led me to self-harm and attempt suicide. This was not necessarily because I was surrounded by homophobes. It was more nuanced than this: society taught me – sometimes explicitly and at other times implicitly – that there was something wrong with being gay. I never saw myself represented in society. I felt isolated, broken and ashamed.

My journey to self-acceptance took a long time, but I can now say that I am very much proud of being gay and incredibly proud to be a part of the LGBTQ+ community.

As we know, the concept of pride is essential to the LGBTQ+ community – we celebrate it once a year. Being part of the LGBTQ+ community, which, through pride, actively empowers its members to take ownership of their identity and celebrate all aspects of who they are, has been empowering. Pride taught me to not just accept my identity, but to celebrate it. Being part of a community that, despite intense persecution which continues to this very day, has managed to build lives that are meaningful, connected, empowered and community-oriented makes me proud. Pride has helped me as an LGBTQ+ person feel comfortable with who I am. But, above all, it has taught me that I have the right to be here and to advocate for myself and my community, which is a lesson I also think that some Jewish people could learn.

BEING A GAY JEW

Reflecting on my own personal experiences of being both gay and Jewish, I have observed some similarities in how both Jews and LGBTQ+ people are perceived by wider society. Specifically, in the way that some LGBTQ+ people and some Jews 'pass' as members of the majority. 'Passing' is the idea that a minority is able to be identified as a member of the majority. A gay person could be perceived as straight, while a light-skinned Jew could be perceived as a white non-Jew, or a Black Jew as a Black non-Jew.

There are those who describe the ability of some LGBTQ+ people and some Jews to pass as a 'privilege'. However, from my experience, this is a specific form of oppression itself. As a young, closeted teenager, I suffered extreme mental health difficulties because I was hiding who I was. That I could pass as straight meant that I could avoid suffering direct homophobic abuse from those around me, but I assure you I did suffer.

Nonetheless, being able to pass does absolutely offer a layer of protection (and certainly allows one to benefit from different kinds of advantages), but the pain and experiences that accompanies it reveals quite clearly that it is not a guarantee for circumventing prejudice – one can simply experience a different version of the prejudice. It also can lead to internalised shame, a false sense of inclusion and safety, and the isolation that can often come once your true identity is revealed.

Similarly, as a light-skinned Jewish person living in a non-Jewish world, I can pass as a non-Jew – which means I am often perceived as a white person. This obviously means I benefit from the advantage of being perceived as white. Yet I remain a Jew. I endure the realities of intergenerational trauma, I am dealing with my own trauma from the multitude of antisemitism I personally have experienced, and my community is also collectively battling modern antisemitism. This is the common Jewish reality, regardless of whether we can pass or not.

It is also true that when you are able to pass, you see the way the world treats you when they think you are part of the majority, as opposed to when they realise you are a minority. The discrepancy is real, and it is something I have experienced several times throughout my life. At this point, any advantages that a passing minority experiences can be revoked when their true identity is revealed. Passing is also something that mainstream society can resent. They can feel they are being deliberately tricked as they interpret your existence as an attempt to make them believe that you are 'one of them'; in my case, a white heterosexual person of European ancestry. When a major antisemitic trope paints Jews as inherently shifty tricksters who often camouflage themselves, a light-skinned Jew passing as a non-Jew can become a specific focus of antisemitic hate.

To many antisemites, Jews – and, in particular, light-skinned Jews – represent the worst kind of threat because they may not be able to detect us until it's 'too late'. Therefore, they must act against us before we're able to 'strike' at them from within.

At this point, I want to offer some thoughts on the word 'privilege' that I mentioned earlier. Unless they are visibly Jewish, light-skinned

Jews benefit from the advantage of being perceived as white, and this is something that should be recognised. Yet, as I also explained, while they benefit from being perceived as white by non-Jewish society, these light-skinned Jews still suffer from the serious and deadly threat of antisemitism and the shame that goes along with it.

So, the question is: how do we discuss these different and complex manifestations of prejudice? I believe that using the word 'privilege' to describe these different manifestations lacks the nuance needed to properly understand prejudice. The word 'privilege' can imply an immovable fixed status, which is not rooted in the reality of these issues. It is also a word loaded with antisemitism when it comes to Jewish people, due to the misconception that all Jews are wealthy and powerful. I believe using the terms 'advantage' and 'disadvantage' not only contains less antisemitic undertones, they are also more reflective of the realities of how prejudice works.

For example, if I am walking down the street holding hands with my light-skinned partner, we are at risk of being attacked for being a same-sex couple. In this instance, we, because of our sexual orientation, are not benefiting from the advantage of being heterosexual. However, we would not be targeted because of the colour of our skin, and therefore benefit from the advantage of being white / being perceived as white. Alternatively, a Black heterosexual person walking down the street with their partner benefits from the advantage of being heterosexual yet can suffer disadvantage due to of the colour of their skin.

In both scenarios, both sets of people experience advantages and disadvantages at the same moment. This is a more nuanced way to discuss and understand these issues. These concepts are moving, fluid and change depending on the context. It is not that the concept of 'privilege' has not been, and cannot be, useful at some points, but I believe we should always be seeking to advance nuance in our conversations.

To me, having faced both antisemitism and homophobia, the notion that these groups are 'privileged' indicates a serious misunderstanding of prejudice. Ranking oppressed groups in a hierarchy of oppression fails to understand that advantage and disadvantage can interact and exist in one person, it also leads minorities to fight one another, instead of our common enemies. What we must instead understand is the different manifestations of prejudice, as opposed to seeing bigotry through a binary lens. Being gay and Jewish has taught me that we must represent and respect each and every community's lived experience in order to understand the full range of human experiences.

REJECTION

Another aspect of my experience of being both gay and Jewish with specific regard to parts of the left, is that my homosexuality is often embraced and accepted, while my Jewishness is often very much not. In fact, it is fair to say that, because of antisemitism, I sadly do not feel comfortable being a Jew in progressive LGBTQ+ spaces.

While it is obviously not a hard and fast rule, there have been several recent examples where members of the so-called progressive community have rejected their Jewish LGBTQ+ brothers and sisters.

For example, in 2019, the Dyke March in Washington banned Jewish symbols. The march organiser, Rai Gaines, was quoted as saying: 'This includes Israeli flags, as well as flags that resemble Israeli flags, such as a pride flag with a Star of David in the middle.'[1] As a gay Jew, it is my right to express the intersection of my two identities as I see fit and for one to try and police the other is deeply disturbing.

I have seen on the left that there are those who are attempting to cause a disconnect between my two identities, despite the historically close relationship between the LGBTQ+ community and parts of the Jewish community, which we will explore in Chapter 12. At first sight, many people might perceive the source of this tension as being my Jewishness. When I say 'Jewishness', I mean it as an identity not solely connected to Judaism, the religion, but rather one that is rooted in the idea of a Jewish ethnicity, religion and people as a whole.

Religious communities (and Jews are often perceived as *only* being a religious community) are often thought of as being intolerant to the LGBTQ+ community. However, in my experience, I have more often than not found myself accepted and respected in Jewish spaces. And I am particularly proud of the Jewish community for providing so many safe spaces for their LGBTQ+ family.

This is not to say that homophobia is not an issue in parts of the Jewish community, it absolutely is – as it is in all communities – and I have experienced it myself. When I was working for a Holocaust education organisation, I was accused by one board member of having a 'gay agenda' because I suggested highlighting the persecution of LGBTQ+ people by the Nazis. Within that same organisation, I was also told to remove any mention of gay people from an online statement which discussed a homophobic attack. After complaining about the latter, several board members sat me down and told me that it was not an expression of homophobia. It was, and their behaviour was nothing but gaslighting.

However, the ultimate source of the tension between two aspects of my identity emanates from the progressive world. Quite simply, being Jewish has led me to being expelled from what David Hirsh, a British academic, terms the 'community of the good'.[2] This idea is rooted in the notion that you believe those with your political beliefs and values are inherently 'good' and everyone else is outside your community and is 'bad'. This has taken many forms throughout history, but, in this case, refers to the fascism of modern-day progressives.

I am a Zionist Jew. This simply means that I support the concept of a Jewish state, in the Jewish indigenous homeland. Yet, sadly, much of the tension between LGBTQ+ progressives and Jews centres on Zionism, and specifically the concept of 'pinkwashing'. This is the accusation that Israel purposefully exaggerates its strong record on

LGBTQ+ rights as a means to diminish its treatment of the Palestinians. These accusations are deeply illogical, hurtful and are a direct attack on my identity as a gay Jew.

Despite the antisemitism of pinkwashing, Tel Aviv is often – and justifiably – described as 'the gay capital of the Middle East'.[3] It is one of the only places in the world where I can comfortably express my two identities at once. It was where I attended my first drag show and where I feel most free as a gay Jew. But when the Eurovision song contest took place in Israel in 2019, it was met with fierce opposition from some on the left, including from within the LGBTQ+ community. For instance, more than 100 'queer and trans liberation organizations from nearly 20 countries across Europe and beyond ... [called] on global LGBTQIA communities to boycott the 2019 Eurovision Song Contest in Israel'.[4]

The fact that my supposed LGBTQ+ brothers and sisters have decided that being a Jewish Zionist is not compatible with fighting for LGBTQ+ rights is not only completely illogical; it is also devastating. This rejection has real-life consequences. It impacts my mental health and undoes the incredibly hard work I have put into feeling comfortable in both of my identities. It also leads to the erasure – through the constant focus on Israel – of LGBTQ+ people in other parts of the Middle East who regularly face legal and violent persecution, including in Palestine.

I am a progressive gay Jew and I believe in progressive values, but because of my Jewishness and my belief in a Jewish state, I am no longer welcome in many left-wing spaces.

It *is* possible to be a Zionist Jew *and* a progressive. These identities are not mutually exclusive. My membership of the progressive community should not depend on me abandoning my Zionism; in fact, it should include me *because* I am a Zionist. Zionism is nothing but the movement to return an ethno-religious minority, a nation and a people, to their indigenous homeland, which should perfectly align with progressive values.

Thankfully, despite the propaganda around pinkwashing, there are still LGBTQ+ people who understand the important part Israel plays in the advancement of LGBTQ+ rights. Tel Aviv Pride, which takes place every June, sees 250,000 LGBTQ+ people from around the world descend on Israel; the only place in the Middle East where Jews and LGBTQ+ people are treated with dignity and respect.

Sadly, I have never made it to Tel Aviv Pride, but one of my closest friends went in 2019 and I spoke to him to understand his perceptions of LGBTQ+ pride in the Jewish state. Grant Thomson, a non-Jewish gay man who lives in London, told me:

> I went to Pride in Tel Aviv to celebrate being gay and to be part of an incredible community of diverse people. It was so meaningful to experience pride in Israel, a country that brings together many people from around the world to celebrate the LGBTQ+ community. LGBTQ+ people are persecuted all over the rest of the Middle East and travelling to Israel to celebrate my community felt defiant and made me feel powerful.

That the wider LGBTQ+ community has not bought into the antisemitic lies of many of the left gives me a huge amount of hope that there can once again be a fusion of my two identities.

Despite the tension that may exist between my two communities, I am determined to remain fearlessly proud of both my identities and create space for them to come together – and, in all honesty, I have to be. What choice do I have? I cannot change my sexuality nor my Jewishness, so I must create a space for both to coexist. One way that I have found to help realign my two identities is by exploring the concept of pride and searching for similarities, rather than focusing on their differences or their areas of conflict. The concept of pride has helped me to not only become more comfortable with my sexuality, but to celebrate it. So, I ask: how can I apply this notion of pride to my Jewish identity? However, to answer this, we first need to better understand identity itself.

IDENTITY

Before we examine the idea of pride in identity, we need to try and examine what identity is and how it is formed. It is important to recognise that the question of identity is a fairly modern one. For example, while having existed since the dawn of time, the idea of LGBTQ+ identity was only formed in the 19th century.

Therefore, when we discuss identity, in some ways we are imposing a modern idea onto historical figures or communities. This can be problematic, particularly if modern definitions do not really fit historical contexts, and it is thus paramount to always understand the historical context of a specific situation before we begin to understand it from a modern context.

We also have to recognise that identity is immensely complex. In a Stanford University draft paper, James D Fearon, a professor of political science, argues that identity 'proves quite difficult to give a short and adequate summary statement that captures the range of its present meanings'.[5] In his paper, Fearon recognises two different perspectives of identity. One is personal and the other is social, so, therefore, 'it refers at the same time to social categories and to the sources of an individual's self-respect or dignity'.[6]

The reason why identity is important, particularly when you are a minority, is that defining your own identity is to state your personal and communal right to self-determination. It ensures the fusion of your personal and social external identities. While outside forces do influence how we see ourselves, allowing others to define who we are does not result in a healthy or happy individual or community. Additionally, from a societal perspective, this often results in tropes and stereotypes being formed around a group that has no bearing in reality – as it does in the case of the Jews.

While there is no one definition of identity, I believe we can loosely and simply understand it to be the formation of understanding the different components that make up one's ideas of the self, based on asking the following questions:

'Who am I?'

'Where did I come from?'

'Where do I fit in?'

'How do I fit in?'

For example, in my case, I am a British, gay, Jewish man whose family fled to the UK from eastern Europe, where they lived as a subjugated people following their expulsion from their indigenous homeland, Israel. This self-identification rejects the non-Jewish world's idea of what it means to be a Jew and allows me as an individual, and as a member of a collective, to define my own story.

Through our journey on Jewish Pride, we will explore the historical formation of Jewish identity, often in the face of intense antisemitism. It is true that identity can be formed – or rather questions can be asked which lead to the formation of identity – based on rejection by wider society. So, for example, Jewish identity is an issue we grapple with, partly because the non-Jewish world has rejected us and we want to define how we see ourselves.

PRIDE

While exploring Jewish Pride, I came across these words by Britain's former chief rabbi, the late Lord Sacks: 'At some stage, Jews stopped defining themselves by the reflection they saw in the eyes of God and started defining themselves by the reflection they saw in the eyes of their Gentile neighbours.'[7] I think this is true, especially when I see the aggressive rejection of Zionism by young progressive Jews, who do not understand their own history and base their role in the modern progressive movement on the perspectives and values of the non-Jewish, often antisemitic, world.

Michael Lerner, the rabbi and political activist, addressed this specific issue in 1993 when he wrote a piece in the *Village Voice* magazine, which argued: 'Lecturing on campuses around the U.S. as editor of *Tikkun*, a progressive Jewish journal, I've met thousands of young Jews who never learned or have conveniently forgotten the realities of their own history.'[8] What Lerner is suggesting is that certain young progressive light-skinned Jews have forgotten the cyclical nature of violent antisemitism faced by their own ancestors and have started seeing themselves as privileged white people whose only role in the progressive world is to support other communities in their fights against oppression.

The question I want to ask at this stage is: how do we define our own identity, *not* through non-Jewish eyes or even through God's, but through our own? How do we create a Jewish Pride movement that defines our own identity in our own terms?

It is important to recognise that some expressions of pride are warped and aim to exclude others. The ADL (Anti-Defamation League) defines 'white pride', for example, as 'a white supremacist slogan appropriated from expressions of ethnic pride by various minority groups in the United States. White supremacists often use the slogan, or variations thereof, to deny any racism on their part, claiming that they are merely exhibiting white pride.'[9] I firmly reject the idea that any expression of pride in oneself should lead to the denigration of another. Stonewall, the British LGBTQ+ rights organisation, defines pride as: 'Pride is about communities coming together in celebration, protest, unity and solidarity.'[10] To me, this is what pride should be about; it has no relationship or impact on any other community.

MINORITY IDENTITIES

As the brief explorations of my own identity demonstrates, identity is complex and each of us has at least two; our internal identity as well as the identity imposed on us by the world, or as Fearon suggested, our 'personal' and 'social' identities.[11] Sometimes they align but not always. My own experience suggests that your internal identity having an impact upon your external identity is generally a good thing. The world sees you as you see yourself. However, issues may arise when your external identity has an impact upon your internal identity.

This is certainly true of minority groups. The impact of prejudice on mental health in the LGBTQ+ community is well documented, with LGBTQ+ teenagers being four times more likely to attempt suicide than their heterosexual counterparts.[12] Trauma caused by prejudice has an impact upon many communities in different ways. In some cases, bigoted societal perceptions of your identities can lead to changes in physiology that can be passed on through the generations. Trauma related to prejudice can be inherited through changes in gene expression, as evidenced through the science and study known as epigenetics. This physiological inheritance of trauma is visible in several groups, including Holocaust survivors.

As a 2015 study, for instance, revealed: 'Genetic changes stemming from the trauma suffered by Holocaust survivors are capable of being passed on to their children, the clearest sign yet that one person's life experience can affect subsequent generations.'[13] Descendants of Jewish survivors of the Holocaust clearly suffer from intergenerational trauma. This is also the case for the majority of Jewish people whose families and ancestors have fled antisemitic murder for thousands of years.

In her book, *Wounds Into Wisdom: Healing Intergenerational Jewish Trauma,* Dr Tirzah Firestone, a rabbi and a psychotherapist, describes intergenerational trauma as 'the residue of our ancestors' overwhelming stresses and life events that they couldn't metabo-lize in their lifetimes, such as the Holocaust or fleeing persecution. It happens on the individual and also on the collective level. And collective Jewish memories are in overdrive these days with the rise of antisemitism.'[14]

Firestone explores an interesting point about the Jewish experi-ence, something I touched on previously. Due to both historical and modern antisemitism, Jews are forced to deal with collective intergen-erational trauma based on our past but also collective and individual trauma based on our present circumstances.

In March 2020, I began planning the last class of my three-month course on the Holocaust, which explores post-Holocaust antisemi-tism. I broke down in tears; I felt distressed, overwhelmed and hope-less that a class on the destruction of 6 million Jews had to end with lessons on modern antisemitism.

While I've always been proud of being Jewish, there was a time in my life, particularly at university, when I was extremely nervous about telling people that I was Jewish. I would not say that I was ashamed, but I definitely felt elements of shame. I remember I met one of my closest friends on the first day of university in September 2005. We attended a politics tutorial together and we went for a coffee after-wards. Fifteen years on, when we were chatting about this very book, he reminded me of how I told him I was Jewish. He recalled that before I told him I hesitated and seemed nervous. He was right, I was nervous. I was bracing for impact, as I often did when I told people I am Jewish. This is unacceptable. It is unacceptable that I should be scared to tell someone that I am Jewish, particularly in a setting that was clearly non-violent. It is true that you cannot control how people react to you, and you always have to be mindful of your safety, but to be afraid of telling people who you really are is a terrible and sad reflection of deeply embedded societal prejudice.

THE PURPOSE OF THIS BOOK

This is not a book about combating antisemitism. The tragic reality is that, more often than not, minority groups cannot influence societal perceptions of them and it is not their responsibility to 'fix' skewed perceptions of their community. Antisemitism is *not* a Jewish problem; it is a non-Jewish problem that has an impact upon Jews. I have learned from years of fighting antisemitism that there is little we can do to combat it on a societal or global level, although we are able to have a dialogue and share our experiences. However, if antisemitism is ever to be eradicated, then it is the non-Jewish world who must embark upon that task. What we *are* able to influence is how we feel about ourselves. The question ultimately is: how can we feel pride in our internal identities when society imposes an external identity upon us that does not relate to the truth of who we are?

This book is ultimately about my attempt to draw from my experiences in the LGBTQ+ community, while exploring and understanding Jewish identities in order to consider how we build a Jewish Pride movement. To me, a Jewish Pride movement is about creating an inclusive Jewish community that represents all its members, draws boundaries on antisemitism, and creates a culture of empowerment so Jewish people never again feel ashamed of their Jewishness.

To my Jewish readers: when reading this, I want you to feel educated, empowered and inspired. I want you to feel proud of and connected to our incredible and diverse community and I want you to feel that you belong. Please also know that your distress over antisemitism is valid. You are allowed to feel frustrated, rejected and dejected about both historical and current levels of antisemitism. You are allowed to point out anti-Jewish racism wherever and whenever you see it. No one should tell you otherwise. I also want you to think about your own expressions of Jewish Pride. Not everyone will express this idea in the same way, it is both communal *and* personal, and it is vital for our mental health and self-esteem.

To my non-Jewish readers: when reading this I would like you to do a few things. The first is to recognise the specific historical and current realities of antisemitism and to understand that it is *just* as dangerous and harmful as any other form of prejudice. Jews desperately need your support. Please also consider how Jews and antisemitism are so often erased and not even recognised in discussions on prejudice. Please acknowledge that antisemitism is an institutional form of prejudice that requires real work in dismantling it. Please allow Jews to place ourselves at the centre of our own stories and experiences. In short, please work to combat antisemitism and support us as we build a Jewish Pride movement.

Lastly, please consider your own identities and whether you feel pride in them. While I am writing about my own experiences as a gay Jewish man, these issues are not specific to just Jewish or gay people. We all have an external identity imposed on us and we all need to feel proud of who we are.

WHO ARE THE JEWS?

Before we start exploring Jewish Pride, let us first explore who are the Jews. I am an educator, so when teaching I always try to start from the beginning of the story I am trying to tell. Context is so important for us to be able to understand our world – and this story is no different.

The Jewish people are an ethno-religious group. Due to misunderstanding, which often results in Jewish identity being erased through Erasive Antisemitism[15], Jews are often mischaracterised as *just* a religion or a race – which, when considering Jewish history, are inaccurate reflections of what it means to be Jewish.

The story of the Jews is extraordinary, and one that began in the Middle East thousands of years ago. The Jewish people originated before the advent of Judaism, the religion, in the second millennium BCE. For the next 2,000 years, Jewish people lived in the Middle East as part of Jewish tribes, independent Jewish states (Israel and Judea) and in Diasporic communities formed through invasions, wars and colonisation.

While the idea of a Jewish Diaspora developed gradually after the first colonisation of the Kingdom of Israel by the Assyrians in around 720 BCE, it took on a new face following the defeat of Jewish resistance fighters by the Romans in the first centuries of the new millennium. It was at this time that the Jews became a 'wholly diasporic people'.[16] It is worth noting that while the non-Jewish world and secular society talk about the Diaspora, Jews traditionally refer to this period as the Galut (or exile), which more accurately represents the Jewish reality of this time period. These colonisations ultimately resulted in the destruction of a Jewish homeland and the dispersal of the Jewish people. This is of vital importance: the Jews only left their homeland en masse because they were forced to do so.

In the Middle Ages, due to geographical separation, sub-ethnic Jewish groups began to form, and these communities eventually settled in their respective regions and developed distinct cultures. However, an incredible thing about the Jewish people has been our continuity. A distinct Jewish identity, nation, tradition and language have survived to this very day, despite our exile and separation from one another. That is not to say, of course, that there have not been enormous shifts and diverse branches in Jewish culture and practice; however, the threads of continuity that bind every single Jew from throughout history are still strong and powerful.

As the journalist and commentator Charles Krauthammer argued in an article in the *Washington Examiner* in 1998: 'Israel is the very embodiment of Jewish continuity: It is the only nation on earth that inhabits the same land, bears the same name, speaks the same language, and worships the same God that it did 3,000 years ago. You dig the soil and you find pottery from Davidic times, coins from Bar Kokhba, and 2,000-year-old scrolls written in a script remarkably like the one that today advertises ice cream at the corner candy store.'[17]

There are currently around 14.7 million Jewish people in the world, we make up just 0.2% of the world's 7.59 billion people – and, for such a tiny community, it may come as a surprise to you that it is incredibly diverse. Due to multiple expulsions from the Jewish indigenous homeland of Israel, four main Diasporic Jewish communities historically emerged. These are Ashkenazi (Jews who settled in central and eastern Europe); Beta-Yisrael (Ethiopian Jews); Mizrahi (Jews who never left the Middle East or North Africa); and Sephardic (Jews who settled in the Iberian Peninsula and then later, due to expulsion, spread through the Mediterranean, parts of Europe, North Africa, the Middle East and the Balkans). Due to migration patterns in the long and complicated history of the Jewish people, it is important to note that there are also smaller Jewish communities in several countries including India, Hong Kong and China. Furthermore, there are inter-ethnic Jewish communities and individuals that have grown out of more modern mixed couplings due to Diasporic migration, which has made our community even more diverse. Various branches of Judaism have also opened up pathways for more people to choose to become Jewish. Each of these communities are important and must be included as part of our Jewish Pride movement.

Due to our status as an ethno-religion and a nation, there are two routes to Jewishness. According to most mainstream Jewish streams, you can either be born Jewish or you can convert to Judaism. In terms of those who are born Jewish, Orthodox Judaism states that you have to have a Jewish mother to be counted as a Jew, while Liberal Judaism says that either of your parents can be Jewish for you to be considered

Jewish. For the purposes of this book, I define anyone who has either a Jewish mother or father as 'being born Jewish'.

Additionally, it is important to note that Jews by choice – like Ruth, the Biblical heroine – are absolutely and fully recognised as Jews, and are just as important to our peoplehood as someone who is born Jewish. While they join our nation specifically through the religion, Jews by choice become full members of the Jewish people once they have converted – and this should never be questioned.

These two routes to Jewishness add an interesting dynamic to the issue of who is and who is not considered Jewish. Although there is a clear religious element – and as it is possible to convert into the people – there are also many Jews who share traceable common ancestry. As a 2010 study published in the American Journal stated: 'The studied Jewish populations represent a series of geographical isolates or clusters with genetic threads that weave them together. These threads are observed as IBD (Identity By Descent) segments that are shared within and between Jewish groups. Over the past 3,000 years, both the flow of genes and the flow of religious and cultural ideas have contributed to Jewishness.'[18]

An explanation as to why Jewish ancestry can be traced is due in large part to what is called endogamy. For most of our history – and for a variety of reasons, including antisemitism as well as religious practice – Jewish communities were isolated. Therefore, for the most part, we have historically married and reproduced within our own community, until more recent times, when isolation of the Jewish people has lessened.

The concept of shared ancestry is complicated and can – and has – been manipulated to demonise Jewish people, as we will explore in the next chapter, so it must be discussed carefully. However, it is also crucial to recognise the existence of shared ancestry because it is also a part of our reality. Light-skinned Jews – most commonly Ashkenazi Jews – often have their indigeneity to the Levant erased.

As such, traceable shared ancestry is incredibly useful to helping those born Jewish understand their roots and their origins. It can also shed more light on how specific diseases impact Jewish groups as well as helping us understand intergenerational trauma, the study of epigenetics. Antisemitism has left genetic, as well as psychological, scars that impact all Jews who share ancestry, and recognising that is vital to understanding their lived and historical experience.

While we must recognise the realities of Jewish shared ancestry, we must also acknowledge that it is one piece of a larger puzzle and is not the be-all and end-all of Jewish identity. Similarly, it is vitally important that it is not used to place a hierarchy on Jewishness that ultimately diminishes the Jewishness of Jews by choice.

When discussing Jewish stories, there are, unfortunately, those who only refer to Ashkenazi Jews and their experiences and who view Ashkenazi Jews as the 'default Jews'. This erases other Jewish experiences, such as Mizrahi, Sephardic, Beta-Yisrael or other. This is known as 'Ashkenormativity' and it is a real issue that we must address when seeking to rebuild our People. While this is damaging, we must seek to understand its context, and as such we must recognise that in the Jewish Diaspora (i.e. outside of Israel) it is not always deliberate – after all, 75% of the world's Jewish population is Ashkenazi[19] – and addressing this imbalance should never lead to a demonisation of Ashkenazi Jews or a misunderstanding of their experience in the non-Jewish world. It is also important not to use Ashkenazi as a synonym for white-passing or light skinned. Many Ashkenazi Jews do not pass as white, and this inaccuracy serves to erase the realities of all of our experiences. It is also important to understand that Diasporic Ashkenormativity is very different to the real and systemic inequality experienced by Mizrahi Jews and Beta-Yisrael in Israel which we will address later in this book. We must address *both* Diasporic Ashkenormativity and different forms of inequality in Israel because Jewish Pride must be based on a celebration of Jewish diversity and inclusion that represents *all* Jewish communities. This is a vital part of working towards a Jewish Pride movement, which is why I have consciously included a diverse collection of Jewish stories to represent us and open the doors of discussion.

Despite a long and complex history, Jewish people – regardless of where we have settled or emerged – are deeply and intrinsically connected, and all Jews today represent a thread within the tapestry of our people.

One of the more tragic threads that bind us together is that Jewish people have endured thousands of years of continuous and intense persecution. To offer brief, non-exhaustive snapshots of the length and breadth of antisemitism in history: note that Jews were oppressed by Antiochus IV, a Hellenistic king, more than 150 years before the birth of Christ. In 1066, 5,000 Jews were murdered during the Granada Pogrom. King Edward I expelled the Jews from England in 1290. In the 15th century, Emperor Yeshaq of Ethiopia, invaded the Jews' autonomous region and forced them to convert to Christianity or face losing their lands. Jews in Spain and Portugal faced cultural genocide at the end of the 15th century. The Jews of eastern Europe were violently persecuted by Tsar Alexander III who implemented the repressive May Laws of 1882 and launched the subsequent pogroms which saw millions of Jews murdered or fleeing for their lives. During the 1940s, Jews were subject to genocidal antisemitism at the hands of Adolf Hitler and the Nazis, which culminated in the Holocaust and the total annihilation of 6 million Jews.

Antisemitism did not end with the Holocaust and even after the Shoah, Jews have continued to be oppressed and persecuted. Already classed as second-class *dhimmis* – a form of subjugation disguised as protection – 856,000 Jews were expelled in the 1950s, 1960s and 1970s from Middle Eastern countries where they have lived for thousands of years. In the postwar period, too, the leadership of the Soviet Union and the Eastern bloc demonised Jews as 'rootless cosmopolitans', while inflicting upon them intense oppression, violence, jailing and assassinations, and refusing them the right to move to the safety of Israel.

Jews continue to be oppressed to this very day; all over the world, they currently fear the resurgence of antisemitic populist parties, while witnessing more harassment, rejection and violence. Antisemitism has existed in every society where Jews live (and in many where they do not due to the popularity of antisemitic conspiracy fantasies), whether that is in the Middle East, Europe, Africa, Australasia or the Americas.

Antisemitism is more than just legal restrictions or genocide. It is, in fact, more than the hatred or mistrust of individual Jewish people. It is an institutional, deeply ingrained and systemic form of hatred. It is a worldview, an idea, that has created a fantastical version of the Jew – based upon antisemitic tropes that we will explore later – that bears *no* relationship with reality.

Once again, *antisemitism is not a Jewish problem*. It is a non-Jewish problem that unfortunately impacts Jews. Jewish people cannot control the non-Jewish external perception of what it means to be a Jew. However, as Lord Sacks said, we must stop defining ourselves in the eyes of our neighbours. We must begin defining ourselves through our own understanding of what it means to be a Jew while we celebrate our Jewish identities.

Jewish Pride is the movement that attempts to do just this.

Chapter 1

UNDERSTANDING ANTISEMITISM

IN EVERY GENERATION

'This is what has stood by our fathers and us! For not just one
alone has risen against us to destroy us, but in every generation,
they rise against us to destroy us; and the Holy One, blessed be
He, saves us from their hand!'[20]

These words – repeated as part of the *Pesach* (Passover) Seder, which
celebrates the Jewish Exodus from slavery in the land of Egypt – are a
truth born out of the Jewish experience of repetitive, violent, murderous and ultimately genocidal antisemitism. Every generation of Jews
has experienced in one way or another the same swelling of antisemitism with very real and devastating consequences. Each and every
time, the story takes on a slightly different context specifically relevant
to that era, with twists on the antisemitic tropes that fuel it – yet, the
roots of this hatred remain unchanged.

This chapter describes the main historical pillars of antisemitism
and how they play out today. Entire books are – and should be –
devoted to these individual forms of antisemitism. This is not, by
any means, an exhaustive or complete account of anti-Jewish racism.
Rather, this chapter is designed to help us to categorise antisemitism
so we can identify it today, while recognising its historical roots,
and also to understand how these specific forms have harmed – and
continue to harm – Jewish people, as a collective and as individuals.

'OH, YOU'RE JEWISH?'

Like most other Jewish people that I know, I have experienced antisemitism throughout my entire life.

My first personal, vivid memory of being made to feel ashamed of being Jewish was when I was just 11. It was my first year of secondary school. I remember very clearly being in class just prior to a school assembly at the local church. Jewish students were exempt from going as we had our own assembly. When the Jewish students left for our own assembly, the boy sitting behind me blurted loudly: 'Oh, you're Jewish? I thought you were normal!'

It was my first experience of Jewish shame.

This shaming continued throughout my school career, but, sadly, it was during my time at university that antisemitism became a part of my daily life. I was one of the only 'out' Jewish students on my politics course at the University of Glasgow. Like many higher educational institutions, the university body is left-leaning. During a class on nationalism, I read an essay on what Israel and the Palestinians could learn from the Northern Irish peace process. After a brief discussion, a student sitting opposite me declared that the UN was right in 1975 when it declared that Zionism was racism.

I was stunned. This was the first time I had ever been accused of being a racist just because I supported Israel's right to exist. It is important to see this interaction for what it was: not a conversation or a dialogue on the Israel-Palestine conflict. Instead, I – a Jew – was being told by a non-Jew in a room full of non-Jewish people that the Jewish movement of self-determination was racist at its core and that because of this I, as a Zionist, was inherently racist. I remember hot waves of anger and shame washing over me. But, as the professor failed to correct him and carried on with the lesson, I felt powerless.

For a progressive Jewish Zionist student, the obsessive antisemitic demonisation of Israel, and revisionism of Jewish history and identity, which this remark demonstrated was deeply painful. I was constantly told that Israel was the worst country in the world and was the epicentre of all evil. My time at university was a baptism of fire and I was forced to learn very quickly how to defend Israel's right to exist. But I should *never* have been placed in this situation and it took a real toll on my mental health.

I realised later that I was experiencing left-wing antizionist antisemitism, which originated in the Soviet Union. As I referenced with regards to the LGBTQ+ community, to this very day, such antisemitism continues to make me feel unwelcome and unsafe in many left spaces. This specific form of left antisemitism – which is the same rhetoric that the former Labour leader, Jeremy Corbyn, espouses – is framed as simple and legitimate criticism of Israel. Yet, what it actually does is superimpose historic antisemitic tropes on to the Israeli state, while demonising, delegitimising, and revising its history, and treating it with double standards.

SOVIET ANTIZIONISM

Although the Soviets officially rejected antisemitism, seeing it as a remnant of Tsarist Russia, antisemitism – in the form of forced secularisation and assimilation – existed in Soviet ideology and policy long before 1948, the year of the creation of the State of Israel. The Russian empire and its successor state, the USSR, both played a major role in fabricating and enacting European antisemitism at different points in history. While the Soviets helped defeat Germany in the second world war, antisemitism was already deeply rooted in their history and simply took on a new guise after the Nazis' defeat.

The Russian empire was the site of some of the most violent anti-Jewish pogroms in European history. For example, 100,000 Jews were deliberately targeted and murdered during the Khmelnytsky Uprising between 1648-1657 and from 1881, there was a wave of pogroms throughout the Russian empire that destroyed countless Ashkenazi Jewish communities and forced Jews to seek safety outside Russia. During the Russian civil war from 1917-1920, an estimated 50,000 Jews were murdered. Antisemitism in this part of the world was a violent and occurred all too often.

Though present in the founding of the Soviet state, Soviet antizionism took on a new face under Joseph Stalin, after the creation of the State of Israel. It then intensified following Israel's victory in the 1967 six-day war. This new brand of post-war Soviet antisemitism equated Israel with Nazism, argued that Zionists had collaborated with the Nazis to destroy the Jewish populations of Europe, and described the Jewish state – rather ironically, given the Soviet subjugation of eastern Europe – as the centre of imperialism.

This antizionist antisemitism was an official policy of the USSR, which produced state-funded propaganda that added a twist to Nazi propaganda: replace Jews with Zionists and it is possible to cover and code your antisemitism. The Soviets had a committee devoted to spreading hate, conspiracy theories and demonisation against Israel using Nazi-inspired messages as their starting point. In 1983, the Anti-Zionist Committee of the Soviet Public – known as AKSO in Russia – produced a document titled *Criminal Alliance of Zionism and Nazism*. During its founding its Chairman, General Colonel Dragnusky stated: 'The sinister role of International Zionism, the ruling circles of Israel, who turned the country into an imperialist gendarme in the Middle East and one of the agents of political colonialism and neo-colonialism is becoming more and more recognised throughout the world. We believe that all honest people of the earth must intensify the struggle against the dangerous intrigues of imperialism, and its ally and weapon – Zionism.'[21]

Through its official antisemitic policy the USSR actively persecuted Jewish people at home and abroad. Soviet Jews faced limitations in higher education and in employment opportunities and could lose their jobs just for being Jewish. In *When They Come for Us, We'll Be Gone: The Epic Struggle to Save Soviet Jewry,* Gal Beckerman suggests: 'You became almost a pariah inside of Soviet society and it led to a whole series of bad things that could happen to you...You'd lose your job, but then it was illegal to be without a job – you would be accused of parasitism. And then you suddenly had people who were former world-renowned scientists working as stokers, shovelling coal or elevator operators, because the government would assign you to a job.'[22]

Jews were legally classed as a nation and their passports stamped with 'Jew', making it virtually impossible to leave the country. There was a heightened sense of awareness of the Jewish community, with an emphasis on the physical features of Jews, leading to verbal antisemitic attacks on the streets. Though framed as a policy directed at Israel, Soviet antizionism made Soviet Jews a very conscious, purposeful and deliberate target underneath its carefully crafted wording.

One important explanation as to why the USSR branded its obvious demonisation of Jews as antizionism lies with the Shoah. As the journalist Jeffrey Goldberg discussed in a 2014 article on the future of Jews in Europe: 'The Shoah served for a while as a sort of inoculation against the return of overt Jew-hatred.'[23] Due to the horrors of the recently discovered Shoah, it was not acceptable to openly persecute Jews as Jews, so another label had to be found. It is also worth noting that the USSR liberated or discovered the Nazi death camps and would have not wanted to have been associated with the horrors committed by their enemies, the Nazis.

'Antizionism' was the label the USSR settled on for their specific post-Holocaust brand of antisemitism and, despite the fact that this officially targeted a sovereign state and not an ethno-religious minority, it masked antizionism as a modern expression of antisemitism.

Despite Soviet denials that they were one and the same, Jews in the USSR felt otherwise. As *The Washington Post* reported in 1979:

'Soviet bureaucrats vehemently reject suggestions that "antizionism" means "anti-Semitism." But to many Soviet Jews, it is a distinction without a difference.'[24]

Despite originating in the USSR, this antizionist antisemitism seeped into the wider leftist community. 'What began as a Stalinist cry was taken up in some of the New Left, which helped shape the world view of Jeremy Corbyn and many of his supporters,' argued Philip Spencer, a professor of Holocaust and genocide studies, in *The Guardian* in 2018.[25] Although, it wasn't just the New Left, it was the vast majority of the left.

Simply speaking, in part due to the left's fixation on anti-imperialism, and its antisemitic perception of the Israeli-Palestinian conflict as the symbol of the battle against imperialism, antizionism has become the *cause du jour*. However, the non-Jewish world's under-standing of this conflict is more often than not rooted in antisemitic ideas imposed on Israel.

My university experience of left antisemitism rooted in Soviet antizionism was just one puzzle piece of a much greater jigsaw. To fully comprehend the scope of antisemitism we have to look at how these pieces come together to form the bigger picture.

This bigger picture is the more general categorisations and mani-festations of antisemitism. It is about recognising that antisemitism is an institutional and systemic form of prejudice – one deeply embed-ded into the structures of our societies – and it has persisted to shame and endanger Jews in every generation for more than 2,000 years.

When I discuss my experiences of antisemitism with non-Jewish people, I am often told that what I experienced was not, in fact, antisemitism. I am gaslit, my experiences are challenged and they are ultimately dismissed. This only deepens the trauma of my experiences.

However, despite constant non-Jewish attempts to define anti-semitism, we are lucky to have a working definition of antisemitism created by world-leading experts in this subject. This can be helpful to both Jews and non-Jews in better understanding what constitutes anti-Jewish racism. In 2016, the International Holocaust Remembrance Alliance (IHRA) adopted the following working definition of antisemitism. The IHRA is an intergovernmental organisation that works to spread awareness of the Holocaust, combat Holocaust denial and antisemitism and defines antisemitism as:

Manifestations might include the targeting of the state of Israel, conceived as a Jewish collectivity. However, criticism of Israel similar to that levelled against any other country cannot be regarded as antisemitic. Antisemitism frequently charges Jews with conspiring to harm humanity, and it is often used to blame Jews for 'why things go wrong.' It is expressed in speech, writing, visual forms and action, and employs sinister stereotypes and negative character traits.

Contemporary examples of antisemitism in public life, the media, schools, the workplace, and in the religious sphere could, taking into account the overall context, include, but are not limited to:

Calling for, aiding, or justifying the killing or harming of Jews in the name of a radical ideology or an extremist view of religion.

Making mendacious, dehumanizing, demonizing, or stereotypical allegations about Jews as such or the power of Jews as collective – such as, especially but not exclusively, the myth about a world Jewish conspiracy or of Jews controlling the media, economy, government or other societal institutions.

Accusing Jews as a people of being responsible for real or imagined wrongdoing committed by a single Jewish person or group, or even for acts committed by non-Jews.

Denying the fact, scope, mechanisms (e.g. gas chambers) or intentionality of the genocide of the Jewish people at the hands of National Socialist Germany and its supporters and accomplices during World War II (the Holocaust).

Accusing the Jews as a people, or Israel as a state, of inventing or exaggerating the Holocaust.

Accusing Jewish citizens of being more loyal to Israel, or to the alleged priorities of Jews worldwide, than to the interests of their own nations.

Denying the Jewish people their right to self-determination, e.g., by claiming that the existence of a State of Israel is a racist endeavor.

Applying double standards by requiring of it a behavior not expected or demanded of any other democratic nation.

Using the symbols and images associated with classic antisemitism (e.g., claims of Jews killing Jesus or blood libel) to characterize Israel or Israelis.

Drawing comparisons of contemporary Israeli policy to that of the Nazis.

Holding Jews collectively responsible for actions of the state of Israel.[26]

These incredibly helpful and illuminating examples, created by the IHRA, allow us as Jews to contextualise our experiences. They also enable our non-Jewish allies to better identify modern examples of antisemitism. However, they are only the first step to truly understanding antisemitism and the impact it has on Jewish identity. To go deeper, we must break down its specific categorisations and explore their historic and modern manifestations.

CATEGORISING ANTISEMITISM

Though there are those who try to define antisemitism solely via its source (e.g. the left or right), this is not the first step we must take when trying to understand anti-Jewish racism. Before one can understand different manifestations of antisemitism, it is important to understand the basic tenets of antisemitism that are common regardless of who is expressing them.

Categorising antisemitism via its source has major limits. It does not take into consideration the shared roots and immense amount of crossover between different sources of antisemitism. Once the roots of these antisemitic accusations themselves are understood, it is then possible to try to understand how they may differ depending on who is expressing them.

In his book, *Trials of the Diaspora*, Anthony Julius, categorises antisemitism into three separate libels: 'the blood libel, the conspiracy libel, and the economic libel'.[27] I will base my own categorisations on Julius's important work. These categorisations are incredibly useful in allowing us to understand antisemitism on a deeper level and identify it in our own worlds.

Furthermore, inspired by conversations with David Hirsh, I have decided to categorise 'conspiracy libel' as 'conspiracy fantasy'. Conspiratorial antisemitism is more than just a libel. It is a hallucination used to pleasure the antisemite. It constructs the diverse Jewish people into 'The Jew' – the money-grabbing, evil, demonic beast trying to control the world and exploit every non-Jew within it.

Additionally, I have also decided to include a fourth classification of antisemitism: the 'racial libel'. While racial antisemitism is often thought to be rooted in pseudoscience that specifically emerged in the 19th century, there has been – and still is – a racial element to how Jews have been depicted for a thousand years. Recognising this is crucial.

Depictions of Jewish money lenders, baby-killers and globalist conspirators all look eerily similar and have common features that intend to demonise and exaggerate perceived Jewish physical features. Though this is not as prevalent as it once was, it does still exist and it is important we understand how Jewish bodies have been and are still depicted. This is an important and damaging method of depicting and shaming Jewish people that continues to this day.

While antisemitism is a deeply complex form of prejudice, these categorisations of the economic libel, blood libel, conspiracy fantasy and racial libel are useful as they allow us to understand antisemitism at its roots, as well as the historical threads that bind each and every example together. They can give us sharper clarity in recognising how this has impacted Jews and Jewish identity. While such categorisations may indicate a separateness to their content, there is one thread that binds each of the examples to the other. The economic libel, blood libel, and conspiracy fantasy all frame the Jews as an evil, self-interested, unnatural, manipulative and perverse monolith who hate non-Jews, while those characteristics are physically depicted through the racial libel.

Modern examples of these categorisations may, on the surface, look different to the original historical accusation, but they are still – at their core – expressions of these three ideas. Furthermore, many examples of antisemitism can be categorised as more than one kind of antisemitism. For example, accusations that Jews control the world can be conspiracy fantasy, economic libel and even racial libel if they include physical depictions of Jews.

THE BLOOD LIBEL

The blood libel is the historic accusation that Jews purposefully murder non-Jews, specifically non-Jewish children, to use their blood in religious rituals. In his 2006 book, *The Changing Face of Antisemitism: From Ancient Times to the Present Day*, the historian Walter Laqueur notes: 'Altogether, there have been about 150 recorded cases of Blood Libel (not to mention thousands of rumours) that resulted in the arrest and killing of Jews throughout history, most of them in the Middle Ages. In almost every case, Jews were murdered, sometimes by a mob, sometimes following torture and a trial.'[28]

The blood libel, as with all examples of antisemitism, has no bearing in reality. The accusation claims that Jews use the blood of non-Jews in our religious rituals, while this is explicitly forbidden by Jewish law. Leviticus 17:12-13 states: 'Therefore I say to the Israelites, "None of you may eat blood, nor may any foreigner residing among you eat blood."'[29]

The irony here being that while Jews are barred from ingesting blood it is actually part, even if symbolically, of Christian ritual.

Accusations of blood libel are clearly unfounded, yet incredibly dangerous, but where did they originate and how did they have an impact upon Jewish people around the world?

One of the earliest known blood libels about Jews murdering non-Jews for their flesh came from the Greek philosopher Democritus and was recorded in the *Suda*, the 10th-century Byzantine encyclopaedia of the ancient Mediterranean world. In it, Democritus suggests: 'Every seven years the Jews captured a stranger, brought him to the temple in Jerusalem, and sacrificed him, cutting his flesh into bits.'[30]

Apion, the Greco-Egyptian author, took this further by claiming that Jews engaged in human sacrifice and cannibalism in their temple, and would sacrifice a Greek and eat his flesh. Socrates Scholasticus, an early Christian historian, also alleged that Jews in Syria got drunk and bound a Christian boy to a cross and whipped him to death.

Though these examples are from the ancient and early Christian worlds, the idea of the blood libel only really took hold following the conversion of the Roman empire to Christianity in 380 CE. On the 27 February 380 CE Theodosius I, the emperor of the Roman empire, published the following statement: 'According to the apostolic teaching and the doctrine of the Gospel, let us believe in the one deity of the Father, the Son and the Holy Spirit in equal majesty and in a Holy Trinity. We authorize the followers of this law to assume the title of Catholic Christians.'[31]

With this statement, the Roman empire was officially converted to Christianity and all other religious practices were outlawed. However, after converting to Christianity, Rome was faced with an uncomfortable truth regarding the death of Jesus. If you cast your minds back to roughly 30 CE, the Romans crucified Jesus. But this small fact became untenable in 380 CE. If the Romans were now Christians, how could they have murdered their own Saviour?

When searching for a new perpetrator of this heinous crime, the Romans turned to the writings in their new Bible, the New Testament. Jesus' disciples and early Christians wrote differing accounts of his life, but one regular theme was that the Jews bore ultimate responsibility for his death. In the First Epistle to the Thessalonians 2:14-15, Paul states, 'the Jews who killed the Lord, Jesus'[32] and, in the Book of Matthew, Matthew writes that when the High Priest asked the Jewish Councils what Jesus' sentence should be, they answered: 'He deserves death.' The account continues: 'Then they spat in his face and struck him.'[33] From these writings, and inspired by their own historical interactions with Jews, the Romans found their new perpetrators.

The idea that the Jews killed Jesus powerfully fuelled accusations of the blood libel. Jesus, the Son of God, was divine, and died for the world's sins – and only the most evil, most monstrous people could destroy something so pure and good. 'The Evil Jew', capable of murdering the Son of God, was also therefore capable of committing any number of untold evil acts – such as the murder of children.

HISTORIC BLOOD LIBEL

While accusations of Jews taking part in ritual sacrifice predate even the Romans, the first recorded example in Europe was in 1144, when a young English boy called William of Norwich was murdered. After William's body was discovered, his cousin claimed she saw a man and William enter the house of a well-known Jew. This accusation, coupled with pre-existing antisemitism in Norwich, led to a life-threatening situation for the city's Jews, who ultimately had to be taken into protective custody in the castle by the sheriff.

Following William's murder, Thomas of Monmouth, a monk, decided to record the story, leaning heavily on the testimony of a formerly Jewish Christian convert called Theobald. Theobald's so-called evidence was used to substantiate blood libel-based conspiracies throughout Europe. Other examples in England include Little Saint Hugh of Lincoln who was murdered in 1255. Under torture, a Jewish man, Koppin, confessed that Hugh had been crucified by prominent English Jews. Koppin and another 18 Jews were hanged for their alleged part in Hugh's death. The king at the time, Henry III, directly benefited from the murder of these Jewish men as, following their execution, he seized their property.

There were also incidents of the blood libel in continental Europe. The first outside of England took place in 1171 in Blois in France, which saw 30-40 Jewish men, women and children burned at the stake, despite no evidence of the blood libel being reported. The first reported Spanish example of the blood libel took place in 1250 in Zaragoza, when Dominguito del Val was found dead. To this day, he is commemorated in the cathedral of Zaragoza. There is no evidence that this boy existed, which suggests the entire story was fabricated after the fact to demonise the Jewish community further. Another tragic example of Spanish blood libel was the case of The Holy Child of La Guardia in 1490. For this crime, two Jewish people, and six 'new Christian' *conversos* – Jews forced to convert under duress – were burned at the stake, after making false confessions under torture.

Though England and Spain expelled their Jews in 1290 and 1492 respectively, these accusations continued in other countries where Jews lived. There were even accusations of the blood libel in the 20th century when Menachem Mendel Beilis was imprisoned in Kiev for the murder of 13-year-old Andrei Yushchinsky in 1913. These continuous accusations of the blood libel have created a world in which Jews represent the ultimate form of evil.

In the rest of this section, we will explore two cases of the blood libel, one historical case focussing on Mizrahi and Sephardic Jews from the Muslim world – chosen as it is not often discussed – and one from the present day.

THE DAMASCUS BLOOD LIBEL

Before examining the story of the blood libel against the Jewish community of Damascus in Syria in 1840, it is important to understand the basic background of Jews in the Muslim world. There is a general belief that Jews, specifically Mizrahi and Sephardic Jews, living in the Muslim and Arab-ruled Middle East and North African region (including Muslim-ruled Iberia) prior to the creation of the State of Israel in 1948, were well-treated, especially in comparison to their cousins living in Europe.

In Andalusian Spain, there was a period when Jews lived and prospered under Muslim rule, referred to as *La Convivencia* and the 'Golden Age'. But Sir Martin Gilbert, the famed Jewish historian, questions this idea of a Golden Age, arguing: 'When there was a lull in persecution – bless them – they called it a Golden Age. It was not a Golden Age. It was an age when Jews were persecuted less.'[34] Challenging the myth that Jews in the Muslim world enjoyed a privileged life free of antisemitism is important because, if we do not, we misunderstand the lived experiences of millions of Jewish people.

This prevailing idea is due, in part, to unnuanced comparisons made with the treatment of Jews in Europe and the incorrect belief that Jews in Europe had it worse. However, this comparison leads people to draw the incorrect conclusion that Jews in the Muslim world were not victims of antisemitism. Mizrahi and Sephardic Jews in the Muslim world absolutely faced antisemitism. They were classed as *dhimmi*, a term of legal inferiority given to non-Muslims living in the Middle East and North African lands that had been taken over by

Muslim colonialists. This came with a set of subjugating laws imposed on the Jewish population that put limits on their everyday lives. Jews in the Middle East and North Africa were also victims of pogroms and, as we will explore in this section, the blood libel.

Writing in the 12th century, Maimonides, the famed Sephardic rabbi (also known as the Rambam) said of Jews living in the Muslim world: 'God has entangled us with this people, the nation of Ishmael, who treat us so prejudicially and who legislate our harm and hatred… No nation has ever arisen more harmful than they, nor has anyone done more to humiliate us, degrade us, and consolidate hatred against us.'[35] This does not sound like a 'Golden Age' to me.

Understanding the realities of Jewish life in the Muslim-ruled world is crucial, as it allows us to better understand the Mizrahi and Sephardic experience as well as further emphasising the idea of a global Jewish experience. In short, no matter where Jews live, and at what time and context, they are victims of aggressive and dehumanising antisemitism.

At this point, Maimonides can once again help us understand how Jews in the Muslim world were certainly not privileged: 'We bear the inhumane burden of their humiliation, lies and absurdities, being as the prophet said, "like a deaf man who does not hear or a dumb man who does not open his mouth…" Our sages disciplined us to bear Ishmael's lies and absurdities, listening in silence, and we have trained ourselves, old and young, to endure their humiliation, as Isaiah said, "I have given my back to the smiters, and my cheek to the beard pullers."'[36]

This oppression continued throughout history. A visitor to Egypt in the 19th century observed that Cairo's Jews were, 'held in the utmost contempt and abhorrence by Muslims in general'.[37] As we will explore in more detail during our conversation with Hen Mazzig, in 1941 the Jews of Baghdad in Iraq, were victims of a violent and deadly pogrom, known as the *Farhud*, that saw the murder of up to 750 Jewish people. The Jews of Morocco faced pogroms in 1948, following the establishment of the State of Israel, leaving 44 dead. The 1950s, 1960s and 1970s saw the expulsion of 850,000 Mizrahi and Sephardic Jews from their respective homes, where their families had lived for thousands of years, simply because of their Jewishness.

Despite the long and distinct history of antisemitism in the Muslim world, Christian and Muslim Jew-hatred began to fuse in the 19th century, during the period of European colonialism in the Middle East. This brings us to the Damascus blood libel of 1840. On 5 February 1840, an Italian friar named Thomas and his Muslim servant, Ibrahim Amāra, disappeared in Syria. Italians in Damascus immediately began spreading the blood libel that both men had been murdered by Jews who aimed to use their blood for ritual practices during *Pesach*. As we have seen in previous cases of the blood libel, Jews were once again scapegoated when a barber called Solomon Negrin was arrested and tortured into making a false confession. Solomon said that the two men were murdered by seven Jews in the home of a Jew called David Harari. All the accused men were arrested, two died during torture, one converted to Islam under duress and the rest made false confessions.

With these 'confessions' – and another forced confession obtained from Harari's Muslim servant – the apparent guilt of the Jews was confirmed. The events sparked a pogrom where a mob attacked and looted the Jobar synagogue, destroying the sacred scrolls of the Torah. Syrian authorities kidnapped and tortured 63 Jewish children to force their mothers to reveal the hiding place of Thomas and Ibrahim's blood.

New communications technology allowed the story of the alleged Jews' guilt to spread quickly across the globe. In June 1840, *The Times* published an editorial article which argued: '[The affair is] one of the most important cases ever submitted to the notice of the civilized world … Admitting for the moment [the accusation to be true] … then the Jewish religion must at once disappear from the face of the earth ... We shall await the issue as the whole of Europe and the civilized world will do with intense interest.'[38]

Following outrage from foreign Jews such as Moses Montefiore, and pressure to release the Jews that remained alive in prison, the Sultan of the Ottoman empire, although he did not actually rule in Syria at this point, issued a *firman* (or edict) proclaiming the innocence of the imprisoned Jews. In it, he declared: 'And for the love we bear to our subjects, we cannot permit the Jewish nation, whose innocence for the crime alleged against them is evident, to be worried and tormented as a consequence of accusations which have not the least foundation in truth.'[39]

But, in a demonstration of how pervasive this antisemitic accusation was, Dr Dov Levitan of Bar-Ilan University recalled that in 1983 – 143 years after the Damascus blood libel – the then Syrian defence minister, Mustafa Tlass, published *The Matzah of Zion* where he reiterated the accusation that Syrian Jews had murdered Thomas and Ibrahim.

Reviewing Jonathan Frankel's account of the 'Damascus affair', the American historian Albert Lindemann argues: 'These reports, as well as the acceptance of them in the west, were the cause of astonishment and profound consternation by Jews in Europe, who had believed that ritual murder trials were a thing of the past, or at least that a belief in them by Europe's educated population was no longer to be expected. Eventually, a different story emerged.'[40]

As Lindemann goes on to suggest, 'as the case unravelled, much was revealed about Jewish consciousness at this time. And much, too, was revealed about non-Jewish attitudes to Jews – much of it not pretty.'[41] This is particularly interesting, as it seemed that, for the Jews of 19th century western Europe, the identification of Jews as 'evil, blood-thirsty murderers' had been consigned to history. However, the Damascus affair led them to the devastating realisation that it was very much a current perception of what it meant to be Jewish. Moreover, for the Jews of Syria and other Middle Eastern countries, their already precarious status would have felt even less secure as a result of this horrific accusation and the events that followed it.

ACCUSATIONS THAT ISRAEL STEALS ORGANS

It is important to understand that, like a virus, antisemitism always mutates to fit the zeitgeist, a notion explored more extensively in the following chapter. Despite appearing different to fit a specific context, traditional antisemitic tropes still persist today. And in the age of the Jewish state, they now focus on demonising, delegitimising or treating Israel with double standards. To be clear: *fair* criticism of Israeli government policy is not antisemitic. A helpful guide to ascertaining as to whether a statement on Israel is antisemitic is Natan Sharansky's 3D test[42]. Ask yourself, does the statement: Demonise Israel, Delegitimise Israel or treat it with Double Standards? If the answer is yes, then it's almost certainly antisemitic.

Sadly, the reality is that the majority of 'criticism' does (either accidentally or purposefully) cross over into antisemitism by superimposing traditional antisemitic tropes onto Israel, which often ends up being directed at Jewish individuals, even in the Diaspora.

This also explains what I experienced at university. No one accused me of murdering children to use their blood in Jewish rituals. However, I did come face to face with ugly, aggressive antizionist antisemitism rooted in the blood libel, which framed Israel as the centre of all evil. In my penultimate year at university, I took part in a debate on humanitarian intervention and, during the course of it, referenced Israel's rescue of Ethiopian Jews, which began in the mid-1980s. In response, a member of the opposing team started ranting about Israel being the most evil country in the world. An argument ensued before we were both hushed by the professor. The student was not chastised for making an egregious and deeply prejudiced claim about the world's only Jewish state. While many people would argue that this student was only targeting the State of Israel – and not Jewish people – that is quite categorically not what he was doing. He had superimposed the antisemitic blood libel that argues the Jews are the most evil demonic people in the world onto Israel. While rarely openly acknowledged or admitted by its most virulent detractors, the sentiment that Israel is the worst country in the world because it is the Jewish state, and the idea that Jews are evil, is deeply embedded in many cultures.

That brings us to the modern manifestation of the blood libel. Instead of solely targeting Jewish people it turns its focus to Israel, which is so often treated as the 'collective Jew'. Looking at this accusation as part of a historical trend, we see a pattern of Jews (including Israel) being accused of innately demonic and evil acts: be it the murder of Christian children so their blood can be used in Jewish rituals, or the murder of Palestinian children so their organs can be harvested. It's the same story, but a different time period, with the narrative placed in a modern context.

In August 2018 in a column for the Belgian *De Wereld Morgen* news website, Robrecht Vanderbeeken, the cultural secretary of Belgium's ACOD trade union and a philosophy of science scholar, wrote of Israel's alleged targeting of Palestinian children: 'Children have been kidnapped and murdered for their organs.'[43] This echoed statements previously made in November 2015 by the Palestinian ambassador to the United Nations, Riyad Mansour, who suggested that bodies of Palestinians murdered by the Israeli Defence Force 'were returned with missing corneas and other organs, further confirming past reports about organ harvesting by the occupying power'.[44]

In 2009, Israeli military officials acknowledged that organs, such as corneas, had been taken from *both* Israelis and Palestinians without the permission of their families by one individual, Dr Jehuda Hiss. Hiss' actions, for research purposes and organ sales, ended in the 1990s and were never government policy. They were obviously reprehensible, but the accusation that the Israeli state *purposefully* kills children to steal their organs is another accusation entirely – and is a blood libel. It is quite a leap to go from individual Israelis committing terrible acts to a state-wide conspiracy at the highest levels of the Israeli government.

These are not simply normal accusations about crimes that have taken place in Israel, they are accusations of the Jewish state being inherently evil – demonstrating how traditional antisemitic tropes that have existed for 2,000 years have been imposed onto the State of Israel as the supposed embodiment of the 'collective Jew'. The awful actions of one person – in this case, Hiss – are blown up and magnified to represent the actions of the entirety of the country and, ultimately, the entire Jewish people.

Throughout the last 2,000 years, there have been countless allegations of the blood libel – all of them false – and this persists to this day. In 2020, Israel was accused of training the police force that murdered George Floyd. While, like other accusations aimed at Israel, this may appear to be a criticism of a specific policy, it is in actual fact steeped in the blood libel. By accusing Israel of training these policemen, it is being held responsible for all the evils of anti-Black racism in the United States, as if it only exists because of Israel. Not only does this lead to a failure to address American anti-Black racism, but this accusation is rooted in Israel – as the 'collective Jew' – being uniquely evil, demonic, blood-thirsty and amoral. This is the blood libel: 2020.

In this section exploring blood libel, we have discussed examples from throughout history. Yes, there are clear differences; the victims have changed from Christian children to Palestinian children or Black Americans. The purpose has changed – blood originally used for Jewish rituals has become organs used for trafficking and sold for financial gain, or the brutal murder of Black people. But, despite these changes, these are ultimately the same accusation of sinister Jewish immorality. As one of my students remarked: 'It's the same soup, different bowl.'

THE ECONOMIC LIBEL

The economic libel, rooted in the accusation that Jews are obsessed with money, is one of the most prevalent forms of antisemitism. As such, it has shamed and endangered Jews for a thousand years and, sadly, shows no signs of abating.

We have seen antisemitic depictions of Jews that focus on this trope in some of the greatest works in western literature. Fagin, from Charles Dickens' *Oliver Twist*, is an archetypal sneaky, money-obsessed Jew who – if there was any doubt as to whether he represents Jews – is referred to more than 250 times in the book's first 38 chapters.[45] Unfortunately, Fagin was neither the first, nor the last, depiction of money-obsessed Jews, but the question is: where did this idea originate?

The connections between Jews and money was forged by Christianity and can be traced back to the murder of Jesus himself. If we recall, Judas – a Jew – betrayed Christ for 30 pieces of silver. This helped set the Christian world on a path of connecting Jews with money. This specific framing of Jews and money was rooted in the idea that they would do anything – including betrayal – for material gain. This idea was eventually extrapolated by the Nazis who declared: 'Money is the God of the Jews.'[46] Thus, according to this libel, Jews are not just greedy, but inherently untrustworthy, sneaky and amoral.

This libel intensified in the Middle Ages when the Church outlawed the act of usury – lending money for interest – by Christians. Interestingly, the passage in the Bible that was the basis for this concept was in the Torah, known to Christians as the Old Testament. In the book of *Devarim* (or Deuteronomy), it says: 'You may charge a foreigner interest, but not a brother Israelite.'[47] Although this clearly refers to Israelites, Christians saw themselves as the 'new Israel', so therefore this Jewish law was applied to Christians.

This religious restriction on Christian people, coupled with the many antisemitic restrictions faced by Jews funnelled them into professions that dealt with finances.[48] Combined with high levels of literacy and numeracy in the Jewish community, these developments filtered Jews into professions dealing with money, which ultimately led to Jews being seen as money-obsessed and affluent. However, this perception existed purely in the minds of Christian society, as the majority of Jews were not wealthy. It also persisted even when Christians disobeyed the Church's ban on usury and began to outnumber Jews in this field.

In roles such as money-lending and tax-collecting, Jews often found themselves in a vulnerable position. Even though society benefited from, and exploited, Jews in these professions, they would be swiftly expelled once the services were no longer needed, necessary, or the ruling bodies required a scapegoat. This was exemplified by the expulsion of the Jews from England in 1290.

Later, as history progressed, historic Jewish involvement in financial services meant certain Sephardic and Ashkenazi Jews were offered specific financial positions in the courts of European rulers. These 'Court Jews' would manage the wealth of the European nobility or even finance them themselves through loans. The financial services that Jews provided to the courts, as well as previous historical instances of economic exploitation, were so great that it is arguable that European wealth was built via the antisemitic victimisation of Jews.

The Court Jew was a direct continuation of the precarious roles that Jews played in the Middle Ages. They were placed in incredibly risky situations as they were still Jews living in an antisemitic world that was ready to dispose of them at will. As the historian Natalie Zemon Davis argues: 'The anti-Jewish suspicion of a Jewish ducal treasurer is ... an expected feature of the historical portrait of the Court Jew.'[49] The story of Joseph Süß Oppenheimer – who was executed after the Duke of Württemberg's death and which was infamously depicted by the Nazis in the antisemitic 1940 film *Jud Süß* – clearly demonstrates the dangers of being a Court Jew. It is clear that though there were certain Jewish people who became wealthy, and even powerful, because of their involvement in financial services, these were ultimately manifestations of deeply embedded antisemitism. Moreover, they were not spared the dangers of antisemitism and these stories have no bearing on the wider Jewish relationship with money.

During the 19th century, Jews, who had effectively been forced into jobs that dealt with money for 900 years by this time, became involved in the development of modern banking. Just as Jews had previously become 'the face' of money-lending and tax-collecting in the Middle Ages, so they once again became linked with modern financial services. This perception then evolved into the accusation that Jews were dominating and controlling the global economy, which eventually helped feed the contemporary conspiracy fantasy.

While these examples reveal the historical roots of the economic libel, there are two different ways these accusations can manifest themselves. One is the accusation of a Jewish global financier; the other is the shady, poor, dirty, stingy Jew. While on the surface these examples appear to be polar opposites – one being wealthy and powerful and the other being poverty-stricken and filthy – they are actually rooted in the same idea. Jews are not merely obsessed with money in this libel, they are also, at root, evil and untrustworthy. Regardless of whether they are rich or poor, if Jews are concerned only with money, then they lack ethics and humanity or are even inhuman themselves. Like all other forms of antisemitism, while this libel took hold due to the specific position of Jews in the eyes of the non-Jewish world, it directly seeks to paint Jewish people as a whole of lacking moral fibre. This forms the basis for two contradictory sentiments. The first being that, through our global financiers, we are responsible for capitalism and all its sins. But, at the same time, through the perspective of the poverty-stricken, stingy Jew, we are also held responsible for communism and all its failings.

The economic libel, and in fact any libel directed at Jewish people, does not see Jews as individuals; it strips Jews of autonomy and diversity by framing all as monolithically immoral. This is why one wealthy powerful Jewish person, like a Rothschild or a Soros, cannot just be a wealthy individual; their own intentions have to be nefarious and symbolically represent all Jews. These ideas are so ingrained in society that I can recall my first experience with the economic libel when I was just a teenager. I was 12 or 13 and was walking home from my secondary school with some friends who asked if they could borrow money. I told them I did not have any and they responded: 'Why not? You are Jewish. All Jews are rich.' At 13 years old, I did not understand why anyone – let alone my friend – would say this to me.

But I understand it now: the antisemitism of the economic libel paints Jews as immoral people who worship at the altar of mammon. We were forced into poverty, and then to get out of it, forced into professions that led some of us to handle money – and for the next thousand years, we have been punished for it.

It is highly unlikely that anyone reading this – Jew or non-Jew – has *not* come into contact with this libel before. It continues, painfully and grossly, to shame Jewish people.

The libel not only erases our humanity and individuality; it also disguises Jewish experience. It ignores how our ancestors had to function in societies which designated to them one specific role only – and then punished them for taking it. It conceals the fact that many of our ancestors lived in abject poverty and did what they could to survive – as do many of our people around the world today.

The reality is the majority of Jews are not wealthy; in fact, many Jews live in poverty. In 2013, the UJA-Federation of New York released research which found that 'one in five New York-area Jewish households is poor'[50] and '45% of children in Jewish households now live in poor or near poor households.' John S Ruskay, executive vice-president and CEO of UJA-Federation of New York, said of the study: 'The sheer scale of Jewish poverty in the New York area is immense.'[51] This is not just a US story. In a 2018 report on poverty in Israel, the Adva

Centre found: 'Today's labor market does not offer all Israelis a decent standard of living.'[52] It is also the case that a quarter of Holocaust survivors in Israel live in poverty.[53]

Despite the reality of our experience, the economic libel has repeated itself for thousands of years regardless of its variants. We can see it in the *Merchant of Venice*, *Oliver Twist* and more aggressively antisemitic texts such as *The Protocols of the Elders of Zion*, Nazi propaganda, Soviet antizionist propaganda, anti-Jewish cartoons from east to west, and in much antisemitic literature today. It can also incorrectly place Jewish people in opposition to socialist ideals as the Jew became a representation of capitalism.

It continues to this day and in 2019, Ewen MacIntosh, the actor who played Keith Bishop in the British version of The Office posted on Facebook that: 'one can see how certain people make the amalgam of Jewish = Genocidal rich evil people who wish to rule the world'.[54] It was also evident in a 2009 poll by the ADL, which found that 31% of Europeans believed that the 2008 financial crash was caused by Jews.[55] However, the modern economic libel does not just focus on Jewish economic conspiracies, it also continues to impact the lives, and cause the deaths, of individual Jewish people.

In 2018, a mail bombing campaign in the United States was initiated by Cesar Altieri Sayoc Jr. For just over a week, from 22 November to 1 December, Cesar sent out packages that contained nail bombs to prominent political and economic figures, several of them Jewish, in the United States. The first package was sent to the New York home of the wealthy philanthropist George Soros.

Soros was targeted specifically because of a noxious mix of the economic libel and the conspiracy fantasy. He is seen as the Jewish spider at the centre of the economic web, snaring all those around him like flies. While other key political figures were targeted, it is not beyond the realm of possibility that Soros was targeted first because Cesar perceived him to be at the heart of the economic exploitation of

America, and thus controlling all other powerful people also targeted in this campaign. He was a major donor to the Democratic party, while Cesar was a Donald Trump supporter. While neither Soros, nor anyone else, was killed during this mail-bombing campaign, he very well could have been.

A more horrifying story of the deadly impact of the economic libel on individual Jews is the murder of Ilan Halimi. On 21 January 2006, Ilan, a 23-year-old Jewish man whose family hailed from Morocco, was kidnapped in Paris in France. A ransom of €450,000 was demanded as the kidnappers falsely believed that because Ilan's family is Jewish, they must have been rich.

For three weeks, Ilan was tortured beyond recognition. No ransom came – because his parents were not wealthy and could not pay it. When Ilan's parents told the kidnappers they could not meet their demands, they were simply told to 'go and ask in the synagogues'.[56]

At just 23 years of age, Ilan's naked and mutilated body was discovered by a passer-by. He died of his injuries on the way to the hospital. Unbelievably, as is often the case in France, Ilan's antisemitic murder, rooted in the economic libel, was not viewed as a hate crime by French authorities. The antisemites who tortured and murdered Ilan were eventually apprehended and sentenced to prison for varying lengths.

Not only does economic libel pose a real danger to Jewish people both as individuals and as a collective, but it has also – along with the other categorisations of antisemitism (barring the racial libel) – shunted Jews down the imagined 'hierarchy of oppression' that has led to the erasure of antisemitism as a 'legitimate' form of prejudice. It is incredibly dangerous to Jewish people, and though it is the foundation of the modern conspiracy fantasy, today's economic libel is just as dangerous an accusation as it ever was. It continues to haunt, harm and put Jewish life under threat.

THE CONSPIRACY FANTASY

The antisemitic conspiracy fantasy is the delusion that the Jewish people are engaged in a concerted conspiracy to control the world by exploiting the global non-Jewish population for Jewish gain. This can be related to economics, politics and media among other things.

The economic libel and the conspiracy fantasy are inextricably linked. For example, when the Rothschilds and, more recently, Soros are accused of financial manipulation and exploitation of the non-Jewish world. These accusations are expressions of both the antisemitic conspiracy fantasy and economic libel.

Take the allegation that Soros provided financial backing for the 2020 Black Lives Matter protests that followed the murder of George Floyd. In the Netherlands, Soros was also accused of financing the 'Kick Out Zwarte Piet' campaign. *Zwarte Piet*, or Black Pete, is Saint Nicholas' Black helper, who is often portrayed by a white person in blackface during the Christmas season. The movement to end the use of this characterisation was created by Black members of Dutch society, yet the antisemitic myth that Jews are using Black people to take over the white, Christian world prevailed in this conspiracy fantasy.

While these accusations are rooted in Soros' billionaire status, the accusation that he was conspiring to disrupt 'white' United States and the Netherlands (among other countries) reveals this type of antisemitism as conspiracy based. Just like with the older, although still prevalent, accusations against the Rothschilds, the focus on one wealthy Jewish man pulling strings among many other non-Jewish wealthy influencers is deliberate and dangerously loaded. It also must be recognised that even *if* a Jewish person is involved in some campaign or another, that still doesn't a) justify the idea that the actions are being taken to destroy society or b) explain the notion that the actions of one can be magnified to represent the behaviour of the entire Jewish people.

Despite modern developments of the conspiracy fantasy, it has always been a part of the expression of antisemitism. Accusations of the blood libel are also accusations against a conspiring Jewish community, such as when Jews were accused of poisoning wells during the Black Death in 14th-century Europe. Jews have historically been viewed as a conspiring, amoral and untrustworthy group. This delusion of Jewish people as inherently conspiratorial, which also pervades the economic and blood libels, evolved into the modern antisemitic conspiracy fantasy, which we will now explore.

THE PROTOCOLS OF THE ELDERS OF ZION

One of the most important documents regarding modern conspiratorial fanaticism is *The Protocols of the Elders of Zion*. This work of fiction was first published in Russia by Sergei Nilus, a Tsarist civil servant, in 1903. The *Protocols* were framed as the minutes of 24 meetings held by world Jewish leaders ('the Elders of Zion') in a graveyard, where they convened to discuss their plans to control the world and exploit the non-Jewish masses. It is hardly subtle. It was also later proven to be a complete forgery.

During and following the French Revolution, Counter-Enlightenment movements blamed the revolution and the Enlightenment on the Jews, who were accused of trying to break the old order and the power of the Church. As 'evidence' of this, the *Protocols* state: 'In all corners of the earth the words "Liberty, Equality, Fraternity," brought to our ranks, thanks to our blind agents, whole legions who bore our banners with enthusiasm. And all the time these words were cankerworms at work boring into the well-being of the Goyim, putting an end everywhere to peace, quiet, solidarity and destroying all the foundations of the Goya States.'[57]

This is the incredible thing about antisemitism: even when societies experience an enormous seismic shift, such as the French Revolution, which upended society and swept away the old order, antisemitism continues to persist in the new and modern societies that emerge afterwards. It is able to shape-shift and evolve to fit with the times. The endurance of antisemitism should not be underestimated.

Following its original publication, the *Protocols* was reprinted several times. During the Russian Revolution and the ensuing civil war, which saw the murder of up to 50,000 Jews, the white Russians seized upon the *Protocols* and blamed the Jews for the revolution and ensuing chaos. This reinforced the idea of 'Jewish Bolshevism', which blamed the Jews for the spread of communism.

The 1920s saw the publication and promotion of the *Protocols* and its antisemitic conspiracy fantasy abroad. In Britain, the *Protocols* were published by Robert Wilton of *The Times* and Victor Marsden of the *Morning Post*, both of whom had lived in Russia prior to the revolution. Due to his knowledge of Russian, Marsden translated the *Protocols* into English, thus allowing it to spread to all corners of the British empire and the English-speaking world. In his introduction, Marsden wrote: 'The Jews are carrying it out with steadfast purpose, creating wars and revolutions ... to destroy the white Gentile race, that the Jews may seize the power during the resulting chaos and rule with their claimed superior intelligence over the remaining races of the world, as kings over slaves.'[58]

The *Protocols* subsequently spread rapidly. This iteration of the conspiracy fantasy was translated into Polish in 1920 and was also used by both the Arab and British forces in Mandatory Palestine to further demonise the Jews who had settled there in order to escape from violent antisemitism in Europe. Many in the United States also bought into the *Protocols*, with Boris Brasol, a former Tsarist officer, encouraging Henry Ford, of Ford Motor fame, to publish an American edition which sold over 500,000 copies.

Unsurprisingly, the Nazis fully embraced the *Protocols*, basing their concept of self-defence against a Jewish threat on the idea that the Jews were conspiring to take over the globe. They positioned Jews as the greatest threat humanity faced while publishing 23 versions of the *Protocols* between 1933 and 1939. The *Protocols* could be seen in propaganda produced by the Nazis that dehumanised the Jews and remade them as spiders and insects scrambling to control the world.

Following the second world war, the *Protocols* were promoted by the Arab and Palestinian leadership, as well as by the Soviet Union, which launched its post-Holocaust campaign to demonise the newly formed State of Israel. As in Nazi propaganda, the *Protocols* can be seen visually represented in antizionist propaganda produced by the USSR, once again depicting the Jews as insects and spiders trying to catch the world in their web of deceit.

A fascinating thing to consider is the universality of antisemitism. 1920s America was a very different place to pre-revolutionary Russia, which was very different to the Arab world – yet, we still see the same antisemitism take hold. We still see it redefining, at least externally, what it means to be a Jew, with a great impact on the lives of millions of Jews all over the world.

Just as Jews were accused of poisoning wells during the Black Death, so we have seen this very notion of Jews causing a pandemic repeated today. I am editing this in 2020, in the midst of the Covid-19 pandemic, when Jews, once again, are blamed for spreading the virus to harm the non-Jewish world. [59]

THE *PROTOCOLS* ENDURE TODAY

In keeping with its historical shape-shifting nature, anti-Jewish racism evolved after the second world war, but it still attempted to impose familiar caricatures and antisemitic identities on to Jewish people. After the horrors of the Holocaust, it was no longer acceptable for broader society to openly denigrate Jews, or publicly claim they were taking over the world or committing evil acts, so a new form of antisemitism emerged. It came to be known as antizionism.

As we know, the Soviets drew from the same source material as the Nazis: *The Protocols of the Elders of Zion*. As previously noted, this demonisation of Israel was a real and prominent policy of the USSR which continued well into the 1980s. Although the Soviet Union was formally dissolved in December 1991, the damage that its campaign of spreading the antizionist conspiracy fantasy lives on today. As Izabella Tabarovsky, a senior programme associate at the US-based Kennan Institute, writes: 'In the course of the campaign, hundreds of antizionist and anti-Israel books and thousands of articles were published in the USSR, with millions of copies entering circulation in the country. Many were translated into foreign languages – English, French, German, Spanish, Arabic and numerous others.'[60]

The USSR's campaign to stoke hatred of Israel worked hand in hand with a concerted effort by the Arab world to libel the Jewish state and place it at the centre of global conspiracies. In May 1998, for instance, the Egyptian daily *Al-Ahram* published an article that declared: 'There is a great Jewish plot to gain control of the world.'[61]

The Protocols of the Elders of Zion is regularly discussed, spoken of as fact and disseminated in the Arab world. In 2017, a Jordanian news programme produced a three-part investigation into the *Protocols*. Its host, Ayed Alqam, opened the programme by reportedly claiming Jews are 'an ostracized and abhorred people' known 'for their lying, fraud, and deception, and their sowing of strife.' He went on to blame the high cost of living in the Arab world on Jews, citing as evidence the so-called fourth protocol. 'The cost of living in all the Arab countries is high,' Alqam suggested. 'Everybody is complaining about the high cost of living, all over the Middle East, as well as about the greed of the traders and their monopoly on food supplies. The [fourth] protocol is being implemented. People have forgotten religion for the sake of money.'

THE 'SMEARING' OF JEREMY CORBYN

Antisemitic conspiracy fantasies are still an issue in other parts of the world as well. As many British readers will be painfully aware, in 2015 Jeremy Corbyn was elected as leader of the Labour party in the UK, thereby occupying the official position of leader of Her Majesty's Most Loyal Opposition. During the Labour leadership election, the British Jewish community began to worry about Corbyn's track record on Jewish issues. It was alarming: for example, he had referred to Hamas and Hezbollah as his friends[62], despite their open genocidal attitudes towards Jewish people. To clarify, Article 7 of Hamas' charter states: 'The time will not come until Muslims will fight the Jews (and kill them); until the Jews hide behind rocks and trees, which will cry: O Muslim! there is a Jew hiding behind me, come on and kill him!'[63]

It is not unreasonable to hope that someone who has their sights set on becoming the prime minister of the United Kingdom would not align themselves with an organisation that seeks explicitly to destroy Jews. On 12 August 2015, shortly before Corbyn's election as leader, *The Jewish Chronicle* posed seven questions regarding his antisemitism.[64] These included questioning his comments on Hamas and Hezbollah, as well as other worrying issues regarding Corbyn's alleged involvement with Holocaust deniers, specifically Deir Yassin Remembered (DYR). DYR is a group that publishes antisemitic material and is run by admitted Holocaust denier, Paul Eisen. In 2008, Eisen wrote an essay titled 'My Life as a Holocaust Denier', in it he stated: 'the notion of a premeditated, planned, and industrial extermination of Europe's Jews with its iconic gas-chambers and magical six million are all used to make the Holocaust not only special but also sacred.' In his answers to *The Jewish Chronicle*'s seven questions, Corbyn admitted that although he attended DYR's meetings in the past, he no longer did.[65] However, in 2018, the *Daily Mail* online revealed that Corbyn lied and in 2014, he met with DYR at Parliament.

After Corbyn ultimately won the party leadership, Labour's antisemitism crisis was kicked up a further notch in March 2018, when he was found six years previously to have defended an antisemitic mural in East London by the Los Angeles-based graffiti artist Kalen Ockerman. The mural featured economic libel, conspiracy fantasy and racial libel in the form of caricature of Jewish bankers sitting at a table supported on the backs of workers. (Ockerman, whose work appears under the name Mear One, denied the work was antisemitic.)

In a 2012 Facebook post, Corbyn expressed confusion as to why the local authority planned to remove the mural. Responding to a post by Mear One which stated 'Tomorrow they want to buff my mural. Freedom of Expression. London Calling. Public Art',[66] Corbyn, then a backbench MP, asked: 'Why? You are in good company. Rockerfeller [sic] destroyed Diego Viera's murals because it included a picture of Lenin'.[67]

To demonstrate just how obviously offensive this image is to Jewish people, when I showed it to a class of students in Hong Kong, they instantly understood how deeply antisemitic it is – yet Corbyn initially failed to recognise how deeply rooted in antisemitic libel and fantasy the mural was.

Another major incident in Labour's ongoing antisemitic firestorm was the party's refusal to accept in full IHRA's definition of antisemitism, which had in 2016 been adopted by a plenary meeting of the 31 countries in the IHRA. Initially, too, in 2016, the Labour party had adopted the IHRA definition. However, in 2018, Labour's governing body, the National Executive Committee (NEC), issued a revised document that removed or amended four of the eleven examples provided by IHRA that referenced exploitation of criticism of Israel as a potential form of antisemitism. In response, the UK delegation to the IHRA issued a statement which made plain its concerns: 'Any "modified" version of the IHRA definition that does not include all of its 11 examples is no longer the IHRA definition. Adding or removing language undermines the months of international diplomacy

and academic rigour that enabled this definition to exist. If one organization or institution can amend the wording to suit its own needs,
then logically anyone else could do the same. We would once again
revert to a world where antisemitism goes unaddressed simply because
different entities cannot agree on what it is.'[68] Ultimately, in September 2018 Labour did adopt IHRA's full definition of antisemitism,
however they simultaneously adopted a statement that the definition
would not 'in any way undermine freedom of expression on Israel or
the rights of the Palestinians.'[69] In essence, this freedom of expression
clause is a get out of jail free card for the Labour Party.

Throughout his leadership, allegation after allegation was made
against Corbyn, such as his presence at a 2014 wreath-laying ceremony at the graves of Salah Khalaf and Atef Bseiso – the masterminds
behind the 1972 Munich massacre, which saw Palestinian terrorists
torture and murder 11 Israeli Olympians as the world watched.

A counterattack to the growing accusations that the Labour party
was institutionally antisemitic was that Corbyn was being smeared
to keep him out of power. Diane Abbott, the then Shadow Home
Secretary dismissed accusations of antisemitism in the Labour Party
as a 'smear campaign against Jeremy'.[70] Indeed, a group was formed
in 2017 titled, 'Labour Against the Witchhunt' (LAW) that stated:
'Those who promote the false anti-Semitism smear, who conflate
anti-Semitism with anti-Zionism and who promote the myth of a
ubiquitous left anti-Semitism, are not welcome in LAW.'[71]

Former Labour MP Chris Williamson, who was suspended from
the Labour party, was quoted in the *Guardian* as saying: 'I'm not
saying it never ever happens but it is a really dirty, lowdown trick,
particularly the antisemitism smears. Many people in the Jewish
community are appalled by what they see as the weaponisation of
antisemitism for political ends.'[72]

Admittedly, neither Abbott nor LAW nor Williamson directly
state that Corbyn was being smeared by the Jews themselves, rather

his political opponents. However, there were those that argued it was the Jews who were behind this campaign. Pete Willsman, a Corbyn ally and member of the NEC was caught on camera stating: 'They can falsify social media very easily' and 'I am not going to be lectured to by Trump fanatics making up duff information without any evidence at all.'[73]

In August 2019, CST (Community Security Trust), an organisation that ensures the safety of the British Jewish community, published a report titled *Engines of Hate* that reported: 'networks of Labour-supporting Twitter accounts endorse or spread the idea that allegations of antisemitism against Labour are a fake smear campaign; allegations that sometimes stray into wider conspiracy theories about a shadowy Israeli, Zionist or Jewish lobby'.[74]

In a Middle East Eye article, journalist, Jonathan Cook took the smear argument up a notch by arguing: 'Mounting evidence in both the UK and the US suggests that the Israeli government is taking a significant, if covert, role in coordinating and directing such efforts to sully the reputation of prominent critics.'[75]

These accusations went far and wide and in December 2019, Leo Panitch, a contributor to the Star, Canada's largest online news site wrote: 'Indeed, there is no way that the anti-Semitic charge can be made any sense of except as a means of deflecting Corbyn's support of Palestinian rights against actions by Israeli governments.'[76]

This specific accusation is an example of David Hirsh's 'Livingstone Formulation', named after Ken Livingstone, the former Mayor of London who ultimately left the Labour Party under allegations of antisemitism. In his book, *Contemporary Left Antisemitism,* Hirsh describes it as 'a means of refusing to engage with an accusation of antisemitism; instead it reflects back an indignant counteraccusation, that the accuser is taking part in a conspiracy to silence political speech.'[77] As a British Jew, seeing my people presented in this way was shocking and terrifying. It is little wonder that almost

50% of British Jews stated they would consider leaving the country had Corbyn been elected.[78]

On 10 July 2019, the Labour party was the subject of a documentary by BBC's *Panorama* programme that argued it had become institutionally antisemitic. In May 2019, the independent Equality and Human Rights Commission launched an investigation into accusations that Labour had become institutionally antisemitic. It is worth noting that the only other full investigation carried out by the EHRC into a political party was the far-right British National Party. Under Corbyn's leadership, Labour lost the 2019 British general election and in April 2020, Corbyn was replaced as leader by Sir Keir Starmer.

On 29 October 2020, the EHRC released the findings of its investigation into antisemitism in the Labour Party. It found that there were 'serious failings in leadership and an inadequate process for handling antisemitism complaints across the Labour Party, and … have identified multiple failures in the systems it uses to resolve them' and 'concluded that there were unlawful acts of harassment and discrimination for which the Labour Party is responsible'.[79] Caroline Waters, Interim Chair of the EHRC stated that this was: 'inexcusable and appeared to be a result of a lack of willingness to tackle antisemitism rather than an inability to do so.'[80]

The EHRC also specifically included that 'suggesting that complaints of antisemitism are fake or smears'[81] were examples of antisemitic conduct that amounted to 'unlawful harassment'.

In a Facebook statement made in response to the EHRC report, Jeremy Corbyn himself reiterated the idea of a smear campaign against him, stating: 'One antisemite is one too many, but the scale of the problem was also dramatically overstated for political reasons by our opponents inside and outside the party, as well as by much of the media.'[82]

Not long after posting this statement, Jeremy Corbyn was suspended from the Labour Party. However, less than three weeks later, he was reinstated. At the time of writing it remains to be seen how Sir Keir Starmer will continue to deal with Jeremy Corbyn and the Labour antisemitism crisis.

THE RACIAL LIBEL

Despite becoming particularly prominent as part of a 19th-century pseudoscientific movement that attempted to use science to define Jews as a distinct and inferior race, the Jewish people have been demonised through anti-Jewish racism for hundreds of years. As it did historically, it continues to have a tangible and real impact on individual Jewish people and our self-esteem. This – as well as its continued prevalence – justifies its inclusion in these categorisations of antisemitism. Simply put: it is rooted in judgements regarding Jewish ancestry and/or our physical appearance.

A prominent example of the demonisation of Jewish ancestry was following the period of forced conversions of Jews in Spain. During this time the idea of *limpieza de sangre,* meaning 'purity of blood', emerged as a term applied to the 'old Christians', while the 'new Christians' (that is, Jews and other groups) were still discriminated against as being impure, regardless of their conversion.

While many of us believe that the Spanish and Portuguese crimes against the Jews were a form of purely religious antisemitism, the notion of *limpieza de sangre* indicates quite clearly that this was not the sole factor at play. This specific experience has *both* religious and racial elements to it. Moreover, the expulsions of the Jews from Spain and Portugal actually took place *after* Jews were forced to convert; in short, we can see that Jews could not simply convert out of being Jewish.

While this depiction of Jews has been a constant for a thousand years, it gained a new lease of life in the 19th century with the rise of pseudoscience and social Darwinism. They attempted to 'prove' that the supposed behaviour of Jews was actually defined through Jewish biology and was thus unchangeable. As we know, the racial libel became an integral part of the Nazis' persecution of the Jews, forming the basis of their antisemitic ideology and policies. Among its other antisemitic measures, the 1935 Nuremberg Laws, legally defined Jews as a race, stripped them of their German citizenship and criminalised *Rassenschande* or 'racial pollution' (i.e. sexual relations between Jews and Aryans). It's important to note that fears over 'race-mixing' are still a common feature of white supremacist antisemitism today.

Following the defeat of the Nazis and the discovery of their crimes, the 'scientific' notion of denigrating Jewish people based on their genetics went out of fashion. Although, they still persist to a certain extent, for example, antizionist Khazar theorists revise history by falsely claiming Ashkenazi Jewish people are all descendants of Khazar converts – a multi-ethnic amalgam of mostly Turkic, semi-nomadic peoples – and are therefore not indigenous to the land of Israel.

Though the Nazi propaganda depiction of Jews is well known, 'Jewish bodies' have been specifically targeted by antisemites since at least the 13th century. Prior to this, depictions of Jews focused on their garb, such as their pointed hats or specific badges that they were forced to wear to mark them as Jewish, or their beards. However, by the 13th century, according to Sara Lipton, an academic author, 'a move toward realism in art and an increased interest in physiognomy spurred artists to devise visual signs of ethnicity.'[83] Thus, the antisemitic depiction of the Jewish nose was born.

These often hideous characterisations portray Jewish bodies, but, more importantly, they represented the physical embodiment of what it meant to stray from Jesus' path. It was an ugly, corrupt and evil life, and, as such, so were Jewish people.

Anti-Jewish racism that targeted Jews and their bodies has long been used to shame and 'other' us. In the 16th century, Francisco de Quevedo, a well-known Spanish poet, wrote *A un hombre de gran nariz* ('To a man with a big nose') about his rival, Luis de Góngora. Quevedo accused Góngora of being a *converso*. The poem is 14 lines long and each line is dedicated to describing Góngora's nose. A translation of the first four lines reads:

> *Once there was a man to his snout attached*
> *Owner of the most unparalleled nose*
> *He was a lively, very lengthy hose;*
> *He was a swordfish dreadfully moustached.*[84]

Though they purported to not be antisemitic, Soviet and Arabic antizionist propaganda also utilised the historical antisemitic racial libel in their depictions of Zionists[85]. Current examples also abound. In 2019, for instance, a Belgian columnist, Dimitri Verhulst, wrote that 'Jews have ugly noses'.[86] We have seen depictions of hooked-nose Jews in far-right antisemitic propaganda that accuses Jews of spreading Covid-19.[87]

While the racial libel may not be as common in the mainstream as the other three categorisations of antisemitism, it still exists to such an extent that it warrants a place in our conversations on categorising antisemitism, particularly as, out of the four, it perhaps has the most tangible impact on the self-esteem of individual Jewish people.

Depictions of Jewish bodies reference not only our appearance but our character as well, making the racial libel a physical manifestation of the other forms of Jew-hatred. Images of Jews are often deformed and hideous, because we, at our very core, are supposedly deformed and hideous. No wonder nose-jobs were once considered – although thankfully less so now – a 'rite of passage' for Jewish teens.[88]

We must not let antisemitism force us to redefine our understanding and perceptions of ourselves. The existence of shared Jewish ancestry does not in any way justify the discrimination against us based on these ideas, nor do they solely define Jewishness. These truths have been exaggerated and warped in order to demonise us and harm us. The abuse, exaggeration and vilification of our physical appearance has long been a part of the shaming of Jews and still impacts our community, often in tandem with other forms of antisemitism. Once we understand the history, roots and modern manifestations of how Jews are depicted, we can reject this specific form of antisemitism and guard against the harm it does us.

PUNCHING UP

As throughout history, modern antisemitism emanates from a variety of sources, including both the right and left of the political spectrum, other minority communities, and Muslim and Arab societies. There is much discussion over which form of antisemitism poses the most serious threat to Jews, but these are reductive conversations that ultimately depend on context.

In different places and times, different forms of antisemitism pose different threats. What is certain, and proven historically time and again, is that all forms of antisemitism endanger the lives of Jews. Despite there being differences to each specific manifestation, they all share the same roots: the economic libel, blood libel and conspiracy fantasy. These libels and fantasies all frame Jews as a perverse, inhumane, supranational, evil group who are often wealthy and powerful, and who maliciously and immorally manipulate and exploit the non-Jewish world. The racial libel is these tropes come to life in the physical depictions of Jewish people.

One crucial aspect of the Jewish experience today is that these specific framings of Jews as an all-powerful group make it difficult for some, particularly on the left, to recognise and address antisemitism. Because they perceive Jews to be powerful and privileged, it also shaped the manner those on the left express their own antisemitism. In other words, antisemitism 'punches up' – Jews are hated for their perceived power.

The difficulty that some people have when recognising anti-semitism as a 'legitimate' form of prejudice and racism stems from the fact that they misunderstand the concept of prejudice itself. There is a view of racism that suggests it is prejudice plus power, which implies that only those in positions of power over others can be racist.

This definition leads to the notion that most forms of racism and prejudice are 'punching down' and that only marginalised groups with less or no power are being oppressed. While this experience is true for certain communities, this specific definition of racism, combined with exaggerated antisemitic perceptions of Jewish power and privilege, can be particularly dangerous for Jews. It thus leads to the erasure of the Jewish experience and of antisemitism as a legitimate form of preju-dice. It can also allow those on the left – and some marginalised groups – to actively target us as representatives of elite power structures.

The view of Jews as powerful is not rooted in Jewish reality. However, that does not stop these irrational ideas persisting. Linda Sarsour, a US activist and former co-chair of the Women's March, has, for instance, suggested: 'I want to make the distinction that while anti-Semitism is something that impacts Jewish Americans, it's differ-ent than anti-Black racism or Islamophobia because it's not systemic.'[89]

In essence, Sarsour is saying that antisemitism is not as bad as anti-Black racism or Islamophobia. She is supporting the notion of a hier-archy of oppression that deliberately excludes Jewish people. Not only is her premise simply untrue – antisemitism absolutely *is* systemic – it is enormously dangerous. It imperils Jews by falsely labelling them as a privileged group not at risk of prejudice and drives a wedge between different minorities, destroying the space for us all to understand the differences and similarities between prejudices. The idea that any one form of prejudice is 'worse' than others simply because it is different must be firmly rejected.

This concept was also exemplified by Melissa Harris-Perry, an American political commentator, when commenting on allegations of Louis Farrakhan's antisemitism. In his 1991 book, *The Secret Relationship Between Blacks and Jews*, the leader of the Nation of Islam, accused Jews of financing the slave trade, which is wholly inaccurate and revisionist. And, after decades of antisemitic rhetoric [90], in a 2018 tweet he referred to Jews as 'termites'.[91]

On this Melissa Harris-Perry says: 'The thing I'm always worried about in the world is power, and how power is wielded in ways that cause inequity ... So if you can show me that Minister Farrakhan has taken his position and used his position to create inequity and inequality for Jewish people, then I will denounce that tomorrow.'[92] However, the reality is that Farrakhan himself has between 20,000-50,000 registered Nation of Islam followers in the US alone. Add to this, celebrities with millions of international followers who have shared his work and Farrakhan's messages hold power and reach.[93] Farrakhan, through his words and his platform, reinforces the foundations of antisemitism that make up the ideological structures of the non-Jewish world. In other words, he is further embedding antisemitism in our society as an institutional form of hatred.

Therefore, to understand antisemitism, and the concept of prejudice more widely, we must begin to understand the specificity of each experience, while recognising that prejudice and racism can manifest itself in a variety of ways, each as dangerous as the next. Antisemitism *is* institutional and it *is* as harmful as other forms of prejudice. Moreover, the reason that some deny this to be the case is an expression of antisemitism in and of itself.

CONTRADICTION

In his 1945 essay on antisemitism in Britain, the author George Orwell wrote: 'What vitiates nearly all that is written about antisemitism is the assumption in the writer's mind that he himself is immune to it. "Since I know that antisemitism is irrational," he argues, "it follows that I do not share it." He thus fails to start his investigation in the one place where he could get hold of some reliable evidence – that is, in his own mind'.[94]

This is something those of us who try to fight antisemitism must recognise. Antisemitism is irrational. Although the notion that a tiny ethno-religious minority can control the world is clearly absurd, this has never caused the antisemite to question their own contradictory beliefs. In fact, they often embrace contradiction as an important part of their worldview.

The Nazis produced enormous quantities of contradictory anti-semitic propaganda. In 1940, for instance, they produced two films *Der Ewige Jude (The Eternal Jew)* and *Jud Süß (The Jew Suss)* that depicted Jews in totally opposite ways: the former portrayed Jews as filthy rodents living in abject poverty, while the latter portrayed a fictional account of the life of the Court Jew, Joseph Süß Oppen-heimer. Through the suspension of their own rationality and logic, the Nazis did not see any problem in the inherent contradiction that Jews are all bad things to all people. It is this suspension that is inte-gral in the 'success' of antisemitism.

Yet these contradictions do not merely apply to the Nazis. In 2019, before Tel Aviv hosted the Eurovision song contest, Salma Yaqoob – who unsuccessfully attempted to become the Labour candidate for the West Midlands mayoralty – spoke at a pro-Palestinian rally. She first stated that Israel is not European and therefore should not be allowed to host Eurovision, before claiming, at the very same time, that Israelis are 'European colonisers'.[95] No one in the crowd, noted how incredibly contradictory this statement was.

You will hopefully have seen a pattern emerging. Regardless of their reality, Jews are depicted as being super-evil, perverse, unnatu-ral and all-powerful. Antisemitism has existed in various places and times; and despite its essence remaining constant, it is always able to fit the zeitgeist, making it relevant to each specific period of time.

Antisemitism is irrational *and* institutional. It is simply not possible for it to have survived and thrived for thousands of years if it were not. It is so embedded in our social structures and norms, that the libels and fantasies survive long after those who first promoted them have died out. It lives on in the perception that Jews are obsessed with money, the demonisation of Israel, the accusation that Jews can smear their so-called political opponents and the shaming of Jewish shared ancestry and physical appearance.

Without understanding these historical roots and patterns, each example of antisemitism may be seen as an isolated incident not necessarily connected to those that came before or after it. Understanding the threads that connect all examples of antisemitism, both past and present, is vital to recognising anti-Jewish racism when confronted with it today. All of this then begs the question I am constantly asked by my students: 'How did antisemitism become so deeply ingrained in so many societies?'

Chapter 2

THE EMBEDDING OF JEW-HATRED
IN THE NON-JEWISH WORLD

WHILE THIS BOOK is not about fighting Jew-hatred, this chapter seeks to explain why it has continued to poison the non-Jewish world against the Jews.

Whenever I begin teaching a new class on the Holocaust, I spend the introduction covering the history of antisemitism. Just as we have done in this book, we begin by exploring the categorisations of antisemitism and seeing how they have been manifested throughout history. This helps my students understand the roots of Nazi antisemitism, but it also brings up confusion in the process.

My students always find themselves asking many questions as they try to understand the roots of anti-Jewish racism, but there is one question I am asked consistently every time: 'Why has it lasted for so long?'

To them, it seems inexplicable that Jew-hatred can still be an issue thousands of years after it first originated, especially when the world has gone through so many fundamental changes.

They ask: 'How can our modern societies bear any similarities to the Romans, the early Christians, or even the Nazis?' As with all things, there is an explanation for this and it lies in understanding how a hatred of Jews became embedded in non-Jewish worlds. This, of course, is not to explain away the Holocaust; it was an unimaginable crime against the Jewish people. Rather, it is to say that without the preceding 2,000 years of Jew-hatred, the Holocaust could never have happened.

As already suggested, the most important concept to grasp when exploring the pervasiveness of antisemitism, is that it is *not* a Jewish problem. It is a non-Jewish problem, which impacts Jewish people. So, to understand its endurance, we do not need to explore the Jewish world, instead, we need to explore the non-Jewish world.

Many brilliant theories have been proposed that offer an explanation as to the nature of Jew-hatred and why it has endured for so long. I will offer my own ideas based on accounts from American historian David Nirenberg's *Anti-Judaism: The Western Tradition*. Nirenberg's work offers an important answer to the central question of why a hatred of Jews has persisted for so long.

DAVID NIRENBERG'S *ANTI-JUDAISM: THE WESTERN TRADITION*

Anti-Judaism, Nirenberg argues, is one of the building blocks of our societies and, at its root, is an ideology, or thought process, that uses ideas of Judaism – and, ultimately, Jews – to make sense of the world and to define non-Jewish identity.

Nirenberg's work focuses principally on a worldview that positions itself against Judaism as an ideology (as opposed to specifically Jewish individuals), which is why he used the phrase, 'anti-Judaism'. However, it is imperative to note that anti-Judaism always results in actual Jewish people being persecuted. As we explored in Chapter 1, antisemitism is based on a fantastical perception of the Jew. Similarly, anti-Judaism is based on the non-Jewish world's version of Judaism which assigns it a meaning based on its own perspective and worldview. Nirenberg argues that this anti-Judaism played a specific role in the foundation of Christian, Muslim and, subsequently, secular ideologies. As Nirenberg suggests, when considering the Jews, the non-Jewish world is simply trying to 'make sense of … their world'.[96]

He argued that anti-Judaism lies deep in the foundations of Christianity and, as such, the foundations of Christian hegemonic western society. In the first centuries of the new millennium, to explain and promote the separation of Christianity from Judaism – and to suggest why the Torah, renamed the Old Testament by Christians, was not discarded – early Christians had to defend why they were no longer Jewish. Paul, one of the early Christians, was instrumental in this parting of the ways and defined Christianity specifically against his perspective of Jewish ideas and values.

According to Paul, if the Jews were seen as old, the Christians were new. If the Jews were physical, the Christians were spiritual. Paul argued against Christians following Jewish practices – as they had done up to this point – and called for a complete separation of Christianity from Judaism. While his own upbringing was that of a Jew, he based Christian practices, in part, on the opposite of what the Jews were doing, to demonstrate that Christianity was the true path to God.

For example, in his Letter to the Galatians, Paul opposed circumcision for gentile Christians (as opposed to Jewish-Christians) as it was a 'physical', not 'spiritual' act. While Paul was certainly defining Christianity and Christian identity, he was not specifically arguing against Jewishness and Jews. However, his writings certainly were interpreted in this way. This concept of describing Christianity against the ideas of Judaism, and therefore Jews, became embedded in Christian culture and eventually became known as *Adversus Judaeos*. This was popularised by John Chrysostom, the archbishop of Constantinople, in the 4th century CE. In his sermons, John denounced both Jews and Judaising Christians (Christians who believed that, to be close to Jesus, one had to observe Jewish practices). In the minds of these Christians, Jews and Jewish action were framed as the antithesis of Christianity.

Included in John's *Adversus Judaeos* was the accusation that the Jews killed Jesus, which we explored during our study of the blood libel. Christianity is the building block of our societies in the west;

embedded in the foundations of Christianity was anti-Judaism, which later evolved to become antisemitism.

As previously suggested, anti-Judaism is not just about the persecution of individual Jews: it is centred on what Judaism and, as such, the Jews represent to non-Jewish culture. This idea is also evident in the 5th century when the theologian Augustine of Hippo outlined the purpose the Jew has for Christians. Describing them as unable to see the true theological path of Jesus Christ, he argued that the Jews, in their blindness, serve a specific role for Christians. They represent, Augustine suggested, what can happen when you do not follow Jesus: you remain blind. He claimed that Jews thus had to be preserved as 'fossils of antiquity'.[97]

Despite this patronising and insulting assignment, some see Augustine as being benign towards the Jews, but this is only because others have been much more violent in their views and actions against Jewish people.

Augustine's own thinking was clear in his words: 'Slay them not, lest my people forget. Scatter them by my might and bring them down.'[98] His argument was that Jews could not be slaughtered simply because they served as a looming reminder to Christians of what would happen if they strayed from the true path. But they could be 'scattered'. It is clear that, to Augustine, the main reason for the existence of Jews is to serve non-Jews – specifically Christians – in understanding their Christian purpose. Hence, they are once more defined using Judaism and the Jews.

Nirenberg's argument is not merely that Judaism, and, by extension, Jews, played a role in the establishment and definition of Christianity, but that they have continued to serve such a related purpose since the time of Augustine.

At this point in my lessons, students will often ask: 'Europe is no longer as Christian as it was, so why has this Christian antisemitism lingered long after the power of the Church declined?'

This is a crucial question. The answer lies in what I call 'cultural Christianity'. Some modern secular European societies, such as the French, have attempted to position themselves specifically against Christianity and adjacent to modernity and secularism. However, some Christian worldviews, such as anti-Judaism, are so deeply embedded that even secularised or those opposed to Christianity can still be governed by their ideologies. Even in the period following the Enlightenment, the culturally Christian majority in the west believed, in Nirenberg's words, that their 'critical tasks [were] ... to be the identification and overcoming of the threat of Judaism from within their ranks'.[99] To them, Judaism and the Jews represented their enemy, their opposite.

Christian institutions were historically so important that they shaped the culture of the countries they dominated. So much so that Christian ideologies persisted long after the power of the Church declined. Ultimately, as Nirenberg argues, 'anti-Judaism should not be understood as some archaic or irrational closet in the vast edifices of Western thought. It was rather one of the basic tools with which that edifice was constructed.'[100]

Nirenberg's work charts the progression of the concept's history, eventually moving on to Karl Marx. In *On the Jewish Question*, Marx argued that Jews and Jewishness represent capitalism so if a non-Jew is capitalist, then they become Jewish. Marx's ideas of Jews were rooted in the economic libel and were not entirely different from Paul's claim 1,900 years previously that they represented the material world. Marx's argument that 'money is the jealous God of Israel',[101] is also similar to the Nazis' belief that 'money is the God of the Jews'.[102]

Once again, this concept of Jewified non-Jews rears its head, recalling Chrysostom's preaching against Judaising Christians. As Marx wrote in 1843: 'The Jew has emancipated himself in a Jewish manner, not only because he has acquired financial power, but also because, through him and also apart from him, money has become a world power and the practical Jewish spirit has become the practical spirit of the Christian nations. The Jews have emancipated themselves insofar as the Christians have become Jews.'[103]

The Marxist concept of Jewishness was, therefore, bigger than individual Jews: it represented capitalism and, ultimately, the oppression of the workers. Marx's Jews served the purpose, like Paul's Jews and Augustine's Jews, of reminding the non-Jewish world of what they should *not* be. To destroy capitalism, you had to destroy Judaism – not because you hated individual Jews, but because of what they represented. Marx thus aimed to ensure 'the emancipation of mankind from Judaism'.[104] These quotes also incidentally demonstrate that a prejudice towards Jews played a foundational role in the creation of Marxism and more widely, Marxist aspects of socialism.

Marx's point was driven home by Ulrike Marie Meinhof, who co-founded the Red Army Faction in 1970, when she argued: 'Auschwitz meant that six million Jews were killed, and thrown on the waste-heap of Europe, for what they were considered: Money-Jews. Finance capital and the banks, the hardcore of the system of imperialism and capitalism, had turned the hatred of men against money and exploitation, and against the Jews ... Antisemitism is really a hatred of capitalism.'[105]

As Nirenberg demonstrates, history is littered with examples of the non-Jewish world defining itself against their idea of Jews and Jewishness long after the power of the Church declined. This has not ceased; as Nirenberg suggests, the western world was able to 'generate so much Judaism out of their own entrails that by the 20th century any domain of human activity could be thought of and criticised in terms of Judaism.'[106]

PROGRESSIVES AND ANTIZIONISM

Fast forward to today and we continue to see the non-Jewish world use Jewish concepts to define and reinforce its identity. An example of this is the manner in which those on the left use antizionism to define themselves as 'progressive'.

The Zionism these progressives declare themselves against follows the same antisemitic rhetoric of the Soviet Union which attacked it as racism, colonialism, white supremacy and even Nazism. To obtain membership to this mythical progressive community of the good, you simply have to reject this fantasy version of Zionism.

Later in this book, we will cover reclaiming the concept of Zionism from non-Jewish people. However, it is important to recognise that just as the antisemitic version of the Jew has no bearing on reality, nor does the antisemitic perception of Zionism or even Israel. These versions exist only in the minds of antizionists as a conspiracy fantasy. Through the suspension of rationale, they are able to ignore the fact that Zionism should actually be a progressive ideal. Zionism simply aims to return a deeply oppressed people to their indigenous homeland, which they were expelled from by several invaders through a process of ethnic cleansing and genocide. Moreover, that expulsion led to millennia of persecution, oppression and genocide as Jews have been forced to live in antisemitic societies ever since. Enduring Jew-hatred has allowed these societies to appropriate Zionism and define it through their own warped worldview, just as they did previously with other ideas of Jews and Judaism.

In a 2019 article from Johns Hopkins' newsletter, Rudy Malcolm, a student at the university, recalled an event he saw being advertised titled 'You can't be Radical without being anti-Zionist'[107] facilitated by the Students for Justice in Palestine (SJP). The assertion that one cannot be left-wing or a 'radical' without being antizionist is obviously deeply antisemitic, but it's actually more sinister than that. Here, we have a modern manifestation of David Nirenberg's arguments on the role that Jewish concepts serve in the non-Jewish world. Modern radicals are using a fundamental and integral Jewish concept, Zionism, to define their own identities as progressives.

It may seem extreme to suggest the non-Jewish world uses Jews in this way, but the proof is in the pudding. During a demonstration for Gaza during the 2014 war between Israel and Hamas, the International Jewish Anti-Zionist Network, displayed a banner which encapsulates this entire concept. It read: 'You're not anti-racist if you're not anti-Zionist'.[108] Again, this is Nirenberg's theory played out in a contemporary context, and, as they say, a picture's worth a thousand words.

The appropriation of Jewish ideas by the antisemitic non-Jewish world has real implications for Jewish people, as it has done historically. In terms of this specific issue, Jews today are forced to choose between their Zionism and progressiveness. As I have already suggested, I am uncomfortable in progressive spaces because of this very trend. Furthermore, it opens Jewish Zionists in the Diaspora and Jews in Israel to being singled out, targeted and labelled as representing today's evil: white supremacy, colonialism and racism. Nirenberg's belief that, historically, 'to the extent that Jews refused to surrender their ancestors, their lineage, and their scripture, they could become emblematic of the particular, of stubborn adherence to the conditions of the flesh, enemies of the spirit, and of God'[109] has a distinct echo in our own times. Jews today who refuse to denounce Zionism become an enemy of morality and progress.

It is fascinating, and terrible, to see this modern manifestation of a historical idea play out on social media. It explains why we see so many people online proudly stating that they are antizionist as a kind of badge signalling their membership of the progressive community of the good. Zionism acts as a form of signal for the non-Jewish progressive world, helping it define its so-called morality, just as Jewish concepts have done for thousands of years.

ANTISEMITISM: UNIFYING THE LEFT AND RIGHT

The Dutch philosopher Desiderius Erasmus is believed to have said in relation to his disagreements with Martin Luther during the

Reformation: 'If hatred of Jews makes the Christian, then we are all plenty Christian.'[110] Historically, as David Nirenberg describes, a hatred of Jews and Jewish ideas can unite even the most violent of enemies – and today is no exception.

Many people perceive the political spectrum to be linear: at one end the far left and at the other, the far right, with the 'centre' in the middle. However, there is a different way of looking at the political spectrum: the 'horseshoe theory'. This supposes that the political spectrum is not linear, but rather shaped like a horseshoe, with the extremes of both political perspectives almost touching. As the British broadcaster Maajid Nawaaz argues: 'If you go far-Left enough you end up at the far-Right and vice versa'[111] The mingling of the far left and right has been evident at different points in modern history. For example, before founding their respective fascist movements both Benito Mussolini and Oswald Mosley, the leader of the British Union of Fascists, were initially involved in socialist politics. Mussolini was a member of the national directorate of the Italian socialists and Mosley was a member of a Labour government.

ANTISEMITISM: THE LINK CONNECTING THE HORSESHOE

In September 1939, the Nazis invaded Poland, thus starting the second world war. What some people forget is that the Soviet Union also invaded Poland and the two powers divided the spoils. This carve-up was preceded by the August 1939 Molotov-Ribbentrop pact, a non-aggression agreement between Hitler and Stalin which the Nazis ultimately broke when they launched Operation Barbarossa and invaded the Soviet Union in 1941.

Unsurprisingly, it was their hatred of Jews that linked and connected these two powers. The Soviet Union never committed crimes against the Jews on the scale of the Nazis, but it did launch its own intensive antisemitic campaigns. The post-Holocaust form of antisemitism – antizionism – was created by the USSR, which based its lies on the same material the Nazis employed when spreading antisemitic propaganda: *The Protocols of the Elders of Zion*. Indeed, prior to the talks which concluded with the Molotov-Ribbentrop pact commencing, Stalin ordered a purge of Jewish ministers to demonstrate to the Nazis that he was open to communication. That the Nazis and the Soviets both utilised the *Protocols* to inspire their antisemitic campaigns indicates their shared value system when it came to the Jews. It is also true that a shared ideology of antisemitism enabled the Palestinian leadership, under Grand Mufti Amin al-Husseini to first ally itself with the Nazis during the 1940s and the Holocaust,[112] and then, after the creation of the State of Israel, the PLO benefited from a great deal of military support from the USSR.[113]

Today, we are once again witnessing antisemitism being used to bridge the political divide. Members of both the far right and far left demonise Israel – indulging in antisemitic conspiracy theories, including Holocaust denial or inversion – and sit together while they do so.

In October 2019, an event was held in Soho, London, organised by the group Keep Talking. Attendees at some of its previous meetings have been described as 'neo-Nazis'[114] by *The Jewish Chronicle*. The October 2019 event was attended by Keep Talking's co-founder, Ian Fantom, a 9/11 truther who supported the idea of a smear against Jeremy Corbyn and wrote on the *UNZ Review*, a far-right media platform: 'The problem is that Zionism is endemically anti-Socialist and that in order to combat Socialism in the Labour Party, the present-day Zionists are doing just what the doctor prescribed.'[115]

Also present at the event was Alison Chabloz, a convicted Holocaust denier described by the judge at her trial as, 'manifestly antisemitic and obsessed with what she perceives to be the wrongdoing of Jews'.[116] One of the event speakers was Miko Peled, an Israeli antizionist whose statements on Twitter, such as that the 'IDF lusts for blood',[117] are rooted in the blood libel. David Collier, an independent researcher and investigator into antisemitism, described the Keep Talking event as 'a marriage between people who would consider themselves of the far-Right and forces that would consider themselves at the far Left.'[118]

In March 2018, Collier published a 290-page report on antisemitism he discovered inside a secret Facebook Group called Palestine Live. Incidentally, Jeremy Corbyn had been a prominent and active member of this secret group for two years.[119] In his report, Collier revealed that when considering antizionist rhetoric, the far-left and far-right are indistinguishable.[120] The secret group was founded by Elleanne Green, a member of the Jewish Voice for Labour, which we will explore in more detail in Chapter 4. And within days of it being set up a copy of *The Protocols of the Elders of Zion* was shared. Despite the number of prominent Labour members (such as Corbyn), posts by far-right white supremacist groups such as Renegade Tribune were also shared.[121]

It's also worth noting that Jeremy Corbyn, former leader of the UK's Labour Party who has been accused of left-wing antisemitism has been supported by Nick Griffin, former head of the British National Party, and a self-confessed, 'lifelong white rights fighter'.[122] David Irving, the infamous Holocaust denier who sued Deborah Lipstadt has also publicly praised Corbyn. Irving has stated that Corbyn was a 'fine man' and 'impressive'.[123] In 2015, David Duke, a former Klu Klux Klan Grand Wizard praised Corbyn's election as leader by stating: 'It's a really good kind of evolutionary thing, isn't it, when people are beginning to recognise Zionist power and ultimately the Jewish establishment power in Britain and in the western world'.[124] On this, Deborah Lipstadt, professor of Jewish history and Holocaust studies at Emory University, wrote: 'David Irving (and former KKK Leader, David Duke) both are impressed with Jeremy Corbyn. Need I say more?'[125]

Often, the union of the far-left and far-right seems to focus on their shared disdain for Israel. In June 2019, Avi Mayer, the global communications director of the American Jewish Committee, tweeted: 'May 25, Dayton: Far-Left activists set fire to an Israeli flag during a KKK rally'[126] and on 'June 8, Detroit: Neo-Nazis urinate on an Israeli flag at Detroit Pride.'[127] You can imagine how devastating it was for proud LGBTQ+ Jews that at a pride celebration the Israeli flag would be desecrated in this way.

In the 2019 European parliamentary elections, Die Rechte, a German neo-Nazi party, campaigned under the slogan: 'Israel is our misfortune.'[128] 'Posters with the "Israel is our misfortune" slogan in bold print, framed by calls in smaller print to "Stop Zionism" and to "Put an end to it!" were proudly displayed wherever the party campaigned in the EU elections,'[129] *Haaretz* reported. Of course, this slogan was simply a modernised, Israel-focused version of an older one, popularised by the Nazi propaganda newspaper, *Der Sturmer*: *'Die Juden sind unser Unglück!'* ('The Jews are our misfortune!').[130]

A DEVIATION FROM TRADITION

Another way the modern non-Jewish world continues to use Jewish concepts to define its identity is through the appropriation of Jewish victimhood. However, in this case, we see an important deviation from tradition. Although still using Jewish ideas to describe its sense of the world, the non-Jewish world also now uses the Jews to define what it *is,* not just what it is *not.*

Through constant attempts to draw comparisons with either the Nazis or Hitler, the non-Jewish world uses this Jewish tragedy to define its own victimhood, or a more general concept of victimhood. Not only does this yet again use Jews to define non-Jewish identity, but it is a continuing and painful reminder to Jewish people of our attempted destruction, while simultaneously erasing the uniqueness of the Shoah and our experience.

In defence, some might argue: 'Well, they are comparing things to Hitler or the Nazis, they're not saying they are the Jews'. Others take it even further by suggesting that 'Jews were not the only victims of the Nazis.' While groups other than Jews were indeed targeted by the Nazis, Hitler left no doubt about his principal enemy and who he believed to be responsible for Germany's alleged failings: the Jews. The attack on the Jews was central, strategic and specific. Nazi policies sharply and openly targeted Jews and most of the other groups were secondary. Jews made up the majority of the Nazis' victims and saw the greatest destruction of their people and civilisations. Therefore, any identification of something as either Hitler or the Nazis automatically casts its victims as the 'Jews'.

In other words, if it is claimed that something or someone is 'just like the Nazis', it is clearly being stated that the group being targeted or harmed are the 'Jews of this context'. This is an almost always inappropriate comparison: most situations are not, in fact, comparable to the systematic and industrialised extermination of 6 million of the world's then 16 million Jewish population. There are universal lessons that our societies can learn from the crimes of the Nazis, but these need to be discussed with huge amounts of care and thought so as not to use the memory of dead, murdered Jews to score modern political points.

I experienced this specific phenomenon while living in Hong Kong during the 2019-2020 protests against its authorities (and, by extension, the Chinese government). As the protests continued for months, I noticed a very troubling trend emerging. Due to the lack of a cultural context regarding antisemitism, it was never a major issue in Hong Kong, which is why what I witnessed took me so much by surprise.

The Hong Kong protesters began describing the Chinese as 'ChiNazis' and spray-painting the slogan, which also regularly trended on Twitter, on street corners and on lampposts. The protesters also began depicting the Chinese flag with the yellow stars arranged in the shape of a swastika.

I found this abhorrent. The Hong Kong protestors' dispute lies with the Chinese government and that is the context in which it should remain. I have taught the Holocaust in Hong Kong and it was shocking that the demonstrators, with very little knowledge of the Shoah, deemed it appropriate to utilise Jewish victimhood to define their own victimhood. If the Chinese were the Nazis, then the protestors were the Jews. Instead of expressing the realities of their own situation, they leisurely and offensively appropriated Jewish pain and trauma to make a point about their own victimhood.

As I am writing this – on 19 April 2020 – 'ChiNazi' is once again trending on Twitter in Hong Kong, with 2,442 tweets using this hashtag. Despite the fact it has become a depressingly familiar part of Hong Kong vernacular, the context of the Hong Kong protests obviously bears no resemblance whatsoever to the Holocaust. Jews in Hong Kong spoke out against this trend online and in articles and were often shut down by supporters of the protests. The emergence of the ChiNazi slogan was a bizarre reminder of how pervasive the appropriation of Jewish victimhood is. It also helps us understand how the non-Jewish world continues to use Jewishness or issues related to Jews to make sense of its world. In this case, it did not just use Jews to define what it is not, rather it used Jewish concepts to define what it is.

Critics of this argument may point to periods in history when Jews have managed to succeed or to gain prominence. This is an important point, but one which does not ultimately support their case. For example, in 1791, Revolutionary France emancipation its Jews. You may ask: 'How is this possible in a world that defines itself against Jews and Jewishness?' But it's entirely possible for anyone – Jew or non-Jew – to want to create a better world. Remember, just as using Jewishness or Jewish concepts is not about individual Jews, it is also not about individual non-Jews.

There are countless upstanding people who aren't Jews and aren't antisemitic but still live in a version of the world that David Nirenberg describes. This is about the conscious and unconscious structures, patterns and mentalities within our societies that are embedded in all of us. It is about a world created through an ideology that used the idea of Judaism – and, by extension, Jews – in a very specific way. An attempt to improve the world does not mean it is no longer dominated by the notions of anti-Judaism and antisemitism.

Ultimately, to understand whether these noble acts undermine this theory, the question is: did the French succeed? Did they usher in a new world order that swept away antisemitism and confined the hatred of Jews to the past? No, they clearly did not. Despite many individuals seeking to make a better world, the ideological roots of anti-Judaism have persisted throughout history and continue to this day.

How else do we explain the 1894 trial of the French Jew Alfred Dreyfus, who was framed for selling secrets to the Germans. When he was falsely found guilty of treason, people cried: 'Kill the Jew!'[131] As we will explore later, the Dreyfus Trial led to a wave of aggressive antisemitism that swept across France. Clearly, under the surface of this supposedly brave new world, where even a Jew could rise through the ranks of the French army to become a captain, antisemitism lurked. That such an event could take place in a France committed to *'Liberté, égalité, fraternité'* meant that the French Revolution was not able to sweep away the deep roots of anti-Judaism and antisemitism embedded in French society.

A more modern example is the post-Holocaust world. After 1945, antisemitism was thought by many to have been 'defeated' following the Nazis' surrender and the discovery of the horrors of the death camps. However, this is not the case.

In an article in *The New York Times Magazine*, the human rights activist Wenzel Michalski recalls growing up in Germany in the 1970s and being told by his father: 'Don't tell anyone that you're Jewish.'[132] Clearly, for a variety of reasons, some believed it was not safe or comfortable to be openly Jewish in Germany, barely three decades after the end of the war and discovery of the Holocaust.

Seventy-five years after the Shoah, we are once again facing the resurgence of antisemitism in Germany. Huge attempts by successive

German governments to eradicate antisemitism have ultimately failed. In a 2016 interview, Deborah Feldman, whose memoir inspired the Netflix series *Unorthodox*, expressed the view that 'Berlin ... is the last bastion against oppression'. But, in an echo of the advice of Michalski's father, she also admitted that she still would not tell people she was Jewish. Feldman says instead that she's from New York. She explains this by saying: 'I still live in Germany.'[133]

Similarly, Felix Kelin, the non-Jewish leader of Germany's first-ever state plan to combat antisemitism, stated in May 2019: 'I cannot advise Jews to wear the kippah everywhere all the time in Germany,'[134] Just five months after those remarks, there was an attack at a synagogue in Halle during Yom Kippur.

Germany's evident failure to combat antisemitism – despite its good intentions – most likely stems from a lack of a true understanding of what antisemitism actually means and what purpose it and anti-Judaism serves. This is about worldviews, ideas and perspectives which use the concept of the Jews and Judaism to define themselves. This is not about individual events, no matter how enormous they are.

What this tells us is that anti-Judaism and, as such, antisemitism is deeply embedded and even major societal shifts, such as the French Revolution, or shocking events, such as the Holocaust, have not been able to break its control over the non-Jewish world. In my opinion, David Nirenberg explains the overarching reason why prejudiced ideas surrounding Jews and Judaism have existed for so long: it is one of the building blocks of western society and no country that has attempted to eradicate antisemitism has ever properly recognised nor addressed this reality.

POLITICAL FOOTBALL

Historically identifying your enemies as Judaizing or even Jewish was a common tactic to denigrate them; such as, when John Chrysostom preached against Judaizing Christians in the 4th century CE. Today, the non-Jewish world continues to use Jews in a similar way. However, as we have seen through the effort to appropriate the concept of Jewish victimhood to describe victimhood more generally, this theory must be expanded to include other ways the non-Jewish world defines itself in relation to Jews and Jewish concepts.

Another modern manifestation of this phenomenon is the manner in which Jews are used as a political football. As the Holocaust is still in living memory, antisemitism is often closely associated with the Nazis, and thus can be viewed as representative of ultimate evil. This means that one would never want to be associated with antisemitism (even if you are indeed antisemitic). Therefore, accusing a political opponent of being antisemitic automatically casts them as 'evil', while the person levelling the charge is, by extension, perceived as 'good', regardless of the truth or indeed their own antisemitism.

Harnessing the non-Jewish world's Nazi-linked version of anti-semitism to demonise a political opponent can take two shapes. In the first, each side of the political spectrum argue the other is antisemitic, while avoiding addressing their own antisemitism. In the second, members of the right, specifically, align themselves with Jews and/ or Israel as a way to position themselves against the left, which they accuse of being antisemitic. Neither of these helps Jews, but both continue to be used to define non-Jewish identities. This in itself continues to harm Jewish people.

A recent example of Jews being used as a political football took place during the 2014 revolution in the Ukraine, as Sam Sokol describes in his book, *Putin's Hybrid War and the Jews: Antisemitism, Propaganda, and the Displacement of Ukrainian Jewry.*

The revolution was a movement to overthrow corrupt politicians and move Ukraine towards the EU and out of Russia's sphere of influence. The impeachment – by a 328-to-0 vote – of the pro-Russian Ukrainian president, Viktor Yanukovych, was seen by the Kremlin as an illegal coup, and led Vladimir Putin to annex eastern Ukraine, including Crimea, in response.

To discredit the new Ukrainian leadership, Russia manipulated the fact that Ukraine has a terrible history of violent antisemitism, including collaboration with the Nazis during the second world war, and among those protesting against Russian influence were far-right groups (such as the radical-nationalist Svoboda party, which holds a handful of parliamentary seats). Against this backdrop, Russia framed all Ukrainian nationalists and protestors as 'fascists'[135] and 'neo-Nazi' and spread misinformation suggesting that Ukrainian Jews were endangered by vicious Ukrainian Nazis. Admittedly, during this period three Jews were beaten in Kiev and a synagogue was vandalised and attacked with Molotov cocktails. Russia's allegations were not helped by the fact that in a response to the conflict, to unify the Ukrainian population against the Russian invaders, memory of the 1940s war against the Soviet Union was promoted.[136] This resulted in Nazi collaborators, Stepan Bandera and Roman Shukhevych, being rehabilitated which ultimately contributed to an increase of violence for Ukraine's Jewish community. However, Russia's framing of all protestors as 'antisemitic' does not represent reality.

Additionally, despite Russia's claims that it alone could save the Jews, the reality is that its attitude towards Jews is one of total indifference. In fact, Putin seems to be more than just indifferent to Jews – reports in the *Times of Israel* in 2019 suggested that the Kremlin's push towards authoritarianism has driven thousands of Jews to leave the country for Israel.[137] Anton Shekhovtsov, a political scientist at University College London, exemplified this when he stated: 'Putin is just using anti-Semitism as a kind of tool to discredit the Euromaidan process. He doesn't care about anti-Semitism … If he had cared about anti-Semitism, he would have acted differently, because anti-Semitism in Russia and neo-Nazism in Russia is a much more significant problem than in Ukraine.'[138]

Shimon Fogel, chief executive officer of the Centre for Israel & Jewish Affairs in Ottawa, explained this situation, stating: 'I think that what we're seeing play out in Ukraine is this tactical anti-Semitism, where the Jew becomes the instrument of trying to advance the agenda ... The agenda on both sides is to discredit and undermine the credibility of their adversaries in the eyes of the international community that's looking on with a great deal of anxiety.'

This is not just a European phenomenon either, both sides of the political spectrum in the United States have also used Jews as a political football to demonise their enemy and to define themselves as 'good'. Ilhan Omar, U.S. Representative for Minnesota's 5th congressional district, has repeatedly been accused of making antisemitic comments. In 2019, she engaged in the economic libel by infamously tweeting 'it's all about the Benjamins'[139] – a slang term for the $100 note – in reference to the supposed power of the AIPAC, the pro-Israel lobbying group. Omar also supports the Boycott, Divestment, and Sanctions (BDS) movement and even introduced a pro-BDS resolution to the US Congress.

BDS encourages an international campaign to boycott Israel over its treatment of the Palestinians. Though it describes itself as a 'Palestinian-led movement for freedom, justice and equality'[140] in reality though, it advocates the destruction of the Jewish state, demonises Israel and Israelis and through its biased perspective on the Israeli Palestinian conflict, derails any chance of peace between Israel and the Palestinians.[141]

On the resolution, Omar stated: 'We are introducing a resolution ... to really speak about the American values that support and believe in our ability to exercise our first amendment rights in regard to boycotting ... And it is an opportunity for us to explain why it is we support a nonviolent movement, which is the BDS movement.'[142] However, many Jewish activists and academics argue that BDS is a form of antisemitism. In a 2016 article titled 'Why BDS is Antisemitic', David

Hirsh, states: 'BDS is a global campaign against Israel and only Israel. It seeks to foment [sic] sufficient emotional anger with Israel, and with only Israel, so that people around the world will want to punish Israel, and only Israel.'[143] In comments about the pro-BDS resolution, Omar compared boycotting Israel to boycotting the Nazis. She utilised memory of the Holocaust to encourage a boycott of the Jewish state, suggesting: 'Americans of conscience have a proud history of participating in boycotts to advocate for human rights abroad including … boycotting Nazi Germany from March 1933 to October 1941 in response to the dehumanization of the Jewish people in the lead-up to the Holocaust.'[144]

When criticised for her comments, Omar's supporters throw the political football back at the Republicans. For example, when Omar was criticised for engaging in economic libel, Jeremy Ben-Ami, the president of J Street, an organisation devoted to bringing about a peaceful end to the Israeli-Palestinian conflict, stated: 'What I see is Republicans who, for partisan purposes, are trying to drive a wedge in the Democratic Party.'[145]

In March 2019, Omar was caught up in further controversy for suggesting that Jewish Americans have dual loyalty. When apologising for her comments about AIPAC's financial power, she inexplicably questioned the 'allegiance'[146] of supporters of Israel. This is a traditional antisemitic trope that paints the Jews as more loyal to global Jewry than they are to the country they reside in. Instead of attempting to deal with her pattern of making antisemitic remarks, members of the Democratic party attempted to deflect the issue by calling out antisemitism on the right. Leah Greenberg, a political activist, tweeted: 'Don't throw the book at a Muslim woman of color while ignoring the many, many white Christian members of Congress who've trafficked in anti-Semitic tropes and tell me you're doing it to protect Jews.'[147] Following Omar's comments, the Democrats announced that they would be bringing a resolution to the floor of the House of Representatives condemning antisemitism, Symone D Sanders, a senior advisor to Joe Biden tweeted: 'Dems doing more to "confront Omar" than Donald Trump. Where is the resolution about the President?'[148]

Using Jews as a political football in this way is obviously offensive to Jewish people, but it is more sinister than that. In reality, it endangers Jews by allowing specific forms of antisemitism to go unchecked. Arguing that one side is less antisemitic or that one side's antisemitism is less dangerous than the other is helpful only to the person arguing the point. Passing the buck and denying that antisemitism comes from a variety of sources, including your own 'side', does not help protect Jewish people from anti-Jewish racism.

While it is prevalent on the left, this phenomenon also exists in the Republican party. In 2016, Trump released, 'Argument for America', his final campaign ad for his Presidential bid. In the Talking Points Memo, Josh Marshall identified that: 'the four readily identifiable American bad guys in the ad are Hillary Clinton, George Soros (Jewish financier), Janet Yellen (Jewish Fed Chair) and Lloyd Blankfein (Jewish Goldman Sachs CEO).'[149] Marshall went on to say that:

'These are standard anti-Semitic themes and storylines, using established anti-Semitic vocabulary lined up with high profile Jews as the only Americans other than Clinton who are apparently relevant to the story... [T]he Jews come up to punctuate specific key phrases. Soros: "those who control the levers of power in Washington"; Yellen "global special interests"; Blankfein "put money into the pockets of handful of large corporations."'

But Trump hasn't only deployed tropes about Soros and other well-known Jews. Like Omar, he has accused Jews of dual loyalty. The president has accused Jews who vote for the Democrats – consistently around 75-80% of the US Jewish population since 1920 – of 'great disloyalty'[150]. In September 2020, just before *Rosh Hashanah* (Jewish new year), Donald Trump told American Jewish leaders that 'we really appreciate you; we love your country also and thank you very much.'[151] Both these examples reinforce the myth of Jewish dual loyalty and, more specifically, the myth that Jewish people are always more loyal to Israel and other Jews; a clear example of an antisemitic conspiracy fantasy.

Like his opponents on the left, when Trump is accused of antisemitism, he deflects by lashing out at the Democrats. He has used Israel to demonise his political opponents, such as the Democratic congresswomen Ayanna Pressley, Alexandria Ocasio-Cortez, Ilhan Omar and Rashida Tlaib. After telling these four women of colour to 'go back'[152] to where they came from, he tweeted: 'When will the Radical Left Congresswomen apologize to our Country, the people of Israel and even to the Office of the President'.[153] Several of these congresswomen have asserted antisemitic messages, but that in no way justifies Trump's racist attack on them. Using Israel – and, by implication, Jews – to justify his racist demonisation of Pressley, Ocasio-Cortez, Omar and Tlaib is not simply wholly inappropriate and prejudiced, it also exemplifies the trend of using an accusation of antisemitism to demonise your opponents, while ignoring your own.

When Donald Trump criticises Omar, and states that she: 'says horrible things about Israel, hates Israel, hates Jews'[154] he ignores – and distracts from – his own record on antisemitism. On this, Deborah Lipstadt, professor of Jewish history and Holocaust studies at Emory University, stated: 'I was disturbed by the president's weaponization of people's indignation about anti-Semitism from some of these women to cloud the accusations of racism against him.'[155]

In a variety of ways Jews still serve the purpose that David Nirenberg describes, albeit they fit – as antisemitism always does – a specific, modern context. The non-Jewish world defines itself against ideas of Jews and Jewishness, uses these ideas to define what it is and what it is not and uses them to define its morality. Each side of the political spectrum tries to score points by using Jewish pain at Jewish expense.

When some on the right align themselves with Jews or Israel, it is not necessarily because they feel any real affinity with Jewish people or the Jewish state, but because they are attempting to use that support as a tool, usually against Muslim or Arab populations. Katie Hopkins, a far-right UK pundit, has openly expressed Islamophobic remarks. She has, for instance, called Sadiq Kahn, the mayor of London, the 'Muslim Mayor of Londonistan'.[156] Many Jewish leaders have rejected Hopkins for her bigotry and her feigned support for Jews under the guise of support for Israel. Hopkins has stated that 'it feels Israel is my kind of natural home',[157] but what is the explanation for this self-proclaimed allyship?

Sadly, it is rooted in antisemitic ideas. Israel is seen as the ultimate oppressor of Muslims. As the commentator Jonathan Freedland suggested in *The Jewish Chronicle*: 'Hopkins, too, recently spent time in Israel, seeing that country as an admirable line of resistance against what she sees as the global Muslim menace.'[158] Support from people who vilify other minorities is not the type of support the Jewish community needs or wants. What's more, such far-right support for Israel can lead to further antisemitism from the left as it reinforces the false notion that Jews and the Jewish state are a symbol of far-right politics. It drives a wedge further between Jewish people and progressive movements because this attempted alignment by the far right leads to Jews once more being expelled from the 'community of the good'.

The same argument can be made of Trump, who has coupled antisemitic remarks with an attempt to portray himself as being overtly supportive of Israel. Just as the left – including parts of the Democratic party – defines itself as progressive through its demonisation of Israel, Trump has aligned himself with Israel as a way to position himself against people on the left.

As Bill Schneider, a political analyst, argues: 'The problem is the Israel issue has become more of a partisan division in the United

States'[159]. The attempt to turn support for Israel into a political football has led to some on the right claiming to be staunch friends of the Jewish state. In truth, they will support Israel and Jews for so long as long as it benefits them. That is not allyship. Jewish people deserve a solidarity movement based on the fact that Jews, like all people, deserve, and need, to be supported while they fight antisemitism.

'THE CLOUD OF ANTISEMITISM'

A simple analogy that I find useful for explaining how a hatred of Jews became so ingrained in society is one that I created for my students called 'the cloud of antisemitism'.

For thousands of years, due to the ideological prevalence of anti-Judaism as one of the building blocks of western civilisation, the cloud of antisemitism has been drizzling antisemitism over multiple societies. It is constantly dampening people with Jew-hatred. It may just stay on the surface of the skin and clothes of some people, while others absorb it until it becomes deeply embedded in their thoughts and perspectives.

It is not always raining the same amount in all places; at different times it can rain harder than at others. Through critical thinking and a pursuit of the rational, some non-Jewish people develop an umbrella protecting them against this rain. Through education we can spread knowledge which leads to individuals opening their own umbrellas. However, this is not the case for everyone – sometimes it pours and most people get soaking wet, not realising until it's too late.

While our discussion focuses on the cloud of antisemitism, it's important to realise that there are multiple 'clouds of prejudice' raining down various hatreds, such as LGBTQ+phobia, misogyny and different forms of racism, at the same time. These showers can also be referred to as 'systems of oppression'. These showers and storms often pit minorities against each other; the only way we can create a society that does not even need umbrellas to protect us, is to work together to dissipate the clouds until they blow away entirely.

Simplifying antisemitism in this manner can help explain how the complexities of Jew-hatred have become so embedded in our society and how everyone – whether they like or recognise it or not – has been exposed to prejudiced thinking. It also demonstrates how people's subconscious bias against Jews are formed and ultimately reinforced. Without realising it, they absorb society's negative perceptions of Jews, which are then buttressed through their own confirmation bias.

This offers an explanation as to why so many people – not merely ardent antizionists, but regular people who just seem to have an instinctively negative reaction to Israel – often hold such strong opinions about the Jewish state. These people ultimately have inbuilt, implicit biases against Jews, leading them to only acknowledge negative information – whether true or not – about Israel as it provides an easy comfort zone for confirming their biases.

CLOUD DISPERSAL

This book is not about fighting antisemitism. It is an exploration of how antisemitism has impacted Jewish identity and how we as a community fight to reclaim our identity through Jewish Pride.

However, I will briefly make three points regarding fighting antisemitism which may help to encourage the opening of umbrellas and, ultimately, the dispersal of 'clouds of prejudice':

First, recognise that fighting antisemitism, or indeed any other form of prejudice is not easy work. I strongly encourage you to align yourself before you take an active stand in this fight. It can also be incredibly isolating. By the very nature of being a Diasporic minority, Jewish people can often live in isolation outside of a Jewish community. Finding a community is really important, whether online or in person. They can support you, bolster and in some ways, protect you. Don't do this work alone.

Please take care of your mental and emotional health. I speak from experience when I say that fighting hate can take a toll on you. Although antisemitism is not a Jewish problem, sharing personal testimony is an important Jewish role in supporting the non-Jewish world in their fight against antisemitism. This itself can be very draining and be aware that you are entitled to step away and repair or restore yourself at any time. You don't owe the world anything.

Second, remember, knowledge is power. Understanding the history of antisemitism is vitally important. Education is the first form of activism – but to educate others we must first educate ourselves. Antisemitism has a long and complicated history and almost every single example can be separated into either the blood libel, economic libel, conspiracy fantasy or racial libel. Understanding these categories and recognising the common threads that connect each example of antisemitism is crucial.

When trying to understand antisemitism, we cannot start at the middle or end of the story, we have to start at the beginning. That does not necessarily mean every person has to become a committed historian, but having a basic understanding of the historical roots, categorisations and manifestations of antisemitism will give us huge power when trying to understand and combat it today. For example, we cannot understand how British Jews experienced some of Jeremy Corbyn's leadership without understanding the antisemitic conspiracy fantasy. What we are experiencing today are all just modern manifestations of what came before. Having this knowledge will help us identify antisemitism, break it down, process it ourselves and clearly explain it to others. Connected to knowledge, is the specific recognition that antisemitism is an institutional form of hate. We must name our experiences and understand how they connect to the system of oppression that is antisemitism.

Third, as antisemitism is institutional most people deserve second chances. If we recognise that the cloud of antisemitism is constantly drizzling over societies, then at some point we have to accept that it is not necessarily the fault of those who have absorbed these constant

drizzles. This is why the 'cancel culture', which calls for the cancel-
ling of public figures if they are deemed to have transgressed, is so
counterproductive. Most people achieve maturity in an antisemitic
culture and have not necessarily been exposed to alternative thoughts
and ideas. When discussing with people, take time to explain your
perspective and position and ensure you have the evidence to back up
what you are saying. Some people may begin to see things from your
perspective. It is not a quick process – remember, we are dealing with
years of conditioning – but, with patience and support, these interactions can begin the process of dispersing the clouds of antisemitism.
It's also true that some people do *not* deserve second chances and
walking away from an exchange because there is no hope of educating
that person is a healthy form of self-care.

The antisemitic libels and fantasies are not rooted in rationality.
However, not everyone is inherently irrational, even if the worldview
they may have been conditioned with is irrational. With education,
they may be able to change.

It is, of course, important to acknowledge that some people cannot
be reached through rational and logical arguments. Some people's
hate is so deeply ingrained that there is almost nothing that we can do
to help them. But that is not the case for everyone. Some people have
simply grown up in an antisemitic world and have no real knowledge
of the world outside their warped and narrow perspective. Those are
the ones who we *may* be able to reach.

Although importantly, we should not ask for acceptance; we should
demand it. We should not ask to be included in the progressive world's
perception of who is and who is not 'oppressed', we should raise our
voices and tell our own stories. We should advocate for ourselves because
we matter. We should never feel guilty or be made to feel guilty for our
advocacy. Our stories deserve to be told. This fight is hard, even if we
do it with pride, but we have a responsibility to future Jews, including
all our Jewish children, to fight antisemitism strategically. In short, if we

can help a few more people open umbrellas to protect them from the constant drizzle of antisemitism then that is progress.

THE ZEITGEIST AND SHAPE-SHIFTING

As we have seen, through the dominance of the Christian Church, anti-Judaism and Jew-hatred became so embedded in western culture that even great societal shifts such as the Enlightenment or the Holocaust could not remove it. Its roots were just too deeply embedded. That it became such an integral way the non-Jewish world defined itself, and because it dominated its worldview, when people's perspectives changed, so did the way they expressed antisemitism. This reveals how antisemitism has always fit the specific context it is expressed in. Despite the clear threads binding all examples of antisemitism, to the untrained eye Christian antisemitism or Nazi antisemitism can look quite different to modern antizionist antisemitism. However, when we understand the common threads of the blood libel, economic libel, conspiracy fantasy and racial libel that bind all examples of antisemitism, we see their connections clearly. To argue modern examples of antisemitism have nothing or little to do with older forms is simply incorrect.

When a cultural shift takes place, a modern iteration of antisemitism emerges (as it did following the French Revolution, the Enlightenment and the Holocaust). Although it fits the zeitgeist, it is not exactly 'new'; it is the continuing trajectory of historical antisemitism. For example, when we argue that antizionism *is* antisemitism, we are not saying that it is a 'new' expression of Jew-hatred, it is simply antisemitism expressed in modern contexts. This is an important distinction. This focus on phraseology may seem pedantic but designating antisemitism as something 'new' implies that it has no historical roots. Recognising the historical continuum of all types of antisemitism is necessary in order to understand it properly.

All examples of antisemitism from history are connected by threads that run through them. Yes, they fit the zeitgeist, but they are in their truest essence the modern expressions of ancient and enduring libels. As the historian Professor Dina Porat of Tel Aviv University suggests, modern antisemitism is just 'a new envelope'.[160]

This new envelope is ultimately rooted in the shape-shifting nature of antisemitism. Ironically, despite the accusation that the Jews shape-shift, are sneaky, manipulative and camouflaged – all expressions of the conspiracy fantasy – it is actually antisemitism that shape-shifts to always fit the context in which it is expressed.

As the great Tunisian Jewish writer and thinker, Albert Memmi argued in his 1962 book, *Portrait of a Jew*, antisemitism is 'a living thing of multiple heads that speaks with a thousand grimacing faces'.[161] Understanding that antisemitism changes its form to fit each specific context is vital to understanding how it came to be so enduring. Each new shape is perfectly suited to serve its central purpose (defining the Jews as the ultimate 'other' and enemy) in its unique context. Shape-shifting thus simply maintains the relevance of antisemitism as a guiding ideology in many cultures.

As we saw repeatedly in the last chapter, while the categorisations persist at their root, they ultimately always represent the time period they are expressed in. For example, leftist antisemitism now tends to fixate on the State of Israel because, after approximately 2,000 years, we once again live in a world with a Jewish state. The Nazis utilised the pseudoscience of racial antisemitism because they lived in an era that focused on science. Christian antisemitism exploited the accusation that the Jews murdered Jesus because the Church was powerful during this period. Jews in the Muslim-ruled Middle East, North Africa and Iberian region were treated as inferior *dhimmis* who must be subjugated due to the power of Islam. The focus of each of these forms of antisemitism may be different but, through their slightly varying lenses, they are saying the same thing: Jews are evil, they are

monsters, they can commit inhumane acts and they are conspiring to take over the world.

TECHNOLOGY

Along with the embedding of anti-Judaism as a non-Jewish worldview, another explanation for how Jew-hatred has become so embedded in culture lies with technology. Throughout history, anti-Jewish racism – like other forms of prejudice – has always been spread and warped by advancements in technology. Of course, technology itself is perfectly neutral with regards to the Jews; rather, it is how antisemites use it as a vehicle to spread their antisemitic hate.

The invention of the Guttenberg printing press in 1439 enabled the printing and dissemination of antisemitic literature throughout the Middle Ages. In a review of David Nirenberg's writings on anti-Judaism, the historian Debra Kaplan argues: 'Luther's ideas about reform and about the Jews gained traction not only because they resonated for readers but also because he was a best-selling author whose writings were accessible in the German vernacular, both in print and in sermons.'[162]

Similarly, the invention of the rotary press in 1843 facilitated the mass publication of *The Protocols of the Elders of Zion* in 1903 in Russia. As we have seen, the *Protocols* was printed and spread all over the world in multiple languages, and embedded the idea of a Jewish conspiracy that inspired both Nazi and Soviet antisemitic propaganda. Antisemitism was thus both enabled and modernised through the use of the printing press.

The Nazis also utilised technology to spread their antisemitic bile. The radio was first invented by Guglielmo Marconi in 1890 and, over the following decades, the technology was improved. In 1933, the year Hitler came to power, his propaganda minister, Joseph Goebbels, introduced the first *Volksempfänger*, a cheap radio that, along with electrification in German villages, brought the Führer and his message into the homes of many German families. In fact, by 1941 65% of German households owned a 'people's receiver'.[163] Nazi propaganda celebrated this, with a 1936 poster declaring: 'All Germany hears the Führer with the People's Radio'.[164] Goebbels himself understood the power of this new technology, arguing: 'What the press has been in the Nineteenth Century, radio will be for the Twentieth Century.'[165]

The Nazis also made use of the cinema to spread their anti-semitism. Films such as *The Triumph of the Will* (1935), which glorified Nazism, were made alongside films such as *The Eternal Jew* (1940) and the *Jew Süß* (1940) to demonise Jews. These dehumanising images of Jews were shown in cinemas around Germany, reinforcing and disseminating antisemitic ideas to the general public.

So important was the German film industry to the Nazis that it was brought under Goebbels' direct control in 1934, making it an official arm of his propaganda ministry. In his book *The Ministry of Illusion: Nazi Cinema and Its Afterlife,* Eric Rentschler notes: 'The Cinema of the Third Reich is to be seen in the context of a totalitarian state's concerted attempt to create a culture industry in the service of mass deception. The Ministry of Propaganda endeavoured to ... remake German Film culture in the service of remaking German culture and the nation's political body.'[166]

The use of cinema to demonise and dehumanise Jews played an important role in Nazi justifications for the attempted destruction of European Jewry. Hitler's use of technology was thus a vital factor in the spread of antisemitism and eventually the murder of 6 million Jews.

Once again, as technology has progressed, so has its ability to spread antisemitism. Despite offering many amazing possibilities, the internet has become a major factor in its dissemination. I have experienced antisemitism on Twitter, such as being told the Holocaust never happened and that Jews are smearing Jeremy Corbyn. The internet has enabled people from all over the world to spread ideas and ideologies, some good and some bad. This has facilitated the cross-contamination of antisemitism from different parts of the world.

While modern European left-wing antisemitism is an amalgamation of classical antisemitism and Soviet antizionism, American left-wing antisemitism is channelled through a focus on dismantling perceived systems of 'white' oppression. US racial binaries have been superimposed on to Israel, framing it as a white colonial state and Palestinians as Black people. As we will explore later, portraying Israel in this manner is a deeply ignorant and antisemitic misreading of history. It is a base and reductive narrative, one lacking in the nuance required to describe a deeply complex situation. However, these two different manifestations of left-wing antisemitism have cross-contaminated and, thanks to the internet, are now basically indistinguishable.

The internet can also lead to the radicalisation of antisemites who are now able to find communities of like-minded people all over the world. Robert Bowers, the perpetrator of the Pittsburgh Tree of Life synagogue massacre, evolved from a conservative into a white nationalist through the internet. A major danger of the internet is that it is a vast ungovernable place where hate is disseminated freely and regularly. The Pittsburgh massacre also underlines that antisemitism that starts in online forums does not necessarily stay online. Bowers murdered 11 Jewish people because he was radicalised online and believed the antisemitic conspiracy fantasy that Jews are funding immigration and refugees and coordinating minority groups in order to replace white people.

On 9 October 2019, Stephan Balliet carried out an attack on a synagogue in Halle in Germany on the holiest Jewish holiday of Yom Kippur, which he broadcast for 17 minutes on Facebook. Like Bowers, Balliet, a far-right extremist, blamed Jews for high levels of immigration and for attempting to destroy the white race. In a 'manifesto', he published online, Balliet said that he aimed to 'Kill as many anti-Whites as possible, Jews preferred'.[167] As *Spiegel* reported two days after the shooting:

'The danger from right-wing extremists is on the rise and there are new forms of radicalization. Even the crimes themselves differ from past attacks – live streams give them the feel of a macabre reality TV show.'[168]

The internet can also be used to spread less violent forms of antisemitism. In Britain, the Community Security Trust produced a report in 2019 that detailed how the internet, and specifically Twitter, is being used to spread antisemitism. It identified, for instance, just 36 accounts that were driving conversations pushing Labour's online antisemitism. 'All 36 of the Engine Room accounts have, at some point, tweeted content arguing that allegations of antisemitism in the Labour Party are exaggerated, weaponised, invented or blown out of proportion, or that Labour and Corbyn are victims of a smear campaign relating to antisemitism,' the CST report suggested.[169]

The report also detailed how hashtags are used to spread hate messages against individual Jews such as the media personality Rachel Riley. Riley, who is interviewed in Chapter 5, was the victim of #BoycottRachelRiley for simply speaking out against antisemitism in the Labour party. In a speech in parliament, Riley stated: 'In the name of Labour I've been called a hypocrite, lying propagandist, tits, teeth and ass clothes horse dolly bird, weaponiser of anti-Semitism, fascist, right-wing extremist, Nazi sympathiser, Twitter cancer, thick Tory, brainwashed, an anti-Semite, white supremacist, hate preacher, Zio political trollster, not a real Jew, a child bully, conspiracy theorist, a paedo-protector minion puppet who my dead grandfather would be disgusted by.'[170]

The internet allows information to be spread far and wide without an official marketing plan. CST carried out research based on words such as 'Jews', 'IHRA', 'antisemitism', 'Zionist', 'smear' and 'Jewish' and noted that 'in some months, the number of articles being shared online in the UK with these search terms exceeded 1,000 and the total number of shares of those articles on UK social media reached almost a million.'[171]

It is quite amazing that just 1,000 articles could be shared and seen by almost 1 million people. It is also incredibly serious. Previously, antisemites without any real power would only have been able to influence their own personal sphere, now they can influence thousands of people across the world.

Ultimately, the internet and in particular social media, is being used as a tool to psychologically condition people into a certain way of thinking and believing. We see this with regards to antisemitism with these ideas perpetuated through social media, such as Instagram and TikTok. The danger is that those already socialised into antisemitic thinking, through the 'clouds of antisemitism' will, through social media be exposed to more material to reinforce these ideas. Eventually, the material they access, or that is thrust upon them will only be in line with their conditioned thinking until such a point that they are only hearing one view and one voice. This highlights why Tech companies must be held accountable to police their sites. In 2019, the French government adopted an important bill that gave social media companies 24 hours to remove hateful content or risk fines.[172]

Technology clearly has changed the face of antisemitism as it has allowed different manifestations to interact and blend to allow antisemitic ideas – including the conspiracy fantasy – to be spread far and wide. However, the internet can also be used to combat antisemitism and promote Jewish Pride. In July 2019, I created a short video with The Orly Project to promote Jewish Pride, which has been viewed nearly 52,000 times[173].

Ultimately, antisemites have always utilised modern forms of technology to spread their Jew-hatred and deepen its roots in society. Antisemites today are no different. The huge reach of the internet is enabling antisemitic ideas to be spread across the world without being challenged. Antisemitism in print, on the radio, in film or the internet does not exist in a bubble. It infects non-Jewish people who pose a real threat to Jewish life.

THE DEMAND FOR A PUBLIC RECKONING

Throughout my time teaching about antisemitism, I have realised that most people do not understand it. They try to relate it to their understanding of other forms of prejudice and many people see it as simply historical, right-wing, or merely related to the Holocaust. This failure to understand the true nature of antisemitism is one of the most fundamental reasons that it has persisted. How can you possibly hope to fight something if you do not truly know what it is?

If any society or organisation is serious about fighting antisemitism, it needs to have a public reckoning on it. Non-Jewish societies must explore its prevalence, deep history and how ideas of Jews and Judaism became a part of the foundations of our societal structures and ideologies. The alternative is that antisemitism will persist, as it has done for thousands of years.

What can we learn from the example of the resurgence of German antisemitism discussed previously? It shows that talking about individual examples of antisemitism is not enough. We have to talk about how the Holocaust could have happened. But that history lesson does not start in 1933, when the Nazis came to power, or even in 1918, with Germany's defeat in the first world war. Instead, it begins in the Ancient world, or with the advent of Christianity or, perhaps, in 380 CE when the Roman empire converted to Christianity and the process of embedding antisemitism into European culture commenced. We have to recognise that antisemitism is an institutional form of hate and ideologies steeped in Jew-hate play a foundational role in the establishment of many global ideologies.

The nature of antisemitism will not be easy to unpack and explore and some people may feel disgruntled at being asked to look inside themselves to explore their own prejudice. However, without this potentially painful process, we are absolutely doomed to repeat the mistakes of our ancestors, and that is something too awful to bear.

Chapter 3

JEWISH RESPONSES TO ANTISEMITISM:
ACCULTURATION

AS WE EXPLORED at the beginning of our journey, we all have at *least* two identities. One is internal and the other external. The external identity is something imposed on us by society, but the internal identity is how we see ourselves. Thousands of years of antisemitism have elicited several reactions from the Jewish community, which ultimately have an internal impact on Jewish identity.

Living with Jewish Pride is sadly not the only Jewish response to antisemitism. Jewish people have had their identities shaped by the bigotry that is constantly swirling around them in 'the cloud of antisemitism'. Unfortunately, due to often being formed against a backdrop of hate, the identities of minorities are not always healthy or positive. However, I want to be very clear that my critiques of various Jewish responses to antisemitism should not be viewed as a criticism or passing sweeping judgment on individuals or communities; these different responses are often survival techniques and should be understood as such.

The Psychologist John Berry created the 'fourfold model' to explain better the different paths minority communities take in relation to how they interact with the wider community. It has four different components:[174]

- *'Assimilation'* – When an individual or a community sheds their own original culture and adopts the dominant culture of the country they reside in.

- *'Integration'* – When an individual or a community keeps both their own culture and adopts the culture of the majority.

- *'Separation'* – When an individual or a community rejects the culture of their host country and maintains their own culture.

- *'Marginalisation'* – When an individual or a community rejects both their own culture and the dominant culture.

This model, also known as 'Berry's model of acculturation', applies to multiple communities, but it can also help us understand the specific experiences of the Jewish community.

All four paths are visible in Jewish acculturation but assimilation, integration and separation are particularly prominent. Assimilation has been seen multiple times in Jewish history, for example, during the 19th century when 100,000 Jews in Germany converted to Christianity following the emancipation of the Jews at the beginning of the century. Integration is also evident in the manner in which synagogues in Britain and the Commonwealth say a prayer for the Queen and the royal family during Shabbat services. Hasidic sects, such as the Satmar, can be classed as engaging in separation; they live in New York City but choose to live their lives separate from American culture.

Unlike those who choose to assimilate, communities which opt to integrate seek to retain part of their original identity – they want dual identities. However, Berry's model makes no reference to the fact that this is not easy. As Jean Phinney, Gabriel Horenczyk, Karmela Liebkind and Paul Vedder have suggested, because of a 'real or perceived hostility towards immigrant groups or towards other particular groups, some immigrants may downplay or reject their own ethnic identity.'[175] Forming one's identity, or opting to integrate, due to pressures from societal and institutional prejudice is unhealthy integration. This is not the same as feeling free to carefully select which parts of the dominant culture you wish to adopt and which parts of your own culture you wish to retain or indeed combine. Combining Phinney's work with Berry's model thus helps to understand the nuanced differences between healthy and unhealthy forms of integration.

ACCULTURATION IN THE JEWISH WORLD.

According to Berry, assimilation can be defined in two ways. The first can be described as 'forced assimilation' when an individual is forced to abandon their own background and identity in order to be accepted by the wider society. Historically, forced violent assimilation has been used to attempt to destroy Jewish cultures. Sephardic Jews, for instance, were forced to converted to Christianity under coercion, duress, threat and torture during the period of the Spanish and Portuguese Inquisitions.

The second form of assimilation comes through non-violent coercion when wider society expects minorities to adopt the culture of the majority. This coercion results in minorities abandoning their own heritage to be accepted.

In my analysis of Jewish acculturation, I am not arguing that Jewish people in the Diaspora should live separately without integrating into their respective societies. I believe that we should integrate, but I believe we should also proudly express both our Jewish and other identities while refusing to subvert our Jewish identity in order to be accepted. Each individual Jewish person should be able to choose exactly how they live their lives – and the choices they make should not be judged, as long as they are making them for 'healthy' reasons. Here is where the work lies in creating individual and communal Jewish Pride: learning what is healthy after millennia of survival techniques.

I am, however, critical of the idea of diminishing, disregarding or changing your Jewish identity in order to circumvent antisemitism and be accepted by the non-Jewish world. If nothing else, history has shown us that this does not work. The non-Jewish world always reminds us that we are Jews.

This sad fact was highlighted by comments made by the former MP Luciana Berger to *The Times* in 2018 at the height of the Labour antisemitism crisis. Despite saying she was 'immensely proud' of her Jewishness, Berger said she never wanted to be defined as a Jewish MP. 'When I put myself forward as a candidate in 2009,' she argued, 'I never thought I'd be described on BBC News as "a Jewish MP".'[176] But, whether she liked it or not, there were those in the non-Jewish world who defined Luciana as a Jewish MP.

19TH CENTURY ACCULTURATION

As always, it is important to root our discussions in history to under-stand how ideas have developed. When they were permitted to, Jews throughout history have tried to acculturate in an attempt to avoid the shame of antisemitism and become accepted as a member of wider society. From 333 BCE to 143 BCE, the Ancient Greeks colonised and ruled the ancient Jewish state. During this period, Jews adopted Greek names and the practice of circumcision was even suppressed. A new form of Judaism emerged called, Hellenistic Judaism, which aimed to incorporate aspects of Greek culture into Judaism. The Jewish state had been colonised by the Greeks so Jews were therefore not an equal player in this relationship. On the ladder of power, Greece was on top and Jews were on the bottom. This power imbalance is not something that Berry considered when he described the process of integration. However, this inequality is something that always must be considered when understanding minority identities, as we are not always looking at two groups with equal power. This power dynamic can influence our identities.

However, Jewish acculturation took on a new form in the 18th and 19th centuries in the Ashkenazi and Sephardic communities in Europe, when the *Haskalah* (the Jewish Enlightenment), and the wider more general Enlightenment, spread across the continent. Prior to this, like Jews in other parts of the world, Jews in Europe had been systematically and continuously subjected to oppressive legal restrictions for centuries. This all began to change with the Enlightenment when non-Jews, such as John Toland, the Irish philosopher, argued for the Jews to be emancipated in Great Britain and Ireland. In 1829, Jews in the United Kingdom of Great Britain and Ireland were legally emancipated which brought them unprecedented freedom. New opportunities now open to them – Jews could, for example, become lawyers and attend university – meant that acculturation became a kind of unofficial policy in this part of the Jewish world.

This is unsurprising: so great was their oppression prior to emancipation, that these 18th and 19th century Jews naturally jumped at the opportunity to free themselves of the shackles of the past. The Enlightenment was thus the promise of a new world, where Jews would be treated equally. It created an opportunity where an ancient dream seemed possible: Jews could now be welcomed into seemingly 'open societies' where – unlike in the past when they were kept legally separate – they could mix freely with non-Jews.

As the Enlightenment developed and modern nation states were born, it was often demanded by these developing societies that Jews give up aspects of their Jewishness in order to become full members of the new nation. This was incredibly coercive and reveals that the non-Jewish world would actually only accept Jews on *its* terms. Those terms were that Jews adopt the external identity that the non-Jewish world allowed them to have. In turn, some Jewish people believed that they should no longer honour their Jewish national identity now that they belonged to another community.

These factors – the mix of coercion and the desire of Jews to free themselves of the constraints under which they had lived – caused new divisions to open within Jewish communities. 'Jewish intellectuals who accepted the values and criteria of the Enlightenment and Christian culture and society,' it has been argued, 'tended to regard the Jewish counterpart as barren and primitive. Their attitude became devastatingly critical.'[177]

In short, some Jews assimilated and rejected Jewishness and Judaism so they could be accepted by the non-Jewish world and escape antisemitism. As the academic Jaroslaw Piekalkiewicz argues: 'For assimilationists, those who championed it as a solution to the stigmatization and marginalization of Jews, it was both desirable and necessary.'[178]

This is assimilation, not integration. The rejection of Judaism was characterised by the German novelist Dorothea Schlegel, the daughter of Moses Mendelssohn (the German-Jewish philosopher who advanced the concept of the Jewish Enlightenment), who said: 'According to my own feeling, Protestant Christianity [is] much purer and to be preferred to the Catholic one. Catholicism has for me too much similarity to the old Judaism, which I greatly despise. Protestantism, though, seems to me to be the total religion of Jesus and the religion of civilization. In my heart, I am completely, as far as I can understand from the Bible, a Protestant.'[179]

While it is possible to criticise the futile attempt by European Jews to gain true acceptance, we must be empathetic. It is all incredibly sad. Jews were a community that had existed in exile for thousands of years but had nonetheless successfully held on to their cultural and national identity. However, that they had been so abused and traumatised by the non-Jewish world that they felt compelled to give up, or warp, their Jewishness to be accepted, is heartbreaking.

This is what antisemitism does to us. It fills us with shame and it forces us to choose between being a member of the wider community or being Jewish – just as Jews today are made to choose between being proudly Jewish or members of the progressive community. This is never a fair choice. 19th-century European acculturation didn't work, but the fault does not lie with the Jews, who tried so hard to be accepted. It lies with the non-Jewish world who forced them into this position and then still persecuted and murdered them anyway.

It is worth noting that these processes did not apply to our Mizrahi and Sephardic brothers and sisters. While the Enlightenment led to a period of new freedoms for Ashkenazi and Sephardic Jews in Europe, this did not extend to the Ottoman empire, which maintained its legalised discrimination against Jews until the empire's demise in 1918. Mizrahi Jews and Sephardic Jews who lived in the Middle East and North Africa were thus not able to acculturate as this was simply not allowed. This lack of integration – one forced onto Jews in the Middle East and North Africa – kept their communities separate until the 20th century. Acculturation was also not an option for our Beta-Yisrael brothers and sisters. They could either convert to Christianity or remain Jewish. Those who remained Jewish actively chose to maintain their Jewishness; they believed they were the last Jews in the world and thus any kind of acculturation meant the end of the Jewish people.

FRANCE

As mentioned in Chapter 2, in 1894, Alfred Dreyfus, a French Jewish army captain, was accused of selling military secrets to Germany. Despite being innocent, Dreyfus was framed and then sentenced to life imprisonment in the infamous French penal colony, Devil's Island. Despite rising to the rank of captain in the French army, Dreyfus was still at the end of the day, just a Jew. Not only did his trial reveal contempt for Dreyfus' Jewishness, it revealed wider antisemitism that pervaded the depths of French society. But none of this is surprising if the 100 years or so that preceded Dreyfus' trial are considered.

In 1785, Abbot Henri Grégoire, a French priest and later figure in the revolution, submitted *Essay on the Physical, Moral, and Political Regeneration of the Jews* to the Metz Royal Academy of Sciences, which had sponsored an essay contest titled: 'The means of making Jews happy and more useful in France.' Grégoire argued that, while the Jews of Alsace, in his view, were disease-ridden and hateful, through emancipation, 'both physically and morally, they will acquire a healthier and more robust temperament, enlightenment, probity: their hearts corrected by virtue, their hands hardened by labor, they will come to profit all society.'[180]

The French Revolution began the process that resulted in the complete and full emancipation of Jews in France on 27 September 1791. However, in 1806, Napoleon, questioning the loyalty of French Jews, created The Assembly of Jewish Notables. This was a committee of Jewish leaders that was to represent French Jews. Thus, just 20 years after their emancipation, the 'Frenchness' of French Jews, had been called into question. On 26 July 1806 the Assembly of Jewish Notables was called, and twelve questions were asked of them, including: [181]

- In the eyes of the Jews, are Frenchmen considered as their brethren? Or are they considered as strangers?'

- Do Jews born in France, and treated by the laws as French citizens, consider France their country? Are they bound to defend it?'

- Do Jews who were born in France, and who have the legal status of French citizens, regard France as their fatherland? Is it their duty to defend it, to obey its laws and to accommodate themselves to all the provisions of the Civil Code?

It is clear from these questions that, despite their legal advances, Jews were still regarded with deep suspicion by French society. In an attempt to be accepted, and to ensure the safety of their community, these representatives discarded aspects of their Jewish identity, as their response demonstrated:

The love of country is in the heart of Jews a sentiment so natural, so powerful and so consonant to their religious opinions, that a French Jew considers himself in England as among strangers, although he may be among Jews; and the case is the same with English Jews in France. To such a pitch is this sentiment carried among them, that during the last war, French Jews have been seen fighting desperately against other Jews, the subjects of countries then at war with France.[182]

In an attempt to escape antisemitism, French Jews declared that their French national identity superseded their Jewish identity. Pre-Enlightenment France stated that Jews had to accept Jesus to be saved, post-Enlightenment France said Jews had to accept 'Frenchness' to be saved. This conditional acceptance dictated that the Jews had to give up their collective or their national identity. As Count Stanislas de Clermont-Tonnerre, a member of the French National Assembly put it:

'We must refuse everything to the Jews as a nation and accord everything to the Jew as an individual. They must be citizens... It is intolerable that the Jews should become a separate political formation or class in the country. Every one of them must individually become a citizen. If they do not want this, they must inform us and we shall then be compelled to expel them. The existence of a nation within a nation is unacceptable in our country.'[183]

This is an incredibly coercive form of acceptance which depended on Jews giving up their membership of the Jewish nation. When I say they gave up their national identity, I mean these Jews abandoned the notion that they belong to the Jewish people; the idea that they were connected to all other Jews around the world – through ancestry, ethnicity, history, culture and language and land – and choosing only to relate to other Jews through the idea of a shared belief system that could be discarded. This act had major ramifications for the identity of Jewish people for hundreds of years to come.

The 'acceptance' that subsequently followed eventually led to a seemingly thriving Jewish French life, which ultimately led to the phrase, *Un juif est heureux comme Dieu en France* ('A Jew is as happy as God is happy in France').[184] On 29 January 1790, the Parisian authority declared that Jews 'shared the honors and the pains of military service'.[185] Pierre Birnbaum, the famed French historian, counted: '171 "State Jews" among the political and administrative elite-members of Parliament and of the Council of State, generals, judges, and prefects-all of whom set great store by the principles of 1789'[186]. He also noted 'twenty-five generals, thirty-four judges and forty-two prefects' were also Jewish. Clearly, Jews were accepted and trusted with the important job of guarding and protecting the French state.

However, the Dreyfus Trial acted like blue touch paper for anti-semitism and an anti-Jewish firestorm spread across France. Newspapers, such as *Le Journal de l'Aveyron*, led the charge, declaring that Jews, 'would come out crushed, annihilated, condemned to be loathed by the entire French population for centuries, and hunted down like wild animals'.[187] Songs with lyrics like the 'sorry figure of the filthy-rich Yids, rooting around to steal the gold of France'[188] demonised French Jews, while, in 1898, antisemitic riots broke out in Paris and other major French cities.

While antisemitism spread across France, there were also non-Jewish French people who declared their support for Dreyfus and the Jews of France, such as the journalist Émile Zola, who published his 1898 open letter to the French president titled, *'J'Accuse!'* ('I accuse!'), which charged the French army with obstruction of justice and antisemitism. Ultimately though, Zola paid a heavy price for supporting Dreyfus and was convicted of libel and forced to flee France. Despite this support, and like so many other periods of Jewish history, the experiment to accept Jews as French was not without its conflicts and difficulties, and, in some ways, it ultimately failed. This specific period of the French Jewish experience should act as a warning from history. Despite the effort that French Jews made to be accepted by wider French society, it did not allow them to escape antisemitism.

GERMANY

One of the most famous examples of Jewish acculturation can be found in the German Jewish community in the 19th century. Prior to unification, German states granted Jews emancipation at different stages. The Grand Duchy of Hesse and the Kingdom of Westphalia emancipated their Jews in 1808, while the Kingdom of Hanover freed their Jews later in 1842. This was the era of Moses Mendelssohn, the father of the *Haskalah* (the Jewish Enlightenment) – whose daughter, as we saw, preferred Protestantism over Catholicism because it reminded her less of Judaism. This Jewish Enlightenment movement argued for Jewish acculturation into non-Jewish culture.

Mendelssohn translated the Torah into German, arguing that Jews could and should become members of wider civil society, and leave their insular separatist communities. Mendelssohn described his translation of the Torah as a 'first step towards culture'[189] for German Jews, clearly indicating that he saw German as true culture or, at the very least, high culture and Judaism and Jewishness as uncivilised. This is a sad reflection on a beautiful culture that had developed over thousands of years. The *Haskalah* thus encouraged Jews to swap Yiddish for German – the language of culture – and to 'be a Jew in your home and a man outside it'.[190]

Another of Mendelssohn's major works that contributed towards acculturation in Germany was *Jerusalem,* published in 1783, in which he argued for a reconciliation between Judaism and modern society. Being Jewish, he declared, was, in fact, compatible with being a good, modern and loyal citizen. While he was clearly passionate about the continuation of the Jewish people, his willingness and eagerness to warp Jewish identity in order to be accepted by non-Jewish German culture demonstrates a deeply unhealthy relationship with the process of acculturation.

Acculturation in the German Jewish community was so strong that they were sometimes referred to as 'more German than the Germans'.[191] Ironically, when we consider the events that transpired in the middle of the 20th century, Germany was seen as a positive place for Jews to live and a safe haven for Jewish refugees. My own mother's family fled from Belorussia to Prussia in the 19th century seeking safety. Due to the commitment of German Jews to live in Germany, there was a belief that it was a kind of homeland for its Jews, who often rejected Zionism – because why would they need a homeland of their own when they had Germany?

Like other places that have been described as safe havens or Jewish utopias, Germany was never a Jewish utopia that allowed German Jews to live freely with their non-Jewish German neighbours. Rather, as throughout history, antisemitism ebbed and flowed until it eventually became a tsunami.

The phrase 'anti-semitism' itself was coined in Germany in 1879 in an attempt to 'scientifically' legitimise Jew-hatred. Certain professions, such as the judiciary, unofficially discriminated against Jews, barring them from promotion. During this period, too, a specific kind of antisemitism known as 'resort antisemitism' emerged, which resulted in Jews being barred from holiday resorts. Signs were hung on doors saying: *Dieses Haus ist judenrein, verdammt soll jeder Jude sein!* ('This house is Jew-free, damned shall every Jew be!').[192] As was the case in other places where Jews tried desperately to acculturate, they were still regarded as foreign by non-Jewish Germans. As Marvin Perry and Frederick M Schweitzer write in *Anti-Semitism: Myth and Hate from Antiquity to the Present*: 'To these Germans, the Jews, lacking in German consciousness, were a malevolent alien force corroding traditional German values and corrupting German culture.'[193]

In this scenario lies the never-ending contradiction of historic Jewish acculturation; on one hand, Jews work incredibly hard to become members of wider society, while, at the same time, that society – in this case, Germany – actively rejects its Jews. It is arguable that this was a form of hope based on the idea that 'if we become palatable and more German and less Jewish then they will like us'. However, in actual fact, it rings truer to the psychological response of denial by those suffering from individual abuse. According to *Psychology Today*: 'Denial is a defense that helps us. There are many reasons we use denial, including avoidance of physical or emotional pain, fear, shame or conflict.'[194]

During the first world war, roughly 100,000 Jews fought for Germany, 1,000 were awarded the first-class Iron Cross and 17,000 were awarded the second-class Iron Cross. But, regardless of the Jewish sacrifice for Germany in that war, the third and fourth decade of the 20th century shattered any illusion of a German-Jewish relationship. In the November 1932 elections, almost 12 million people voted for the Nazis despite their overt antisemitism. By 1945, 6 million Jews were murdered by the Nazis and their allies. This includes an estimated 180,000 German Jews, out of a total Jewish population in Germany of 214,000 at the outbreak of the war.

This discussion on acculturation is in no way intended to blame the victims. The circumstances they found themselves in make it clear why so many Jews wanted desperately to be accepted by their wider societies. I tell these stories simply to highlight the inherent challenges of acculturation for Jews, of giving up or changing your identity in order to circumvent antisemitism and fit in.

This story has happened time and time again. The tragedy is that, despite real attempts by Jews to fit in, the non-Jewish world would not allow it. Acculturation has consistently failed to allow Jews to escape antisemitism. This is not the Jews' fault; it is the fault of the non-Jewish world's refusal to accept Jews.

The thought I continuously return to during my research is: it seems that the only way to integrate in a healthy way, that honours both your Jewish and other identities, is through Jewish Pride. Jewish Pride asserts our Jewishness as an equal partner to our other identities while refusing to subvert it for acceptance.

The question of how Diasporic Jews acculturate into their respective societies is not just a historic Jewish issue. It is a question with which every single generation of Diasporic Jews must wrestle. For a period, the experience of Jews in the United States appeared to many to be the greatest achievement in Jewish acculturation. However, while there is much talk of American Jewish exceptionalism, the reality is that the American Jewish experience resembles other Jewish Diasporic experiences rather more closely than some may care to admit.

AMERICA

There have been Jews on the American continent since long before the Declaration of Independence in 1776. These Jews acculturated and were proudly American. They fought in the war of independence and in 1784, Gershom Mendes Seixas – a mixed Ashkenazi and Sephardic *Hazan* (cantor) at the Spanish and Portuguese synagogue in New York City – wrote a Hebrew prayer for George Washington and the New York state governor, George Clinton. Thus, as in other Diasporic Jewish stories, Jewish loyalty to the United States has been a prominent theme throughout the course of this relationship. From its conception, the Jews of the new United States demonstrated that they were loyal citizens of this new enterprise. This effort to form good relations with their leadership is understandable, considering these new-American Jews would have either fled persecution or been the descendants of those who did. Mendez Seixas' grandfather, for example, was a *converso* who fled Portugal under threat when he was accused of continuing his Jewishness in secret.

In 1790, just six years after he wrote the Hebrew prayer for Washington, Gershom Mendez Seixas' brother, Moses, was selected to deliver a letter from the Jews of Newport, Rhode Island, to the president regarding the issue of tolerance of minorities. Clearly aware of his community's vulnerable position Moses Seixas, wrote: 'Deprived as we heretofore have been of the invaluable rights of free Citizens, we now with a deep sense of gratitude to the Almighty disposer of all events behold a Government, erected by the Majesty of the People – a Government, which to bigotry gives no sanction, to persecution no assistance – but generously affording to all Liberty of conscience, and immunities of Citizenship: deeming every one, of whatever Nation, tongue, or language equal parts of the great governmental Machine.'[195]

In August 1790, Washington responded, saying: 'The Citizens of the United States of America have a right to applaud themselves for having given to mankind examples of an enlarged and liberal policy: a policy worthy of imitation. All possess alike liberty of conscience and immunities of citizenship. It is now no more that toleration is spoken of, as if it was by the indulgence of one class of people, that another enjoyed the exercise of their inherent natural rights. For happily the Government of the United States, which gives to bigotry no sanction, to persecution no assistance[,] requires only that they who live under its protection should demean [conduct] themselves as good citizens, in giving it on all occasions their effectual support.'[196]

A year later, in 1791, the Bill of Rights was added to the US constitution. The first amendment famously states: 'Congress shall make no law respecting an establishment of religion, or prohibiting the free exercise thereof.'[197] This explicit commitment to religious freedom in the newly formed United States had a deep impact on the identity of American Jews for generations to come.

Between 1820 and 1870, 197,000 Jews emigrated to the United States. But while this 50-year period saw what seems like a huge amount of Jewish migration to America, it was nothing compared to what was to follow in the next half-century, in which 2.4 million Jews fled the intense antisemitism and deadly pogroms of the Russian empire. By 1930, there were 4 million Jews in America. These Jews arrived in an America that guaranteed religious freedom, so they understood that, to be accepted in America, they had to engage primarily with the religious aspect of their Jewish identity and downplay, or even discard, their Jewish national identity. In their eyes, identifying as a religious community guaranteed them a kind of protection that was not afforded to them as a nation. This may not have seemed to be such a difficult decision as Jewishness, as we know, is a nation, an ethnicity *and* a religion. Many new Jewish immigrants may have felt comfortable in identifying more closely with Judaism as a religion if it guaranteed them freedom from the horrendous and enduring antisemitism they had experienced previously.

There is often a view – and one that I was certainly told growing up – that American Jews did not face antisemitism. I remember understanding this specific point as a child watching *An American Tail*, where Fievel Mousekewitz, a mouse from the Russian empire, sings with his family: 'There are no cats in America, and the streets are paved with cheese.'[198] Even my young mind registered that Fievel, like members of my own family previously had, was fleeing antisemitism. But while America was a place of refuge for millions of Jewish people from Europe who fled murderous antisemitism, it is a myth that it was devoid of Jew-hatred.

As Jonathan D Sarna and Jonathan Golden argue in *The American Jewish Experience in the Twentieth Century: Antisemitism and Assimilation*: 'More recently, scholars have pushed back the history of American antisemitism, discovering that no period in American Jewish history was free of this scourge: Jews encountered it from their earliest days on American soil.'[199]

Thus, to understand the current resurgence of American antisemitism, we have to understand this point: antisemitism has been, and is, a component of the American Jewish experience and, despite it having periods of less prominence, it has always existed.

While the narrative suggests otherwise, and the contexts differ, the American Jewish experience is not so different from that of European Jews. Understanding the major similarities of Jewish experiences from around the world is as important as understanding their differences. One of many major similarities is that, tragically, all Jews, regardless of whether they are from Egypt or England or Algeria or America, experience antisemitism.

Examples of American antisemitism include Order No. 11, given in 1862 by Major General Ulysses S Grant. Grant, the civil war general and later president, stated: 'The Jews, as a class violating every regulation of trade established by the Treasury Department and also department orders, are hereby expelled … within twenty-four hours from the receipt of this order.'[200] With that order, Grant ordered the expulsion of all Jews from the areas of the Confederacy under his control, including parts of Tennessee, Kentucky and Mississippi.

While Grant later apologised and repented for his antisemitism, saying that 'I have no prejudice against sect or race, but want each individual to be judged by his own merit,'[201] this doesn't detract from the realities of his own, or indeed America's, antisemitism. Indeed, up until the mid-20th century, there were quotas on how many Jews could enter university and they were barred from certain kinds of employment, while certain establishments would even refuse Jews service. Jews also faced violent antisemitism in parts of the US – for example, in 1915, Leo Frank, a 31-year-old Jewish man, was lynched in Atlanta, Georgia, having been falsely accused and convicted of the murder of an employee.

Unsurprisingly, the massive influx of migrants fleeing Europe led to questions about the status of Jews in the United States. While the majority of these new immigrants worked in very specific fields, such as clothing manufacturing, a few prominent Jews successfully established investment banking firms. Again, rooted in the economic libel and conspiracy fantasy, this led to a rise in antisemitism focusing on perceptions of Jewish power and financial wealth. In reality, Jewish bankers made up only a small percentage of the nation's bankers, but the myths perpetrated by the libel and fantasy stuck. For example, during the depression of the 1890s, Jews were blamed for declining farm prices. The American Jewish experience demonstrates just how cyclical antisemitism is and how we see the same accusations made against us over and over again and become the projected symbols of financial power.

In the 1930s, Father Charles Coughlin preached antisemitic sermons on his weekly Sunday night radio broadcasts and, following the devastating destruction during Kristallnacht in Nazi Germany, he defended this orgy of violence and encouraged a Nazi rally in Madison Square Garden in 1939. These are just a few examples of antisemitism in the United States, but there are many more, including the failure of the United States to help Jewish refugees on the St Louis escaping Nazism in 1939, Senator Joseph McCarthy's 'red scare' in the late 1940s and early 1950s, and the executions of Julius and Ethel Rosenberg, the only two American civilians to be executed for espionage-related activity during the cold war.

This echoes the situation of German Jews in the 19th century who, despite believing they were at home in Germany, still faced the realities of antisemitism. American Jews attempting to acculturate were also doing so against a backdrop of rejection and antisemitism.

Like many Jews in other places, American Jews have worked hard to be accepted by non-Jewish American society. As many of them could pass as white Christian Americans, they were – to a *certain* extent – able to acculturate. Many Jews who immigrated to America changed their names (as they did in other parts of the Diaspora) to sound less Jewish, and like their German brethren, they embraced Reform Judaism, which, according to its German founder, Abraham

Geiger, focused on reconciling 'Judaism with contemporary life and harmonising it with emerging currents in Western thought.'[202]

Writing in 1870, James Parton suggested that American Reform Judaism resembled Christianity to such a degree that, as he wrote of a service at Temple Immanuel: 'A stranger coming in by chance ... might suppose he had strayed into an Episcopal church where three professors from Oxford were conducting the service to a style recently introduced in England, but not yet known in America.'[203]

I grew up in the Reform community in Britain and love and identify with many of its values, but I have to question how healthy this concept was in practice. While I agree, to a degree, with harmonising Judaism with the societies in which Jews live, we have to ask if the Jews promoting this form of Judaism were doing so out of Jewish Pride and the desire to see Judaism evolve, or from external pressure from the non-Jewish world. The willingness to warp or change Judaism to fit in cannot be considered without also recognising the trauma Jews faced from antisemitism, whether personal or intergenerational. Asking these questions does not mean I do not value Reform Judaism; I believe that all communities have to evolve and grow. My question is: was that evolution based on pride or shame? And if it was based on shame, then how can we refocus it to be based on pride?

This effort to integrate Judaism may have been popular in America, but it certainly wasn't unique to American Judaism. As we saw in France, Jews shed their national identity and adopted a solely religious or secular one, at least externally. If internal dialogue and conversations lead to changes of Jewish culture or religious practice, that is one thing, but changing identity to fit in with the wider culture is not healthy and leads to a diminishing of one essential part (usually the minority part) of your identity.

This shedding of Jewish national identity and the move towards Judaism the religion has long been a part of the process of Jewish acculturation. In 1885, the Pittsburgh Platform was adopted by the

American Reform Movement which stated: 'We consider ourselves no longer a nation, but a religious community,'[204] and expect 'neither a return to Palestine, nor a sacrificial worship under the sons of Aaron, nor the restoration of any of the laws concerning the Jewish state.'[205]

Given the Bill of Rights' guarantee of religious freedom, it is understandable why the American Reform community made this statement. This fundamental altering of the Jewish identity has influenced modern American Jewish perspectives on what it means to be a Jew, thus making it difficult for some American Jews to understand the true nature of antisemitism which ultimately targets Jews regardless of their religious affiliation.

This shift in Jewish identity further allowed American Jews to integrate, but it clearly came at a cost. As a collective, American Jews, especially those in the Reform community, had to fundamentally change their identity to be accepted into American society, only to be shown time and time again that this acceptance was conditional.

As with German Jewish acculturation, the American Jewish commitment to life in the United States led parts of the Reform community, at one point, to officially define themselves as anti-Zionist. However, it is important to recognise that this was long before the establishment of the State of Israel in 1948, and that the Reform community was against the *concept* of a Jewish state, not against *a living breathing state* with millions of citizens. This is an essential distinction.

This history also suggests that, as with German Jews who felt so attached to Germany, American Jews at this point believed they had found their promised land, and, as such, why would they need a specifically Jewish state? This idea is exemplified by how American Jews often refer to synagogues not as *'shul'* or *'beit hamikdash'* but as 'temple'. In fact, underlining the similarities between the 19th century Germany community and the American community, the first permanent Reform synagogue in the world was opened in Hamburg in October 1818 and was referred to as the Hamburg Temple. Hamburg was the Jerusalem of the German Reform Jews, just as America was the Jerusalem of the American Jewish communities.

Nonetheless, the 1897 declaration by the Central Conference of American Rabbis (CCAR) stated that they 'totally disapprove[d] of any attempt for the establishment of a Jewish state'[206] was an incredibly heartless and particularly narrow-minded action by the American Jewish leadership. It was released in the middle of the period when multiple Jewish communities, including the Beta-Yisrael and Yemenite Mizrahi Jews, were attempting to flee subjugation by escaping to Ottoman-ruled Palestine. It was also issued during the first wave of Ashkenazi *Aliyah,* from 1882-1903, when Jews from the Russian empire fled to Palestine to escape incredibly violent European antisemitism. An estimated 35,000 Jews reached the indigenous homeland of the Jewish people and it seems uncharitable that American Jews would choose to define themselves as anti-Zionist at this time. This specific form of American antizionism is something we continue to see to this very day. Antizionist American Jews often feel safe in the United States and have lost sight of the wider Jewish historical experience and they disregard the possibility that other Jews may continue to need a Jewish state to ensure their survival.

It is interesting to note that this hopefulness can be found in Bundist pre-Holocaust Jews in Europe. Bundism was a secular left-wing Jewish movement that argued against Zionism and advocated for Jewish life in Europe. Sadly, history has proven that no society has been willing to eradicate its antisemitism in order to allow Jews to safely integrate without losing their identities.

But while late 19th and early 20th century pogroms could not alter the antizionism of the American Reform community, Nazi antisemitism did, and in 1937 the CCAR endorsed the concept of a Jewish state. In seeking to understand CCAR's decisions, we must recognise that they were dealing with real intergenerational trauma, a fear for survival, and an overwhelming desire for it to finally work out *this time*. Despite this history, the overwhelming majority of American Jews still identify Zionist today.

The echo of American Jewish intergenerational trauma was also seen during the second world war. It is known that certain members of the American Jewish community, such as presidential speechwriter Samuel Rosenman, advised President Roosevelt not to allow Jewish refugees fleeing Europe in the wake of Kristallnacht to find safety in the United States. As Michael Laitman describes in his book, *The Jewish Choice: Unity or Anti-Semitism*, Rosenman 'opposed such a move because it would create a Jewish problem in the US'.[207]

Rosenman's opposition took place against the backdrop of growing pre-war antisemitism: 100 new American antisemitic organisations were created between 1933 and 1941. During this period, inspired by Coughlin, an Irish Catholic group known as the Christian Front terrorised Jews in New York and Boston, which the authorities did very little to combat. It is clear that, as these events unfolded, certain members of the American Jewish community began to feel the precariousness of their seemingly stable position in American society. Wider public opinion was not sympathetic to the plight of European Jews either. In a 1938 Gallup poll, 79% of Americans said the US should not allow 'a larger number of Jewish exiles from Germany to come to the United States to live'[208].

This is the reality of Jewish attempts at acculturation. While some Jews could prosper (and some certainly did in France, Germany or the United States) and feel safe to a point, their positions have never truly been secure. There was always the risk that wider society would remember they were foreigners with their own identities; that wider society would remember that they were Jews, not just religiously but nationally too.

It is also true that Roosevelt himself held antisemitic views that ultimately doomed thousands of Jewish people to their deaths through inaction. In his book, *The Jews Should Keep Quiet: Franklin*

D. Roosevelt, Rabbi Stephen S. Wise, and the Holocaust, Rafael Medoff writes: 'Roosevelt's unflattering statements about Jews consistently reflected one of several interrelated notions: that it was undesirable to have too many Jews in any single profession, institution, or geographic locale; that America was by nature, and should remain, an overwhelmingly white, Protestant country; and that Jews, on the whole, possessed certain innate and distasteful characteristics.'[209]

While Roosevelt did have Jewish advisors (similar to the Court Jews of yore) such as Rosenman, his views on Jews would surely have had an impact on how these people spoke up in defence of admitting more Jewish refugees. We can judge Rosenman – and perhaps we should – but we can't ignore the fact that he was a Jew living in a time of growing antisemitism in America who did not want to upset the Jewish American applecart. As the essayist and author Steve Bayme argues: '[Jewish leaders were] engaging in an unrequited love affair with a president who was, at best, indifferent, and at worst cynical about the pleas of the Jews.'[210]

Despite the effort, American Jews had made to acculturate, this was not always deemed as being sufficient. In an anonymous 1939 article titled, 'I married a Jew', the author remembered that, when she announced her impending nuptials, her mother told her: 'Bethink yourself what this means. Married to a Jew, you will be barred from certain circles. They can say what they like about Germany, but democratic America is far from wholeheartedly accepting the Jews. Remember that Ben couldn't join a fraternity at his university. Remember there are clubs and resorts and residential districts that bar Jews. Remember there are a dozen other less tangible discriminations against them.'

The author herself stated her beliefs that 'Jews are alien' and 'what keeps the Jew alien is his alien culture, his alien tradition, his fierce pride in belonging to what he believes a superior race.'[211] Reading this primary historical source is fascinating. The author may have married a Jew, and she may have loved him, but it is clear that she loves him for being the 'right kind of Jew' as she still discriminates against other Jews who live their desire to stay as Jewish as they are. She sees Jews through her warped antisemitic perception of them – note her comments about Jews believing they are a superior race – and expresses the conspiracy fantasy. She argues that to be accepted, Jews need to acculturate; but no matter what Jews could do to fit in, the non-Jewish world will never really allow them to forget the fact they are Jewish and only accept them if they shed their Jewishness. If the non-Jewish world constantly attempts to define what it means to be an acceptable Jew, and if we adopt their definition, how can we ever be proud of who we are?

Despite continuing antisemitism, the second half of the 20th century saw the American Jewish relationship reach its peak. In the wake of the discovery of the full horror of the Holocaust – with American soldiers liberating the camps confronted by the realities of the Nazis' attempt to annihilate European Jewry – overt American antisemitism declined dramatically. However, this decline in American antisemitism and the acceptance of Jews was based on post-Holocaust guilt. Through inaction, America – and other countries, including Britain – bears some responsibility for the number of Jews murdered by the Nazis. While American antisemitism did not totally disappear after the Holocaust, it did become less vocal, with the historian Leonard Dinnerstein recording that the number of Americans who heard 'criticism or talk against Jews' declined from 64% in 1946 to 12% in 1959.[212] In 1950, the *American Jewish Yearbook* wrote: 'Organized anti-Semitic activity, which began to decline after the war, continued at a low ebb during the year under review.'[213] However, we can't disregard the fact that acceptance based on guilt is a dangerous thing. When the guilt disappears, so does the acceptance.

Moreover, even in this period where Jews were allowed to further integrate into American society, antisemitism did not disappear. Synagogues in the south of the country were still attacked. On 12 October

1958, for instance, the Hebrew Benevolent Congregation, the oldest synagogue in Atlanta, was targeted with 50 sticks of dynamite. Nonetheless, the director of the ADL, Benjamin R Epstein, has described this post-war period as both a 'period of tremendous progress' and a 'golden age' and he stated that American Jews, 'achieved a greater degree of economic and political security and a broader social acceptance than had ever been known by any Jewish community since the [ancient] Dispersion.'[214]

During this period, legal discrimination against Jews was lifted (Yale University placed quotas on Jews until the early 1960s) and a select number of Jews were able to rise towards the upper echelons of American society, *seemingly* free of antisemitism.

Yet we should remember that other eras considered to be a 'Golden Age' for Jews – the Enlightenment in Europe, *La Convivencia* in Iberian and Andalusian Spain, the *dhimmitude* of the Middle East and North Africa and the Persian region – proved not to be so golden after all. In the years preceding this American 'Golden Age' period, the Jewish community in the US continued to work hard to be accepted by the non-Jewish society that surrounded it – and, for the first time, it seemingly was. This specific period – of change and acceptance – forms the backdrop of life for today's American Jewish community.

We have discussed how antisemitism and rejection forged Jewish identities through acculturation, but what happened when Jews felt they had succeeded in integrating? Through the shedding of Jewishness as a nation or a people, many American Jews began to perceive themselves as just members of *just* a religion or even as secular cultural Jews. Set against the civil rights movement and the continuing complexities of race relations in the United States, this resulted in some light-skinned Jews viewing themselves as white.

When discussing the whiteness of light-skinned Jews, I am referring specifically to Jews by birth, and not those who chose to become Jewish. This is not to erase their Jewishness, rather it is to address the specific nature of the conversation around whether light-skinned Jews by birth are, in fact, white. Furthermore, there are many Jewish people in the United States who do not pass as white. Their experience is just as valid and important but, while they face their own unique challenges in being Jewish and possibly of another ethnic minority, this discussion centres on the light-skinned Jews by birth as those Jews are the ones commonly referred to as 'white'. We will explore issues relating to non-white passing Jews later on in this book.

THE COMPLEXITIES OF JEWS IN THE US RACIAL BINARY

As a Jewish man from Scotland, I did not grow up navigating the complexities of the US race hierarchy and the Black-white binary, and clearly this experience is not my own. However, during my research, I have concluded that two aspects of US identity have had an impact on both internal and external Jewish identities: the concepts of white supremacy and misconceptions and inaccuracies about Jews that lead to both erasure and misidentification within ideas of racism in the United States.

White supremacy as defined by Professor of Law at the University of Tennessee; France Lee Ansley is: 'A political, economic and cultural system in which whites overwhelmingly control power and material resources, and in which white dominance of non-white subordination exists across a broad array of institutions and social settings.'[215]

Both white supremacy and its successor, white nationalism – which, according to Eric Ward, seeks the 'complete removal of Jews and people of color from the United States altogether'[216] – actively discriminates against Jewish people, Black people and other ethnic minorities.

Ward, who heads the Western States Centre, is a Black non-Jewish American who has attended white nationalist rallies in order to research this phenomenon. He states very clearly that 'Antisemitism forms the theoretical core of White nationalism.'[217] White nationalism frames Jews as the puppet master of other groups who are orchestrating the destruction of white America. It specifically believes the conspiracy fantasy that Jews camouflage themselves secretly as white people in order to rally Black people to overthrow the white race.

As previously discussed, it is the fact that light-skinned Jews can pass as white and this, believe white nationalists, is what makes them so dangerous: they can hide in plain sight while orchestrating the destruction of white culture and society. As has been the case historically, we once again see the non-Jewish idea of the Jew serving the purpose of helping the non-Jewish world – in this case, white supremacists – make sense of the world.

Ideas that attempted to explain anti-Black racism, such as 'critical race theory', were developed to explain the impact of white supremacy on US society, specifically on Black Americans. It is a theory that aims to 'combine progressive political struggles for racial justice with critiques of the conventional legal and scholarly norms which are themselves viewed as part of the illegitimate hierarchies that need to be changed'.[218] Essentially, this theory explains how anti-Black racism in the United States is systemic.

Critical race theory has been taken up by many in the progressive world as the principal means to explain American manifestations of racism. However, as it is primarily focussed on identifiable skin colour, it fails to take into account expressions of other forms of racism, such as anti-Jewish racism. As such, it has inadvertently led to light-skinned Jews being identified as white, while missing critical nuance.

Richard Delgado and Jean Stefancic, authors of *Critical Race Theory: An Introduction,* acknowledge that perceptions of Jewish identities have changed over time. 'Early in our history ... Jews ... were considered non-white' they argue.[219] But, as Ward describes, around the time of later developments in understanding white supremacy and racism, 'a discourse developed around anti-racism so strict, it no longer allowed a self-identity for Jews, except to assume the primary role of the "white ally".'[220] This then contributed to the creation of the progressive hierarchy of oppression; as Ward suggests: 'How could a supposed "white ethnic" group's suffering compare to what was happening to communities of color or women?'[221] Light-skinned Jews were then forced to deny the historical and current reality of antisemitism.

Jews by birth – along with other peoples from the Middle East and North Africa – occupy a complicated space in the American racial hierarchy and both groups have, at specific times, been legally classed as non-white and white in the United States. Two specific 1987 court cases, *Saint Francis College v. al-Khazraji* and *Shaare Tefila Congregation v. Cobb*, stated that while Arabs and Jews can legitimately claim to be victims of racial discrimination (as protected by 42 U.S.C. Section 1981. Equal rights under the law) they were still legally classed as white.

To add to the complexity, it is worth noting that 42 U.S.C. Section 1981 'was intended to protect from discrimination identifiable classes of persons who are subjected to intentional discrimination solely because of their ancestry or ethnic characteristics'[222], which the court ruled unanimously applies to Jews. An explanation as to how this can be the case is ultimately rooted in the idea that whiteness cannot be simplified to mean European heritage, which is how it is often portrayed in the US progressive notion of race. While these cases ultimately aimed to protect both peoples from discrimination, they do not take into account, nor define, the precarious racial position that these often-passing minorities, such as light-skinned Jews, occupy in American society.

Despite the fact that these rulings focused on both Jews and Arabs, the attempt by some progressives to erase Jewish indigeneity to the Middle East, and force people to take responsibility for white crimes, is only aimed at light skinned Jewish people. In fact, Arabs and others from the Middle East of all skin tones are often classified as 'people of colour' by progressive movements, while light-skinned Jews are not.

Regardless of legal rulings, assigning only light-skinned Jews – and not Arabs – whiteness is problematic because in parts of the left whiteness is identified as the main cause of suffering for non-white people. Thus, rooted in antisemitic ideas of Jewish power and wealth inspired by the economic libel, blood libel and conspiracy fantasy, Jews can be portrayed as the ultimate oppressor. When Jews are described as white, without nuance, it assigns them responsibility for all the crimes of whiteness – even though we have long been victims of white supremacy. Progressive ideas of 'white' Jews also erase light-skinned Jews by birth indigeneity to the Middle East (which is also used to portray Israel as a white colonialist state) and incorrectly qualifies and revises their ancestry as European. It is here we see some progressives use their ideas of light-skinned Jews, as David Nirenberg argues, to make sense of the oppression they see in the world.

The complex racial structure of the US requires adopting whiteness in order to rise up in the racial pyramid. This is not so different from France in the 19th century forcing Jews to warp their identities in order to be accepted as French. In the United States, this struggle is not unique to only Jews, it applies to anyone who can pass as white.

When Jews attempt to define their own identities in progressive spaces, light-skinned Jews are told that they are unable to cope with their 'white privilege'. In June 2020, a 'Jewish privilege' hashtag was started by white nationalists on Twitter and then picked up by hard-left activists. Hen Mazzig, a Mizrahi LGBTQ+ activist, rallied Jewish voices to swamp the hashtag with stories of their own individual examples of antisemitism, to demonstrate the falsities of 'Jewish privilege'. I myself shared one describing that the day before an Instagram user told me that I should be gassed. Ward himself dismisses the concept that light-skinned Jews are white, arguing: 'The notion that Jews long ago and incontestably became White folks in the U.S … is a myth that we must dispel.'[223]

Ultimately, light-skinned Jews are not white, not because of the colour of their skin, but because of their historical and current experiences as well as specific ancestral heritage. Moreover, we have never been fully able to assimilate into white society because of our Jewishness and persistent antisemitism. In fact, it is often when Jewish people seem to have acculturated most that the huge hammer of antisemitism comes down hardest.

Like all people, including other minority groups, Jews must be mindful of the societies in which we live and how they may influence our participation in various forms of prejudice. No community is immune to the disease of prejudice. However, this does not mean non-Jews are allowed to dictate Jewish identity, particularly when defining Jews through inaccurate binaries, out of context of our experience, and with a lack of knowledge of Jewish history as an ethno-religion.

Theories which seek to understand anti-Black racism, such as critical race theory, were developed in an American context and have clear limits in understanding and explaining the American Jewish experience. Furthermore, using it to understand the *non-American* Jewish experience is deeply inappropriate. Quite simply, it is a form of American cultural colonialism. Forcing American values and ideas on non-Americans is an attempt to impose a cultural hegemony on a global scale and, as such, must be rejected.

Relying on non-Jews to define Jewish identity never results in accurate or nuanced definitions of Jewishness, which is why Jews – not white supremacists nor non-Jewish progressives, antizionists, or the US legal system – should be the ones to define their own Jewish identities.

THE WHITENESS OF LIGHT-SKINNED JEWS

I believe that the adoption of a solely religious Jewish identity has had serious consequences in terms of American Jewish identity. Many light-skinned Jews now see themselves as white Americans who happen to be religiously or culturally Jewish. Certain progressive Jews on Twitter and social media regularly apologise for their white privilege without acknowledging their own realities as members of a targeted and threatened community. They often describe themselves as 'privileged white Jewish people'. This simply opens the doors to antisemitic libels and suggests Jews have a responsibility for white supremacy, while ignoring the continued targeting of Jews by white supremacists, among others.

Such Jews tend to align themselves with left-wing or progressive antisemites who only take up the cause of other minority groups and often only reference antisemitism when discussing its prevalence on the right, or using it for the benefit of others (for example, using Holocaust memory as a means of promoting advocacy for other at-risk communities). Many base their Jewish identity on the notion of *Tikkun Olam* (a Jewish concept translating to 'repair the world'), which is about 'repairing' the Jewish community to act as a light unto other nations. They see it as a call to social justice that supersedes the needs of their own community.

Their association of Jewishness with a purely religious or secular identity, leaves them vulnerable to adopting society's narrow, monolithic and stereotyped perception of what a Jew is. This, along with perceived whiteness – as well as antisemitic tropes around Jewish wealth and power – have persuaded these young American light-skinned Jews that they are merely privileged white people, as opposed to being Jews who can benefit from the advantage of being perceived as white.

In May 2020, Gazi Kodzo, a Black social media influencer, wrote a deeply offensive tweet describing Anne Frank as a 'Becky'. Becky is a stereotype for a white woman, especially one who is unaware or takes advantage of her social privilege. Frank was a victim of racial genocidal antisemitism, but Kodzo's tweet demonstrates just how dangerous and pernicious it is to frame light-skinned Jews as white.

In a response to Kodzo's tweet, the author Lux Alptraum wrote: 'More often than not, Black anti-Semitism hurts Black people more than it hurts white Jews.'[224] Because light-skinned Jews are 'white', she suggested, they are not allowed to discuss the genuine threat and harm posed by antisemitism because it does not fit in with the progressive movement's perceptions of Jews. Anti-racism work in America is rooted in the Black-white binary, but this narrative does not account for the fact that Jews simply do not fit this binary. It is a square peg in a round hole as it mis-assigns white identity, without nuance, to light-skinned Jews both because of their white-presenting appearance and antisemitic libels that frame Jews as privileged and powerful.

This term 'white Jews' is used regularly, however, as Michael Lerner wrote in the *Village Voice*: 'In the context of American politics, to be "white" means to be a beneficiary of the past 500 years of European exploration and exploitation of the rest of the world — and hence to "owe" something to those who have been exploited. So, when Jews are treated as white in the United States, the assessment is not a crude physical one but a judgment of Jewish culture and civilization, history and destiny.'[225]

Lerner's insight is key: attributing whiteness to light-skinned Jews is not about the colour of their skin, but what their skin colour represents. To many, particularly those on the left, whiteness means not only power and freedom from oppression, but also the oppressor.

It is worth noting that perceptions of light-skinned Jews are related to political leanings. 'These are rough sketches of two camps, concentrated at the margins of U.S. political culture,' suggested an article in *The Atlantic* in 2016. 'On the extreme right, Jews are seen as impure – a faux-white race that has tainted America. And on the extreme left, Jews are seen as part of a white-majority establishment that seeks to dominate people of color.'[226]

But these perspectives do not only exist on the margins of US political culture. Modern populism has also moved them to the centre. As Joe Biden and Bernie Sanders battled for the Democratic party's presidential in spring 2020, *Common Dreams*, a progressive news outlet, published an article under the headline: 'Not Just "Two Old White Men," This Democratic Primary Is Now a Serious Fight Between Joe Biden and Bernie Sanders'.[227] Incredibly, the article makes no mention of Sanders' Jewishness. That a member of a tiny ethno-religious minority (in America, Jews make up less than 3% of the population) which has been persecuted continuously for over 2,000 years does not qualify as diversity is beyond me.

There are countless American Jews, such as the historian Deborah Lipstadt and journalist Bari Weiss, who are deeply aware of the existing and rising tide of antisemitism in the United States and who continuously speak out publicly against it. But, it seems, there are certain progressive North American Jews who have forgotten the fact that they belong to a persecuted minority.

The Holocaust, the expulsion of Mizrahi and Sephardic Jews, and the persecution of both the Beta-Yisrael and the Ashkenazi Jews in the USSR all occurred in living memory. So, too, did the Munich massacre and multiple attempts to destroy the State of Israel.

The idea of Jewish privilege denotes a severe misunderstanding of the experience of *all* Jewish communities. It is insulting to Jewish communities who continue to face antisemitism today. Even in North America, it is lunacy. The emphasis on light-skinned Jews as privileged white people both misunderstands the deadly violence which has historically been directed at them and can erase the mere existence of other Jewish people.

No Jew by birth is white, but many Jews aren't even white-passing. By simply framing Jews as white, without adding the nuance of specifically addressing the identity of light-skinned Jews, the lives of non-white passing Ashkenazi Jews, Beta-Yisrael, Mizrahi and Sephardic Jews, as well as Black, Brown and Asian Jews, are ignored.

It is tragic that the majority of American Jews felt they had to warp their own identity to acculturate. There is also no denying that they benefited from being perceived as white. But while they believed that they had been fully accepted by and totally integrated into American society, rising antisemitism tragically paints a different picture – not just of the present but, in retrospect, of the entirety of the American Jewish relationship.

ANTIZIONISM, PRO-PALESTINIANISM AND BLACK CIVIL RIGHTS

Not only have the realities and nuance of Jewish identity been erased through the American Black-white racial binary, but, in recent years, members of the US progressive community have joined forces with pro-Palestinian activists against their perceived shared enemy: white supremacy – which, from their perspective, includes Jews and Israel.

Much of this rhetoric echoes the Soviet antizionist-infused antisemitism that we explored in Chapter 1. This ideological union is a result of certain American civil rights campaigners, such as Angela Davis, working with the Soviet Union during the 1970s. These were important partnerships and in 1971, the CIA estimated that 5% of the Soviet propaganda budget was dedicated to promoting Davis.

In 1972, on a trip to the USSR, she was quoted as saying: 'Everything we have seen in the Soviet Union will inspire us in our own struggle. Our devotion to Marxism-Leninism and Communism and our own ideological convictions have been greatly strengthened.'[228] Along with accusations of Jewish wealth and privilege (and the perception that all Jews were white), this fed the superimposing of the US Black-white racial binary and accusations of white supremacy on Israel and the Palestinians. This is a form of cultural colonialism – an American is imposing their specific and narrow worldview onto other unique and distinct experiences.

While some civil rights voices, such as Martin Luther King, have been raised in support of Israel, the union of certain Black campaigners and Palestinian rights advocates continues to this day. In 2015, for instance, activists from the Movement for Black Lives went to the West Bank to connect with Palestinian activists. As Ahmad Abuznaid, a co-organiser of this delegation, explained: 'In the spirit of Malcolm X, Angela Davis, Stokely Carmichael and many others, we thought the connections between the African American leadership of the movement in the US and those on the ground in Palestine needed to be re-established and fortified.'[229]

The attempt to frame the Israel-Palestine experience in this manner is rooted in leftist antisemitism and the effort to portray Jewish people as white and therefore responsible for white supremacy. During her trip in 2015, Black Lives Matter movement co-founder Patrisse Cullors, an American, described Israel as 'an apartheid state' and stated: 'We can't deny that and if we do deny it, we are a part of the Zionist violence.'[230]

Antisemitism was also visible during the 2020 Black Lives Matter protests. The official Twitter account of the British Black Lives Matter organisation, for instance, published information promoting BDS and in support of the Palestinians, who they see as their ideological cousins. BDS is also an official part of the platform of the Movement for Black Lives. In return, Palestinian activists issued a supportive statement that there was a 'joint struggle between Blacks and Palestinians.'[231] In a June 2020 article, journalist Osama Al-Sharif argued that 'BLM has found an ally in pro-Palestinian activists, including the BDS movement'.[232]

As we saw previously, at different times both Arabs and Jews have been legally classed as both white and non-white in the US. However, while light-skinned Jews are seen as white, the fact that Arabs (including Palestinians) are framed as not white in progressive movements means that they are seen as 'legitimate' victims of prejudice. Meanwhile, antisemitism, specifically that related to antizionism, is delegitimised.

This places Black Zionist Jews in a very difficult situation: it erases their existence and denies their lived experience. It also puts Jewish social justice activists in a very precarious position. Either they abandon a community they wish to support or they have to ignore the realities of antisemitism. It is an injurious choice.

THE RESURGENCE OF AMERICAN ANTISEMITISM

For American Jews, antisemitism has once more become a major threat. In 2019, AJC Global Jewish Advocacy conducted a survey asking American Jews: 'How much of a problem, if at all, do you think antisemitism is in the United States today?'[233] Staggeringly, 88% answered that it was a problem (38% saying it was a very serious problem and 50% saying it was somewhat of a problem). In the same poll, 43% of Jews said that antisemitism in the United States has greatly increased.

These fears are not unfounded. In October 2018, there was the devastating antisemitic mass shooting at The Tree of Life Pittsburgh synagogue where 11 people were murdered on a Shabbat morning. In April 2019, a shooting in a synagogue in Poway in California resulted in the death of Lori Gilbert-Kaye, who threw herself between the gunman and Rabbi Yisroel Goldstein.

Orthodox Jews are regularly physically and verbally assaulted on the streets of New York. During Hanukkah 2019 there were numerous violent acts perpetrated against Orthodox Jews and their property in both the city and neighbouring New Jersey. These acts have been committed by people with various ideologies, far-left, far-right, antizionist, as well as various ethnic groups.

As this violence demonstrated, the Jews most likely to be consistently physically attacked in America are Orthodox Jews or visibly Jewish Jews. With regards to this, I have seen internalised victim-blaming taking place on social media, where American Jews, who are not members of the Orthodox community, vent their frustrations about the Orthodox community. But Orthodox Jews are particularly vulnerable: with only 10% of American Jews identifying as Orthodox, they are a minority within a minority.

Some progressive Jews, it seems, resent the fact that Orthodox Jews have not acculturated into American society and are obstinately Jewish. They stand as a reminder of how different Jewish culture can be in the non-Jewish world. The Orthodox world is often framed as monolithically backwards, homophobic, misogynistic and racist – and having no other characteristics. The author of 'I Married a Jew', for instance, contrasted her husband to his Orthodox parents, writing that: 'Like a large percentage of modern and intelligent young Jews, [he] looks with affectionate tolerance on these parental habits but eschews them for himself.'[234] Note her use of the words 'modern and intelligent'. She is making very clear her views on Orthodox Jews.

Eighty years on attitudes do not seem to have changed. The Satmar community in Netflix's *Unorthodox* are portrayed as backwards, archaic, unevolved and deeply prejudiced. Germany is, by contrast, given a redemption story and shown as a secular, welcoming society. Anyone who recognises the current level of antisemitism in Germany will view this as absurd.

I am not suggesting the Orthodox world cannot work to make themselves more inclusive – as a proud Jewish gay man, this is also something particularly important to me – but there is also much beauty in the Orthodox communities and they are defiantly and proudly Jewish. Jewish Pride is about accepting and loving all parts of the Jewish world, not just the ones we agree with. This does not mean simply accepting things we disagree with. Instead, we should aim to enter into dialogue to support change where possible and, at the very least, attempt to understand those with whom we have differences. For example, I have many disagreements with the Satmar Hassidim, but I understand that much of their way of life has been constructed in a post-Holocaust world where they are trying to understand, and come to terms with, the horror that befell and practically erased them.

Another major issue facing American Jewry is antisemitism on university campuses. My own time at university was incredibly difficult due to antisemitism. Disturbingly, though, antisemitism continues to drastically intensify for young Jews, especially in the United States. I have seen Jewish students from around the world on Twitter trying to raise awareness of this issue. To understand what is happening to Jewish students today, I interviewed Rafaella Gunz, a Jewish American student, to understand her experiences at the City University of New York (CUNY).

RAFAELLA GUNZ AND CUNY

Rafaella Gunz is a young passionate activist who has spent many years writing about, and advocating for, women's issues, the LGTBQ+ community and, more recently, Jews.

I wanted to speak with her because she has had the immense courage to be very open about the incredible and orchestrated antisemitic campaign she experienced for six months at CUNY. During our conversation, Rafaella told me her heartbreaking story. Although it is personal to her, it is also our story and the story of countless Jewish students on university campuses around the world.

Before starting law school at CUNY, Rafaella attended the New School, a university in New York, where she minored in Gender Studies. Interestingly, the New School used to be known as the 'New University in Exile', as it was one of the only institutions in America to give Jewish professors fleeing Nazi persecution a place to work. Her time at the New School was not marred by anti-Jewish racism, although she did experience one particularly memorable instance of antisemitism. Rafaella worked on the school paper and, following her first trip to Israel, was inspired to write about the intersection of being

LGBTQ+ and Jewish. Rafaella herself identifies as bi-sexual and inter-viewed LGBTQ+ Jews to highlight their experiences. The focus of this article was on American Jews but it obviously mentioned Israel and she interviewed one Israeli.

After this article was released, Students for Justice for Palestine (SJP) defaced a physical copy of the article using big red markers with the words: 'Stop pinkwashing apartheid' and then posted it on social media. Pinkwashing is the accusation that Israel highlights its record on LGBTQ+ issues to silence criticism of its treatment of the Pales-tinians. This concept is an attack on nuance. This was the first time Rafaella had been open about her Jewish identity on campus and left-wing antisemites – under the guise of Palestinian solidarity – sought to silence her merely because she was a Zionist Jew.

In June 2019, Rafaella applied to, and was accepted by, CUNY's Law School. Ironically, given her later experience, CUNY was set up as a response to the quotas which limited the number of Jewish students at Ivy League institutions such as Harvard. Rafaella took up her place at CUNY in August 2019. She left the university less than six months later due to her horrifying and deeply upsetting experience there.

Prior to the start of the new academic year, Rafaella went on an open day to visit the CUNY campuses. She recognises that what unfolded that day should have been a red flag, but it underlines the continuous feeling of hope of the Jewish community that she none-theless went ahead and joined the University.

While she was on the tour, she spotted a bulletin board that adver-tised a Jewish students' group. Clearly feeling safe, she remarked: 'Oh I am so happy there's a Jewish student group, I don't usually talk about my Jewish identity because it's very divisive.' Her guide responded with the words: 'Well, we don't hate Jews, just Zionists.' While this is obviously very shocking, being a progressive, Rafaella tried to engage her guide in dialogue, which he seemed open to. His respectful engagement with her perspective gave Rafaella hope that, even if she

encountered leftist antisemitism, there might be real and productive
opportunities to hold these difficult conversations.

Despite her open mind – and her simple desire, like all students,
to make friends and feel safe – the targeting of her because of her
Jewishness began immediately.

Rafaella is one of the key voices of young Jewish students on Twitter;
she adds nuance to complex conversations and regularly receives antisemitic comments in return. As soon as the new academic year started,
Rafaella was stalked online and screenshots of her defending herself
against antisemitic trolls were circulated by SJP. However, this tweet was
inexplicably and maliciously interpreted as a threat to Muslim students.
Once again, Rafaella was marked as a bad Zionist Jew.

At the beginning of each new school year, the student organisations hold a fair to advertise themselves to new members. At the
2019 fair, Rafaella spotted the SJP table and was shocked to see a
woman wearing a sweatshirt that featured a map of Israel and the
words 'Free Palestine'. Understanding the importance of document-
ing antisemitism, Rafaella took a photo of the sweatshirt, taking great
care to ensure that the woman wearing it could not be identified.
Rafaella then shared this photo on Twitter, under a locked account,
informing her followers – myself included – of what she was experiencing at university. Screenshots of her tweet – and other tweets
shared in the CUNY community – once again described Rafaella as
a 'threat to Muslim students'. A clear narrative was taking shape: if a
Jewish student speaks out against leftist antisemitism, they must be
right-wing, racist and Islamophobic. But, for Rafaella, who has always
identified as progressive, nothing could be further from the truth.

In October 2019, the SJP, along with organisations, set up a bake
sale next to the escalator, which Rafaella had to pass by multiple times
a day to get to her locker. As an isolated and targeted Jewish student,
she was forced to pass by this antizionist propaganda repeatedly. Once
again, Rafaella photographed the stall. 'In the back of my mind,' she

says, 'I am very much aware that Jews are not believed when they speak out against antisemitism and I wanted to gather evidence.' She did not share the photograph online and, once again, she made sure that no one was identifiable in it. As Rafaella came down the escalator one day, the teaching assistant from her criminal law class who was at the SJP stall accosted her and said, in a very pointed and threatening tone: 'Do you want to buy anything?'

It is important to remember that the assistant was in a position of authority, yet still felt justified in speaking to Rafaella in a biting way. Later that same day, the teaching assistant followed Rafaella, found her classroom, and waited for her after the end of her next class. Though she was with friends, the assistant asked to speak to her 'in private', thus isolating her from those who could support her. This was clearly an abuse of power because, Rafaella, who was already feeling threatened, wouldn't have agreed if the woman had not been a teaching assistant. Rafaella was being abused not only by the student body but also by those in positions of authority who were meant to protect her.

The teaching assistant found an empty classroom and quickly said: 'What's your issue with us?', not being able to recognise for one second – due to her belief that the left has a monopoly on good – that her antisemitism and that of the SJP students was what was bothering Rafaella. As we have seen on numerous occasions, she couldn't see her own racism because she identified as an anti-racist.

The teaching assistant was aggressive and threatening, telling Rafaella: 'You knew what you were getting into by coming here.' Thus, this was – in some perverse universe – all Rafaella's fault: the Jewish student is to blame for seeking an education. In this conversation, she proceeded to tell Rafaella that Zionism was inherently anti-Palestinian and she would protest against any Israeli if they spoke on campus. She couldn't see that it was not Rafaella who had any real issue with her and SJP, it was SJP that had an issue with Rafaella because she was a Zionist Jew.

Understandably, Rafaella burst into tears because of this aggressive conversation. Rafaella, as a young Jewish student, had been targeted in an unacceptable, deeply antisemitic way.

The following week, the SJP held their bake sale again and, to avoid any further confrontation, Rafaella felt forced to take the back staircase. Let's just take this fact in, for a moment. A Jewish member of this academic community felt compelled to isolate and demean herself due to threatening leftist antisemitism. It is disgusting, and at this point during our conversation, the emotions of this incredibly traumatic experience overcame Rafaella and she had to take a moment to compose herself. Seeing the pain these antisemites have caused her is incredibly difficult, but this is the realities of antisemitism. Jewish people all over the world continue to be deeply traumatised by the immense antisemitism they experience from all parts of society and all sides of the political spectrum.

Throughout this experience, Rafaella did the responsible thing and reported this abuse to the dean of students – four times. The dean sent Rafaella to the guidance counsellor but when she said that being Jewish was her ethnicity, not her faith, received the response: 'Well, that's debatable.' Rafaella was stunned. The non-Jewish dean was bluntly telling Rafaella that her ethnicity and identity were up for debate. The dean abused her power and abused her duty of care. Can you imagine many other minorities having their identity disregarded and twisted in this way?

Around Thanksgiving in November Rafaella bravely began writing an article detailing her experiences at CUNY. The article, titled 'Campus Antisemitism Made Me a Zionist', was published in January. In response to her honesty, several of her classmates commented under the article accusing her of Islamophobia, harming Muslim students, and asserting that complaints were being made about Rafaella to the dean.

In response to this, one of her professors (yes, her *professor*) spent 30 minutes telling the class that 'students had come up to her asking her to reprimand a certain student' – a clear reference to Rafaella.

It is hard for people who haven't experienced this to imagine just how incredibly isolating and upsetting it is for a Jewish student to be targeted in this way by both staff and peers.

Following this sustained abuse, Rafaella was forced to take a leave of absence for her mental health. Despite no longer being on campus, a petition was created and circulated decrying the fact that 'a subset of Zionist activists choose to weaponize the genuine threats of anti-Semitism elsewhere in our society as a tactic to repress activism and harass and threaten Palestinian students and Muslim students more broadly'.[235] The petition, targeted at Rafaella and only Rafaella, also stated: 'This tactic of conflating a critique of Judaism with critiques of Israel as a nation-state is on the rise around the country.' Given their former track record, it is unsurprising that Rafaella's former classmates signed this deeply antisemitic petition, but shockingly, so, too, did 20 members of CUNY's staff, including her professor, the dean of students and the teaching assistant who had accosted her.

In response to Rafaella, a Palestinian Solidarity Day was also staged – despite its target no longer being on campus. One of the accusations that Rafaella faced when her article came out, is one that is regularly deployed against Jews who speak out against leftist anti-semitism, regardless of their political persuasion. They are described as right-wing. The attempt to compare Rafaella to Donald Trump is an example of the external world's antisemitic characterisation of Jews that assign evil to a delusional caricature they have created. It is particularly offensive and hurtful to someone like Rafaella, who has made it her life's work to champion groups that Trump harms. She is a fierce advocate for many social justice issues including women's rights and LGBTQ+ issues. She only became an active participant in the fight against antisemitism in 2017, when she saw that the Chicago Dyke March excluded women who carried Jewish symbols. Like many others and I, Rafaella was expelled from the 'community of the good' because she simply believed that Israel has a right to exist.

Rafaella is incredibly courageous for standing up against the antisemitism she encountered – but it was not without an enormous personal cost. After taking a leave of absence in January, she has now decided not to continue her education at CUNY. Rafaella will now pursue social work at New York's Yeshiva University and I know she will make a wonderful social worker who will help protect vulnerable people. But none of this detracts from, or makes up for, the hugely traumatic experience she suffered at CUNY.

In September 23 2020, the CUNY Law Twitter account wrote a since deleted tweet stating: '@CUNYLaw stands against hate and antisemitism. We stand for the law to promote the rights and dignity of all human beings and to train lawyers whose work advances justice and equality.'[236]

It's just a pity they didn't promote the rights and dignity of Rafaella during her time at CUNY.

PRECEDENT MATTERS

In John Berry's model of acculturation, we can find a way to understand how Jewish communities throughout history have responded to antisemitism. We see its impact upon their identities and we can learn from their experiences while we seek to build a Jewish Pride movement. There is much to praise about Jews from France, Germany and America. But, despite their serious effort and sacrifices to acculturate, they were not able to escape antisemitism. This chapter is not intended to unduly criticise these Jewish communities. The purpose is to highlight the historical precedent of Jewish people being forced to fundamentally alter their identities to accommodate the non-Jewish world's delusional perceptions of their identities. Any ramifications from this accommodation essentially remains the fault of society at large. When considering how Jewish identities were formed in each of these countries, it is important to understand this context and nuance.

We have seen this time and time again. Despite Dreyfus being able to become a captain in the French army, he was still a victim of an antisemitic plot. Despite German Jews reaching the highest levels of acculturation in their history, antisemitism hammered down on them with deadlier force than any other in modern history. Despite American Jews experiencing a 'Golden Age' of acceptance and working hard to integrate, they are currently facing a crisis of antisemitism reminiscent of so many other periods of Jewish history.

Every day that I teach, I tell my students: 'You are perfect as you are, you don't need to change to fit in.' Why then do we as Jews make so much effort to give up and change our identities to become part of societies that ultimately reject us, despite our repeated attempts? And, if that is the case, then surely there is a way to focus our attention less on fitting in and more on creating a strong and proud Jewish community that integrates in a healthy way.

I am not advocating for the Jewish community to follow the route of separation described by Berry's, and to live in isolated and ghettoised communities. I believe that it is both possible and important to integrate with the societies in which we live.

But integration should mean that we engage as equals – with pride in our beautiful identity, heritage and culture – and not as people begging to be tolerated, accepted or respected.

Chapter 4

JEWISH RESPONSES TO ANTISEMITISM: INTERNALISATION

PRIDE AND THE DIFFERENT forms of acculturation explored in Chapter 3 are not the only ways in which groups can respond to their minority status. Sometimes they can internalise the hate that swirls around them in the 'clouds of prejudice'. The issue of internalised prejudice is not a strictly Jewish phenomenon and it can be identified in other targeted and vulnerable groups as well.

Unfortunately, I have my own experiences with internalised prejudice. When I was a young closeted gay man, I did not have a healthy relationship with my sexuality. My multiple mental health difficulties were the result of internalised homophobia, and I believed that being gay was not something I should be proud of.

At one point, after being a victim of homophobic abuse in the street, I even considered pursuing conversion therapy: a pseudo-scientific and enormously damaging form of 'therapy' that attempts to turn gay people straight. It doesn't work because homosexuality is not a disease, an illness or something people need to change.

After years of working hard to accept myself, I am now a very proud gay man. Yet, I still witness this internalisation of homophobia within my community. For example, there are gay men who regularly denigrate other gay men they deem to be too feminine. These gay men adopt toxic masculine traits which shame anything not perceived as traditionally masculine – such as femininity – as a weakness. Toxic masculinity persecutes those in the gay community who embody what are perceived as 'negative stereotypically gay characteristics', such as being effeminate. I know gay friends who are worried they aren't masculine enough, that their voices sound 'too gay', and, from my experience, gay men spend more time in the gym trying to hone a 'traditionally masculine physique' in an attempt to demonstrate that they are indeed 'real men'. This internalisation of homophobia is very damaging and has a deep impact on the mental health of LGBTQ+ people. As I stated previously, LGBTQ+ people are four times more likely to attempt suicide than their heterosexual counterparts. Simply put, a negative and oppressive external identity can be internalised and can damage you psychologically and even lead to forms of self-harm.

Internalised prejudice is a concept rooted in psychological theory. The 'minority stress model' explains the trauma of prejudice, and is described as:

> A social research and public health model designed to help us better understand the lived experiences of people of oppressed communities. The model posits that within the social structure of a particular culture or society, certain (oppressed) groups experience greater incidents of minority stress (based on race, sexuality, gender, disability, etc.) in the form of prejudice and discrimination. As a result of those experiences, members of oppressed communities experience greater negative health outcomes than majority group communities.[237]

As with my own experience, 'incidents of stress, prejudice, and discrimination related to one's oppressed identity leads to serious negative consequences for both physical and mental health'. Considering how little positive representation of LGBTQ+ people I saw growing up, combined with the overt homophobia I witnessed and experienced, it was little wonder I struggled so much with my mental health. Over time, incidents of prejudice and a lack of positive representation can lead to 'negative internal responses for those who experience those events, such as … internalized negative beliefs about their own race, gender or sexual identities'.

This is why we see gay men sometimes railing against other gay men who seem to conform to society's homophobic perception of what it means to be gay. This phenomenon is revealing because an internalised prejudice does not necessarily lead you to always hate yourself, but rather to be ashamed of and/or hate other members of your minority group who you see as conforming to stereotypes. This is why 'self-hater' is not an appropriate or useful way to understand this issue. Understanding different responses to prejudice are vital as it helps the wider world to see how prejudice impacts the psychology of those it targets – as well as allowing targeted communities to better guard themselves against this type of response, for example by engaging in activities which boosts the group's sense of pride in itself.

The issue of internalised prejudice in America's Black community is well-documented. In the *Encyclopedia of Multicultural Psychology*, for instance, the psychologist Yo Jackson references 'Uncle Tom syndrome'.[238] This syndrome is a psychological theory which sees members of a minority become subservient to the majority when threatened (or when living under direct threat). The term 'Uncle Tom' is drawn from Harriet Beecher Stowe's novel *Uncle Tom's Cabin*, in which the titular figure of Tom is portrayed as an elderly Black man who was incredibly subservient to white people. This is not just a historic issue in the American Black community. As the diversity consultant and trainer Donna K Bivens states: 'This internalized racism has its own systemic reality and its own negative consequences in the lives and communities of people of color.'[239]

While much of the original research on internalised prejudice focuses on the American Black community – and some of it is specific to their particular experience – it can also be helpful in understanding this issue in the Jewish community. This is not meant to appropriate important research that focuses on this issue in the American Black community. However, there is simply much less research on this issue in the Jewish community, so, to understand it, we have to look to research conducted among other communities. We should, of course, always be mindful and respectful of the specific nature of each individual community's experiences.

As stated, describing someone as 'self-hating' is unhelpful and inappropriate. The issue is much more complex than that. It is much more accurate to describe someone as having internalised prejudice. Writing about the American Black community, Bivens suggests: 'Internalized racism is systemic oppression, it must be distinguished from human wounds like self-hatred or "low self-esteem", to which all people are vulnerable. It is important to understand it as systemic because that makes it clear that it is not a problem simply of individuals. It is structural.'[240]

Due to the institutional nature of antisemitism, this is also true for the Jewish Diasporic world. It has to be recognised, though, that proving someone has 'internalised antisemitism' is very challenging and obviously depends on your own definition of what it means to be a proud Jew. My definition of being a proud Jew is based on the rejection of antisemitic notions of what it means to be Jewish. If I believe someone has adopted them, I would describe that person as having internalised antisemitism. For example, I believe that being a Zionist (that is, believing in the concept of self-determination in a Jewish state in the indigenous homeland of the Jews) is a fundamental part of Jewish Pride and of Jewish life. If a Jew identifies as an antizionist in the age of the Jewish state, or if they do not recognise Israel's right to exist, then I would describe them as having internalised antisemitism. If a non-Jew who treats Israel with double standards or delegitimises and demonises the country can be termed antisemitic, then this can also be said of Jews who behave in the same manner. Jewish people, like other groups, do not need to agree on every single issue and conflict is natural. However, there are certain things – such as the existence of the

State of Israel and of the people who live there – that should not be 'up for debate', whether you are Jewish, or not.

Bivens argues that internalised racism in the American Black community can function in four different ways:

- inner, where it 'affects the inner lives of people of color';

- interpersonal where individuals 'continually facing racism and white privilege can negatively impact the ability of people of color to maintain healthy and fulfilling relationships with each other or with those who have white privilege';

- institutional where 'people of color often question or subvert' their 'power in white-controlled institutions';

- and cultural, where 'dehumanizing relationships, systemic racism decimates cultures—clearly those of its victims, but ultimately also those of its perpetrators'.

While the Jewish and American Black communities' experiences are in some ways different to one another, antisemitism can manifest itself along similar lines. For example, it can be argued that antizionist Jews who demonise Zionist Jews or Israel are exhibiting interpersonal internalised antisemitism. The distinction between these two manifestations is important. However tragic the roots of their internalised antisemitism, Jews with interpersonal internalised antisemitism are posing an active danger to our community by validating and enabling antisemitism, whereas Jews with inner internalised antisemitism are primarily harming themselves (which is tragic enough).

This is a complex issue with many layers. However, based on psychological theory and the experience of other communities, the issue of internalised antisemitism is clearly one that has an impact upon the Jewish world. Jews with interpersonal internalised antisemitism not only have an internalised response to institutional antisemitism but, as we will see, they have weaponised their Jewish identity to harm other Jews. This doesn't mean we should blame any Jewish person for having absorbed the non-Jewish world's perceptions of what it means to be Jewish. As Bivens suggests: 'internalized racism is systemic oppression'. But this means to tackle this issue we do have to understand the threat Jews with interpersonal internalised antisemitism pose to the rest of the Jewish community, especially considering the levels of external antisemitism we face.

HISTORICAL JEWS WITH INTERNALISED ANTISEMITISM

Because Jews have faced intense persecution for thousands of years, internalised antisemitism has been a feature of Jewish identity for just as long. There are countless examples of this form of internalised prejudice throughout Jewish history. Although the following examples are clearly historical, I am analysing these figures through modern psychological theories. Due to differences in context, it is not always right to impose modern ideas onto the actions of historical figures. However, it is appropriate in this context in order to better understand the historical precedent of internalised antisemitism. These historical figures represent different points of an unbroken chain of Jewish reaction to antisemitism. Though each example is separated by a thousand years and differing contexts, they all exhibit a similar response to being Jewish in a non-Jewish world.

An example of a Jew manifesting internalised antisemitism was Tiberius Julius Alexander, a governor and general in the Roman empire, who has been labelled 'the Jew who destroyed Jerusalem' by *The Jerusalem Post*.[241] This is in reference to Tiberius' role in the first Jewish-Roman war, which resulted in the destruction of the Second Temple and, ultimately, the end of an independent Jewish state for 2,000 years. Tiberius' internalised antisemitism was so great that even

Flavius Josephus, the infamous Jewish historian, criticised him in *Antiquities of the Jews* because he 'did not remain in the religion of his country'.[242] Interestingly, Flavius Josephus himself has been accused of having internalised antisemitism due to his defection to the side of the Romans during the first Jewish-Roman war.

Tiberius was born in Alexandria, then a Roman Egyptian province, in roughly 14-16 CE. His family were one of the few Jewish families in Egypt to hold citizenship. His father, Alexander, held the office of *alabarch* – traditionally the head of Alexandra's Jewish population – and was one of the richest men in Alexandria. Tiberius' uncle was Philo, the famed Hellenistic Jewish philosopher. Despite being 'Hellenised', Tiberius' family maintained a strong Jewish connection and identity. This is evident in Philos' writings, who, when attempting to combat antisemitism, is said to have 'preferred to extol the virtues of Judaism than to fight against the adversaries of Jews, as we can see in the extant fragments of his Hypotetica'.[243] Alexander, moreover, 'was famous for his gift of gilded gates to the Jerusalem Temple'.[244] In a tragic twist of fate, these are the same gates that his son, Tiberius, would help destroy.

Despite this Jewish upbringing, events that unfolded during Tiberius' youth seem to have left deep scars. In 38 CE, devastating anti-Jewish riots took place in Alexandria. The only remaining eye-witness testimony is from Philo, who later travelled to Rome to plead the case of the Jews to the Emperor Caligula. These riots demonstrated the precarious situation for Jews living in the Roman empire. As Rabbi Marisa Elana James suggests, at this time it was 'perhaps becoming true that Jews could only achieve the highest roles in society if they ceased to publicly practice their Judaism'.[245]

Due to the lack of historical records, much of what we know about the riots is speculation. However, we can assume that this ancient pogrom, and the humiliation of his uncle at the hands of the Roman emperor, would have led Tiberius to see his Jewishness as a hindrance to his future career plans.

Aged 30, Tiberius became the procurator of Judea, a position he held until 48 CE. Twelve years later, he became procurator of Egypt, remaining in that role until 70 CE. In 66 CE, he failed to quell the Alexandrian riots, which were caused by Greek attacks on Jews during a public discussion about sending a mission to Emperor Nero. As Flavius Josephus reported: 'They rushed out, and laid violent hands upon the Jews, and as for the rest, they were slain as they ran away. There were three men whom they caught and hauled along, to burn them alive.'[246]

While the Jewish community threatened violence in return, Tiberius urged Jews to remain calm in case they provoked the Roman army. But the Jewish community 'reproached him for so uttering threats'[247]. The consequences were devastating, with Tiberius sending in 5,000 Roman troops to destroy the Jewish community. Flavius Josephus described the events that followed:

[Tiberius] then let loose among them the two Roman legions, and with them 2,000 soldiers who happened to have come from Libya, with fearful consequences for the Jews. He gave the men leave not merely to kill them but also to plunder their property and burn down their houses. The soldiers rushed into the area called Delta where the Jews were concentrated, and proceeded to carry out their orders, but not without bloodshed on their own side; for the Jews stood shoulder to shoulder with their most heavily armed men in front and held their ground magnificently, but when once the line gave they were destroyed wholesale. Death came upon them in every form; some were overtaken in the open, others driven into their houses, which the Romans first looted and then burnt down. They felt no pity for infants, no respect for the aged; old and young were slaughtered right and left, so that the whole district was deluged with blood and 50,000 corpses were heaped up: even the remnant would not have survived had they not begged for mercy till Alexander, pitying them, ordered the Romans to retire.[248]

In short, Tiberius, a Jew from Alexandria, oversaw the murder of 50,000 Alexandrian Jews.

Following his time in Egypt, Tiberius was appointed as the chief of staff to Titus, the son of Emperor Vespasian. Once again, he was brought into direct conflict with Jewish people when he travelled with Titus to Jerusalem to take part in the siege, after which the Second Temple – which was built by King Herod and adorned with the golden gates donated by Tiberius' father – was destroyed.

As the highest-ranking officer at Titus' headquarters, the historian Aryeh Kasher has written, Tiberius 'participated in the siege of Jerusalem, and he may even have been responsible for burning the Temple down'.[249] After the siege, all Jerusalemites became Roman prisoners and, according to Flavius Josephus, 97,000 were enslaved. Some were eventually forced to build famous Roman structures like the Colosseum. As he had been in Alexandria, Tiberius was thus an active participant in the destruction of his own people.

As the story unfolded 2,000 years ago, it is important to treat any historical record, such as that of Flavius Josephus, with caution. But, his career suggests that Tiberius considered himself to primarily be Roman and, through conjecture, we can assume that this led him to abandon his Jewishness. It seems impossible for him to have maintained any kind of Jewish identity while he participated not just in the murder of more traditional Jews in Jerusalem, but the Hellenised Jews of Alexandria.

It is difficult to truly understand Tiberius' motives for his crimes against the Jewish people. Yet, despite his ability to rise to positions of political power, it is worth remembering that he was still a Jew in the Roman empire. While, as the historian Martin Goodman argues, 'ethnic origins could be ignored if someone was sufficiently talented,'[250] the incredibly tense relationship and the constant wars between Jews and the Romans prior to the siege of Jerusalem cannot be ignored. It is entirely possible that Tiberius believed that the only route to real political power was not simply to shed his Jewishness but to prove how 'good a Roman he really was' – by murdering Jews and helping destroy symbols of Judaism.

If we fast forward roughly 1,000 years, we encounter another historic example of a Jew with internalised antisemitism. In Chapter 1, we briefly encountered Theobald of Cambridge, a Jewish convert to Christianity who testified to Thomas of Monmouth for his work, *The Life and Miracles of St. William of Norwich,* regarding the Jewish proclivity for murdering non-Jewish children to use their blood. Thomas indeed made much play of Theobald's Jewish ancestry, writing at one point: 'These words – observe, the words of a converted Jew – we reckon to be all the truer, in that we received them as uttered by one who was a converted enemy, and also had been privy to the secrets of our enemies.'[251] Underlining his attempt to use Theobald's Jewishness as evidence of his trustworthiness, Thomas also suggested: 'As a proof of the truth and credibility of the matter we now adduce something which we have heard from the lips of Theobald, who was once a Jew, and afterwards a monk.'

Theobald offers an incredibly clear example of a Jewish person who had, due to the high levels of surrounding antisemitism, absorbed this prejudice and weaponised his own Jewish identity (or, in this case, former Jewish identity) against the rest of the Jewish population. Using Bivens' model of understanding internalised racism, we can argue that Theobald exhibited both internal and interpersonal internalised antisemitism; his conversion to Christianity serves as a rejection of his Jewishness and his testimony to Thomas was a direct attack on Jewish people.

Theobald's testimony rested at the heart of The *Life and Miracles of St. William of Norwich* and his Jewishness made him a star witness in this literary trial of the Jews. When he lied to Thomas, he did so not simply to vilify the Jewish people, but also to ensure his status as a 'good Christian'.

It is hard to believe how, regardless of which religion they ultimately identified with, someone who was born a Jew could turn so viciously on their own historic community. Yet we cannot underestimate the psychological impact of antisemitic prejudice. This becomes clear when placed in the context of the period in which Theobald lived. Fifty years previously, England had fought and won the First Crusade and the ascendancy of Christianity was viewed as a divine right. Theobald's expressions of Jew-hate were deeply influenced by this domineering Christian narrative, which was embedded with anti-Judaism.

Theobald had no pride for the people he came from; instead, the overarching might of Christianity had produced within him an internalised shame. It is not difficult, given this backdrop, to imagine why he would reject his Jewishness and work hard to curry favour with Christianity by demonising Jewish people – and, make no mistake, this is exactly what Theobald did.

Not only did he accuse Jewish people in Norwich of murder, but he fabricated the idea of an international Jewish conspiracy centred on the murder of innocent children. Examining exactly what Theobald is meant to have said is important. He does not merely argue that Jews need the blood of non-Jewish children for *Pesach* or some other religious ritual – a terrible accusation in and of itself – but he also creates a scenario where Jews are purposefully targeting and attacking the very roots of Christianity – Jesus. Using Theobald's testimony, Thomas wrote: 'Hence it was laid down by them in ancient times that every year they must sacrifice a Christian in some part of the world to the Most High God in scorn and contempt of Christ, that so they might avenge their sufferings on Him; inasmuch as it was because of Christ's death that they had been shut out from their own country, and were in exile as slaves in a foreign land.'[252]

Thus, according to Theobald, this alleged child sacrifice was an attack on Jesus and the entire Christian world. In his bid for acceptance in the dominant Christian world, he used his proximity to Jewishness and Judaism to affirm Christian antisemitism. Theobald helped cause generations of irreparable harm to the Jewish community in England and Europe more widely, with his testimony repeatedly used to justify accusations of the blood libel across the continent.

MODERN INTERNALISED ANTISEMITISM

One thousand years later and we find ourselves in the 20th century, where, sadly, we are still dealing with the issue of Jews and internalised antisemitism. As they have throughout history, the specific manifestations of both antisemitism and internalised antisemitism are based on the context of the era surrounding the individuals involved. Tiberius' antisemitism reflected Jew-hatred in the Roman empire, while Theobald echoed wider Christian antisemitism.

Since the establishment of modern political Zionism in the late 19th century, there have always been Jews who decided not to support the recreation of a Jewish state. Prior to 1948, those Jews who opposed the idea of a Jewish state were arguing against a then-theoretical concept, not campaigning against an actual, existing sovereign state nor the destruction of an actual country, Israel, and its people.

There is one exception: the Yevsektsiya. The Yevsektsiya, created in 1918 following the October 1917 Russian revolution, pledged to support the 'destruction of traditional Jewish life, the Zionist movement, and Hebrew culture'.[253] Despite the clear antisemitism inherent in this statement (let alone any of their actions), these Jews claimed they were simply antizionist, not antisemitic. It is an argument that is parroted by antizionist Jews today.

The Yevsektsiya was created to encourage Jews to join the revolutionary movement. As Semyon Dimanstein, chair of the Yevsektsiya, stated: 'When the October revolution came, the Jewish workers had remained totally passive ... and a large part of them were even against the revolution. The revolution did not reach the Jewish street. Everything remained as before.'[254]

The Yevsektsiya advocated for the destruction of Zionist organisations and Jewish communities and, as the historian Richard Pipes argued, in time, 'every Jewish cultural and social organization came under assault'[255] – not just from the new Soviet government, but from Jewish communists specifically.

With a promise of acceptance from the non-Jewish world, these Jews turned against other Jews, in order to prove themselves worthy of belonging to the new world order of their home, the USSR. The Yevsektsiya legally destroyed Jewish community organisations and the offices of these organisations were burned down. The Yevsektsiya raided the offices of Zionist organisations in Ukraine and arrested all their leaders. Schools that taught the ancient Jewish language of Hebrew were shut down, as were the rabbinical schools, and thousands of Jews were subjected to show trials.

Unsurprisingly, this Jewish bid for acceptance failed. The Yevsektsiya was disbanded in 1929, and, as is so often the tragic lot of tokenized Jews, many of its leaders – including Dimanstein – were eventually murdered by Stalin. The Yevsektsiya Jews caused real and irreparable damage to Jewish communities in the Soviet Union, helping to destroy Jewish life and culture, all in the hope of being accepted. Yet, in the end, it did nothing to protect them.

Unlike the Yevsektsiya, we live today in the time of a modern Jewish state and Israel, as previously discussed, is often targeted as the 'collective Jew'. Modern antizionism, which demonises, delegitimises and subjects Israel to double standards, dominates much of the leftist worldview today as a form of antisemitism. It is through this specific lens that we will explore modern Jews with internalised antisemitism.

Jews who fairly, and even harshly, criticise Israeli government policy or actions are not antisemitic and don't harbour internalised antisemitism. However, those who delegitimise and demonise the

Jewish state, and treat Israel with double standards they do not apply to other countries, do harbour internalised antisemitism.

Some Jews, of course, believe antizionism is not a form of antisemitism. In March 2019, the American journalist Peter Beinart argued in a piece for *The Guardian*: 'Anti-Zionism is not inherently antisemitic – and claiming it uses Jewish suffering to erase the Palestinian experience.'[256] I disagree.

Antizionist Jews have absorbed antisemitic perceptions of Israel and, instead of rejecting this antisemitism, they have internalised it and, in turn, rejected Israel, the Jewish state. To be clear, when I say, 'antizionist Jews', I do not mean the majority of Jews who identified as antizionist prior to the establishment of the State of Israel in 1948 who were against the *idea* of a state, not an actual, living state. Nor do I include those ultra-Orthodox Jews who identify as antizionist. While I vehemently disagree with them, and believe that they harm other Jewish people, their antizionism is more complicated than that of progressive Jews, as their beliefs call for a return of the Jews to their homeland, but not until the coming of the Messiah. Of course, some partner with antisemites and actively work against the Jews of Israel, so it could be reasonably argued that they exhibit signs of modern internalised antisemitism. However, theirs is a more nuanced situation that requires a more in-depth examination.

For the avoidance of doubt, references in this chapter to 'antizionist Jews' apply only to modern, left-wing, antizionist Jews. To demonstrate that this is an issue which impacts Jews from all over the world, we will explore case studies from both the United Kingdom and the United States. Nonetheless, there are countless other examples of Jews with internalised antisemitism in both the UK, US and indeed the rest of the world.

CASE STUDY ONE: BRITAIN

In July 2017, during the midst of the Labour party antisemitism crisis, a new group called Jewish Voice for Labour (JVL) was formed. JVL said its aim was to 'uphold the right of supporters of justice for Palestinians to engage in solidarity activities' – including boycotts of Israel – and to oppose 'attempts to widen the definition of antisemitism beyond its meaning of hostility towards, or discrimination against, Jews as Jews'.[257]

JVL also claimed it was established to offer an 'alternative voice for Jewish members of Labour'.[258] The alternative voice it is referring to is the Jewish Labour Movement, which has been officially affiliated with the Labour party for 100 years.

JVL's real purpose, argues JVLWatch, an organisation dedicated to monitoring and investigating its work, appears to be to 'lend legitimacy to modern antisemitism by giving it a Kosher seal of approval' particularly in reference allegations of Corbyn's antisemitism.[259] Their support for Jeremy Corbyn, throughout his period as leader was absolute and unquestioning, and they strenuously defended Labour's handling of antisemitism. In February 2019, for instance, they published an open letter that praised Corbyn's 'lifetime record of campaigning for equality and human rights, including consistent support for initiatives against anti-Semitism, is formidable. His involvement strengthens this struggle.'[260]

But JVL has been described as a 'fringe voice'[261] in the Jewish community. One month after the organisation published its open letter, a poll of British Jews found that 86% of respondents believed that there were 'high levels of antisemitism among Labour Party members and elected representatives'[262] and 87% thought Corbyn himself was antisemitic. Based on this poll, the vast majority of British Jews believed that Corbyn was antisemitic. If JVL believe him not to be and to actually be strengthening the fight against antisemitism, then we can understand its perspective does not reflect the majority of British Jews.

JVL's prominence however, is based on its Jewish identity and that of some of its leading figures. Because of this, they are given a platform, invited on TV and radio, and interviewed by newspapers. The non-Jewish world sees these Jews as Jewish voices that deserve as much representation as other Jewish voices – say, Zionist Jews.

In July 2019, Euan Phillips, spokesperson of the Labour Against Antisemitism group, wrote to the BBC to complain about an appearance by Naomi Wimborne-Idrissi on BBC radio. In his complaint, Phillips noted that Wimborne-Idrissi 'was not accurately described: she represents a tiny faction within the Jewish community and her organisation is not an official affiliate to the Labour Party, unlike the much larger Jewish Labour Movement.'[263]

On the programme, Wimborne-Idrissi suggested proposals for Labour to establish an independent complaints process to investigate allegations of antisemitism within the party 'means bring[ing] in the pro-Israel lobby to make sure that nobody says anything about Israel'.[264] This is an example of the antisemitic conspiracy fantasy.

Wimborne-Idrissi's claims were not challenged by either the host of the programme, Jeremy Vine, or his other guest, the former Labour cabinet minister Lord Falconer. This is perhaps understandable. Many non-Jewish people would feel incredibly uncomfortable about describing something a Jewish person has said as antisemitic. Thus, Wimborne-Idrissi, a Jewish member of JVL, was able to spread antisemitic conspiracy fantasy to the millions of people listening at that time to BBC radio.

While its membership includes a number of non-Jewish people, JVL has many members who identify as Jewish, including Jackie Walker. Walker was expelled from the Labour party in May 2019 due to 'prejudicial and grossly detrimental behaviour against the party'.[265] Her expulsion came after an initial suspension in 2017 following comments she made about Holocaust Memorial Day only commemorating Jewish victims of Nazi persecution. As David Hirsh writes in his book, *Contemporary Left Antisemitism*: 'Jacqueline Walker also spoke about Holocaust commemoration as though it had become a Zionist-owned enterprise whose primary function is to increase the victim-power which it bestows on Jews by creating a hierarchy of victimhood and by obscuring and downplaying other "Holocausts", as she calls them.[266]

This is a post-Holocaust form of antisemitism, whereby Jews are accused of using the Shoah to dominate the global victim narrative, with the aim of ultimately seeking to downplay and minimise the experiences of other communities. However, the violence perpetrated against other minority communities is regularly commemorated during Holocaust Memorial Day in Britain. I took part in Scotland's official commemoration several times and witnessed the commemoration of the Roma community and the Cambodian genocide.

This incident was not Walker's first suspension from the Labour party. The previous year, she was also suspended following antisemitic comments about the alleged role of Jews in the slave trade. 'Many Jews (my ancestors too) were the chief financiers of the sugar and slave trade which is of course why there were so many early synagogues in the Caribbean,' she is quoted as saying. 'So who are victims and what does it mean? We are victims and perpetrators to some extent through choice'.[267]

By claiming that Jews were collectively financers of the slave trade, Walker is repeating the antisemitic lie propagated by Louis Farrakhan in his 1991 book, *The Secret Relationship Between Blacks and Jews,* in which he claims to have 'irrefutable evidence that the most prominent of the Jewish pilgrim fathers [sic] used kidnapped Black Africans disproportionately more than any other ethnic or religious group in New World history.'[268]

David Brion Davis, a historian and leading authority on the slave trade, demolished this lie, writing:

Much of the historical evidence regarding alleged Jewish or New Christian involvement in the slave system was biased by deliberate Spanish efforts to blame Jewish refugees for fostering Dutch commercial expansion at the expense of Spain. Given this long history of conspiratorial fantasy and collective scapegoating, a selective search for Jewish slave traders becomes inherently anti-Semitic unless one keeps in view the larger context and the very marginal place of Jews in the history of the overall system. It is easy enough to point to a few Jewish slave traders in Amsterdam, Bordeaux, or Newport, Rhode Island. But far from suggesting that Jews constituted a major force behind the exploitation of Africa, closer investigation shows that these were highly exceptional merchants, far outnumbered by thousands of Catholics and Protestants who flocked to share in the great bonanza.[269]

Another Jewish JVL member who uses her Jewish identity to legitimise criticism of Israel is JVL co-founder Jenny Manson. While Manson was born and raised a Jew, she publicly stated in 2018 that she 'began to identify as a Jew in order to argue against the State of Israel'.[270] While Israel is a sovereign state, it is the Jewish state and is home to the world's largest Jewish population. Manson seems well aware that her Jewish voice would be seen as more legitimate in the fight against Israel than if she was perceived to be a non-Jew.

But Manson hasn't just used her Jewish identity to denigrate the Jewish state. She has also supported and defended individuals who had been accused of making antisemitic comments. In 2016, the former Labour mayor of London, Ken Livingstone (who Hirsh's 'Livingstone Formulation' was named after), was suspended from the Labour party for stating that Hitler supported Zionism. Livingstone was basing this fallacy on his misreading of the 1933 Haavara Agreement between the Nazi party and the Zionist Federation of Germany. It allowed Jews fleeing Nazi antisemitism to transfer some of their assets to British

Mandatory Palestine. From this agreement, Livingstone attempted to create an ideological connection between Hitler (and the Nazis) and Zionism. Livingstone's inaccurate assertion thus frames Zionism as akin to Nazism. This argument was often utilised in Soviet anti-zionism to denigrate Israel and the Jews.

During Livingstone's Labour party disciplinary hearing in 2017, Manson appeared as a defence witness and said of his comments: 'I remember saying to myself, "it's not a good idea to mention Hitler" but I was not offended because I knew that what Ken Livingstone said was true.'[271] Not only did Manson back up Livingstone's claims about a connection between Hitler and Zionism, but she also delegitimised the idea that someone could be offended by it.

Manson also stated during this hearing that 'nothing that Ken has ever said, in my experience, is offensive or antisemitic and there has to be, I think, much more freedom than we are currently having on the subjects of Israel or the Jews'.[272]

It is, of course, fantastical to suggest that there isn't 'free speech' on Israel when it is routinely and freely demonised and criticised throughout the world. The United Nations' Humans Rights Council, for instance, seems to have an obsession with Israel. As Hillel Neuer, director of the group UN Watch suggests: 'No other country in the world is subjected to a stand-alone focus that is engraved on the body's permanent agenda, ensuring its prominence, and the notoriety of its target, at every council meeting.'[273] Thus, in the first 10 years of its existence through to June 2016, the UNHRC adopted 135 resolutions criticising countries and 68 of those were against Israel.[274] The UNHRC is reflective of the UN's work more generally. According to UN Watch, from 2012 to 2015, the United Nations General Assembly adopted 97 resolutions criticising countries with Israel the target in 83 of these. [275] The notion that there is a lack of free speech regarding Israel is simply risible. Moreover, what *exactly* does Manson mean when she calls for more freedom of speech on the Jews?

Since its founding, JVL has consistently acted against the interests of the mainstream British Jewish community as well as the global Jewish community. Its members spread antisemitic conspiracy fantasy. Its Jewish members weaponise their Jewish identity. And they support individuals in the Labour party who are openly antisemitic.

This phenomenon became so great that during the Labour antisemitism crisis the term 'AsaJews' entered into the lexicon of Jewish activists against antisemitism. Originally coined in the early 2010s, 'AsaJews' are Jewish people who use their Jewish identity to shut down accusations of antisemitism or to legitimise demonisation of Israel. In this case, they generally begin their defence of Corbyn with the phrase, 'As a Jew…' before dismissing accusations of antisemitism or expressing support for him. These Jews do not hate their own expressions of Jewishness, in fact, they appear quite comfortable in publicly identifying as Jews. However, it may be argued that their actions imply that they suffer from internalised antisemitism.

Cast your mind back to Theobald of Cambridge, whose antisemitic lies helped reinforce the concept of the blood libel. Thomas of Monmouth wrote of his testimony: 'As a proof of the truth and credibility of the matter we now adduce something which we have heard from the lips of Theobald, who was once a Jew, and afterwards a monk.'[276] As it was then, so it is now.

CASE STUDY TWO: AMERICA

As discussed in Chapter 3, the transformation of the American Jewish identity from a national to a religious or secular one has had enormous ramifications. It has contributed towards the perspective that light-skinned Jews are white, and, by extension, share the guilt of white America's crimes against minorities, particularly ethnic minorities. This fundamental shift in Jewish identity – along with the antisemitic demonisation of Israel – has led some young Jewish progressive Americans to no longer see Jews as a legitimate minority. They have also bought into the notion that Israel is the worst country in the world. The impact is startling: for example, a 2018 survey found that 'only a minority of young Jews in San Francisco's Bay Area believe a Jewish state is important'.[277]

These attitudes are epitomised by If Not Now (INN), a Jewish American organisation that has positioned itself against Israel. Its name is derived from the end of a quote, taken out of context, by Hillel the Elder: 'If I am not for myself, who will be for me? But if I am only for myself, who am I? If not now, when?'[278]

INN was founded by radical left-wing Jews and Christian antizionist Evangelicals in 2014 during Operation Protective Edge – that summer's conflict between Israel and Hamas. It was founded in response to what they perceived to be the overwhelming support for the war from Jewish American organisations.[279]

As its mission statement demonstrates, INN claims to root its activism in Jewishness. Its website also states: 'We celebrate Jewish cultural diversity as a source of resilience. We connect our movement to Jewish traditions, languages, rituals and practices, knowing that there are as many ways of being Jewish as there are Jews.'[280]

The rooting of INN's work in Jewish values could be interpreted as a deliberate political tool. Just as is the case with JVL, INN's Jewishness is often used to silence accusations of antisemitism and to legitimise antisemitic attacks on Israel. Yet here, through misunderstanding Jewish values, Jewishness is not just being used to change the conversation on Israel – the conversation on Israel is also being used to attempt to fundamentally alter Jewish identity.

While the transformation of the American Jewish community began in the 19th century, antizionist Jewish-identifying organisations, such as INN, now appear to be bringing about another fundamental shift in what it means to be a Jew; this time, basing Jewish identity solely on support for the Palestinians and other minorities.

In her 2019 book, *Days of Awe: Reimagining Jewishness in Solidarity With Palestinians*, Atalia Omer, associate professor of religion, conflict, and peace studies at the University of Notre Dame, 'considers how a new generation of Jewish activists is making solidarity with Palestinians a central feature of their Jewish practice and identity – and is thus transforming the very meaning of contemporary Jewishness.'[281]

For example, Jewish antizionist activists removed the iconic, ancient promise of *l'Shana Haba'ah B'Yerushalayim* – 'next year in Jerusalem' – from their *Pesach* Seders. INN itself organised a 'Liberation Seder' in Boston in 2016 that aimed to portray the Palestinians as the ancient Hebrews. As we will see, INN says *kaddish* for members of the terrorist group Hamas who have been killed. They have also misinterpreted the concept of *Tikkun Olam* (meaning repair the world) and have promoted it as a fundamental Jewish value and described it as a: 'central tenet of Judaism'.[282]

First mentioned in the Talmud, *Tikkun Olam* traditionally meant repairing the self through acts of *Halacha* (Jewish law). *Halacha* can be observing Jewish law or even carrying out *mitzvot* (good deeds) and there are many *mitzvot* about treating others with kindness. While it is perceived to be the instruction to 'repair the world', in reality, Jews were given no mandate to 'repair the world'.

Instead, as Rabbi Josh Yuter argues, '*Tikkun Olam* is the explanation given for why the Rabbinic sages legislated certain enactments.'[283] There is no evidence to suggest that *Tikkun Olam* was an instruction for Jews to repair the non-Jewish world, and it is certainly not about sacrificing Jewish people at the altar of social justice – it is specifically about repairing Jewish people. As *Vayikra* (Leviticus) states: 'You shall not take vengeance or bear a grudge against your countrymen. Love your fellow as yourself'.[284] From a religious perspective, loving and accepting all Jewish people is a *mitzvah* and, according to tradition, was an instruction from God. That is not to say that Jewish law does not mandate compassion and empathy towards non-Jews, but we must not appropriate Jewish concepts, especially taken out of context, in order to demand that Jews follow calls for self-sacrifice in the name of progressive values.

As Eric Ward suggests, when Jews are assigned the role of white-ally in the progressive world, it leaves progressive Jews very few options than to adopt as their main role the defence and service of others, while being silenced, and prohibited, from advocating for themselves. All of these examples, and many others, indicate another fundamental shift in certain progressive Jewish Americans' identity: basing their *entire* Jewish identity on serving other people. I would argue that this is incredibly dangerous and threatens to erase Jewish identity.

In a 2013 Pew survey, 56% of Jews suggested that 'working for justice and equality is essential to what being Jewish means to them.'[285] While this is not necessarily a bad thing, it seems that, to some Jews, their Jewishness is based on self-sacrifice at the altar of social justice. INN and other organisations that seem to follow Omer's line of thinking represent a deeply unhealthy relationship with, and a bastardisation of, their Jewishness. It is also true that, while they state, 'we are all proud Jews who know the history of anti-semitism. We love ourselves and our community'[286], one of the INN directors and founders, Seth Woody a Christian evangelist antizionist, who has proselytized on Twitter.

In 2019, a report published by Canary Mission, a website that compiles a dossier of anti-Israel activists on North American campuses, revealed that INN has partnered with American Muslims for Palestine (AMP), a group whose members have been accused of spreading antisemitism. In 2011, Neveen Ayesh, executive director of AMP-Missouri, tweeted: '#crimesworthyoftherope being a Jew.'[287] In 2014, she tweeted: 'I want to set Israel on fire with my own hands & watch it burn to ashes along with every Israeli in it. Call it what you want to call it idc.'[288]

According to the Canary Mission, INN has included AMP in training its activists, and collaborated on events and protests. In 2017, for example, INN invited Taher Herzallah, AMP's associate director of outreach and grassroots organising, to train its members. Taher has called for the destruction of Zionism, arguing: 'We cannot envisage a future, a beautiful bright future for the Palestinian people as long as Zionism exists ... the only language that the State of Israel understands is that of resistance.'[289]

He has also engaged in antisemitic conspiracy fantasy by suggesting: 'In a world where Zionism is slowly eating away at the crippled Muslim world, the Palestinians have essentially become our last line of defense. If Israel were to take over the entire compound or possibly even destroy al-Aqsa, it would be the death knell of the Muslim world.'[290]

Herzallah supports the destruction of the State of Israel and superimposes traditional antisemitic tropes on to the country, yet INN deems him to be an appropriate partner for a Jewish organisation and has allowed him to train young Jewish activists.

While INN states that it does not take a position on Zionism or 'statehood', it seems that, through its partnerships with antizionist organisations and individuals, it has made clear where it stands. Moreover, as it actively does not partner with Zionist organisations, it can be assumed that, at least in part, it has an ideological connection with those who wish to destroy the State of Israel.

In February 2013, Max Berger, co-founder of INN, tweeted that he would, 'totally be friends with Hamas'.[291] Hamas, as previously stated, is an organisation that quotes antisemitic literature and has sworn to murder all Jewish people, regardless of where they are from. My youth leader growing up, Yoni Jesner, was murdered in the Allenby Street bus bombing in Tel Aviv in 2002. His death was orchestrated by Hamas. Yoni was a 19-year-old Scottish student, who was going to be a doctor, before his life was tragically cut short during the Intifada. This is the organisation that Berger said he would 'totally be friends with'. To openly state support for Hamas is thus to support those who wish to bring about the end of Jewish life.

Antizionism is one of the most common forms of post-Holocaust antisemitism and is how modern internalised antisemitism is often expressed today. Declaring yourself a proud Jew does not mean you do not have internalised antisemitic notions about Israel.

In 2018, INN organised *kaddish* to be said for Palestinians who had been killed in Gaza. Alongside a video of them taking part in this traditional Jewish prayer for the deceased, INN tweeted a quote from the Mishnah: 'Whoever destroys a single life…is considered by Scripture to have destroyed the whole world.'[292]

While any death of a civilian is a tragedy, INN ignores the fact that 80% of the Palestinians killed in the Gaza border crisis were reportedly terrorists.[293] Questioned about the organisation's actions, INN co-founder Yonah Lieberman stated: 'We do not organize Kaddish prayers for "Arab terrorists" or "Hamas members". We say kaddish and mourn the unconscionable Israeli violence on Palestinian protesters.'[294]

However, INN did indeed say *kaddish* for terrorists who attempt to murder Jewish people. They are even reported to have listed the names of the dead during these vigils. INN also referred to the death of Imad Mohammad Nseir, a member of the Kataeb Humat al-Aqsa terror organisation, as 'heartbreaking'.[295] INN does not condemn terrorists; in fact, it sanctifies their names and mourn their deaths. Using Jewish prayers and Jewish values to glorify those that wish to destroy Jewish people indicates a deeply troubled relationship with Jewishness.

More recently, in a September 2019 tweet, INN asked: 'What's the most absurd accusation of antisemitism you've seen against legitimate criticism of Israel?'[296]

INN's question to their 50,000 plus followers is a direct example of David Hirsh's 'Livingstone Formulation'. In *Contemporary Left-Wing Antisemitism*, Hirsh lists its key elements as follows:

1. To refuse to discuss the content of the accusation by shifting focus instead onto the hidden motive for the allegation.

2. To make a counter-accusation that the accuser is not mistaken, has not made an error of judgment, but is getting it wrong on purpose.

3. To collapse everything, some of which may be demonization of Israel, support for boycott, or antisemitism, into a legitimate category like 'criticism'.

4. To allege that those who raise the issue of antisemitism are doing so as part of a common secret plan to silence such 'criticism'.[297]

INN's tweet suggests that Jews weaponise antisemitism to detract from Israeli crimes against the Palestinians. INN's tweet is guilty of the second and fourth element of Hirsh's formulation. They imply that Jews purposefully exploit antisemitism: they are acting in bad faith and are not 'mistaken in their accusations' but rather are making them on purpose. It also implies that there is some kind of Jewish plot to silence legitimate criticism of Israel by weaponising antisemitism.

Hirsh often concentrates on non-Jewish people or organisations that utilise the 'Livingstone Formulation' to deflect charges of antisemitism. However, in this case we have a Jewish organisation accusing other Jews of weaponising antisemitism. They are attempting to silence Jews raising their voices and drawing attention to Jew-hate, which is deeply manipulative. These statements actively harm the fight against antisemitism. It creates a situation whereby all accusations of antisemitism are to be treated with suspicion and thought to be made in bad faith.

INN's *raison d'etre* is the demonisation of Israel, which is not in fact a necessary component of advocating for the Palestinians. They partner with and support antisemites as they engage in modern leftist antisemitism. They are warping Jewish identity, forming it around advocating for Palestinians, while ignoring and erasing the Jewish connection to Israel, Jewish history, Israeli history and the history of Jews in the region.

Advocating for Palestinian liberation is incredibly important, and it is possible to be a Zionist while advocating for Palestinian self-determination. Yet INN does not agree this is possible. While they do not take a position on Zionism officially, they interact with those who vigorously oppose it and work with them to demonise, rather than criticise, Israel. This was evident when they doctored a video of one of their members asking Senator Bernie Sanders about Israel. In his answer, Sanders stated: 'The fault is not all with Israel. You got very poor and corrupt Palestinian leadership ... The goal of the US needs to be to bring together people of the region, the Palestinians and the Israelis and create a workable peace.'[298] He also said: 'We respect Israel'.[299] But these parts of Sanders' answer did not fit INN's narrative, so in a tweet about the exchange they simply deleted it – which tells us everything we need to know about If Not Now.[300]

From this we can understand that they are not interested in nuance and are willing to doctor the truth to continue to delegitimise the Jewish state. They are a fringe minority of radicals who, through social media, have amplified their voice as they attempt to fundamentally alter Jewish and Jewish American identity. We must not allow them to succeed. There is beauty in the Jewish American identity and community and INN threatens it.

While the first and last of the four examples of Jewish internalised antisemitism we have explored in this section are separated by 2,000 years, there are common threads running through each of them.

Ultimately, it seems they believe that being proudly Jewish is not compatible with being a citizen of the societies they live in or wish to be a part of. Tiberius Julius Alexander grew up in a Roman Alexandria that had absorbed the Egyptian ideas of what it means to be a Jew.

Although it remains conjecture, it is reasonable to assume that he fully shed his Jewish identity and adopted a solely Roman one, which brought him into direct conflict with the Jewish people. The Romans saw themselves as part of a tradition of civilised peoples. They represented morality, culture and society and the Jews were foreigners who bastardised religion and had strange ways. To join the society of civilised peoples, Tiberius shed his Jewishness.

Theobald left the Jewish community to become a monk in 12th century England, where Christianity was the established and dominant religion and it was perceived as the only path to heaven. To be Jewish meant living outside of the Christian community in sin, so when Theobald joined the Christian faith, he joined the 12th-century version of the 'community of the good'.

In the early 20th century, the Yevsektsiya destroyed Jewish communities in the new Soviet Union to demonstrate that they were good Soviet citizens.

JVL and INN exploit their Jewish identities to demonise Israel and other Jews. They demonstrate the notion that being a proudly Jewish activist is incompatible with being a member of the current 'community of the good', the left.

Dr Andreas Zick of Bielefeld University in Germany argues that internalised antisemitism exists because, despite their best efforts to be accepted, Jews are not 'viewed as an integral part of society, but rather as foreigners'.[301] Just as the Jews of the Yevsektsiya desperately wanted to be included in the new Soviet Union, all people want to belong to the communities that surround them. Jews were always regarded as foreigners and now Zionist Jews who retain their Jewish identity are seen as foreigners to more abstract communities, such as the progressive world. Expulsion from these communities still hurts nonetheless. However, when a community you want to belong to rejects you, you have two choices: you change to make yourself palatable or you reject their demands and strengthen your bonds with your own community.

As previously stated, I reject the term 'self-hating' Jews. While some Jewish people may hate themselves, 'internalised antisemitism' tells a more nuanced story. We must also, as Donna K Bivens has done, distinguish between the different forms of internalised prejudice.

Each of the Jews discussed in this chapter embody their own prejudice towards other Jews in a way that imitates the antisemitic context of the wider world: Tiberius' reflected the prejudices of the Roman empire and Theobald that of the Medieval Christian world, while JVL and INN echo the intolerance and bigotry of 21st century hard left politics. The Jews involved in JVL and INN may not hate themselves at all – particularly as we see members of INN stating they are basing their activism on their Jewish values – but they certainly endanger other Jews.

Even being harshly critical of Israel does not mean you have internalised antisemitism or that you exhibit interpersonal internalised antisemitism. Israel is a sovereign state locked in a long-running conflict and as such must be open to criticism.

However, we must all recognise that this is not what JVL or INN are doing. As the American academic Alvin Hirsch Rosenfeld correctly argued in his 2006 essay on progressive Jewish thought and the new antisemitism, a 'number of Jews, through their speaking and writing, are feeding a rise in virulent antisemitism by questioning whether Israel should even exist'.[302] JVL and INN do not criticise Israel fairly; they spread antisemitic tropes while demonising, delegitimising and treating the country with double standards.

It is important to reiterate that this is not a specifically Jewish issue. As I have personally experienced, and as Bivens' work shows, this is an issue that has an impact on all groups. While I disagree with his terminology, the German Jewish philosopher Theodor Lessing's statements in *Der Jüdische Selbsthaß* ('Jewish Self-Hatred') still ring true today: '[Self-hatred] is a phenomenon of the whole human race!'[303]

So, what is the solution? Internalised antisemitism poses a clear and present danger to the Jewish community. Each of us is ultimately responsible for our own actions, yet antisemitism leads some Jewish people to use their Jewish voice against the wider Jewish community. They, in turn, legitimise and spread antisemitism, and, despite being a fringe minority, these Jews seek to promote themselves, and are accepted by some, as legitimate representatives of the Jewish people. The non-Jewish world will never question these Jews as it is both afraid of being accused of policing Jewish voices and happy to use Jews to legitimise its own antisemitism.

I believe the solution is Jewish Pride. Antisemitism is all around us and, in all likelihood, it won't go away. Instead, we can form a buffer from it by educating, inspiring and empowering Jewish people all over the world to feel pride in their Jewishness. To not be afraid of identifying as Jewish. To not be afraid of prioritising the Jewish people in progressive activism. To recognise the incredible beauty and diversity in the Jewish people, while not being afraid to help Jewishness and Judaism evolve, but through internal, rather than external, conversations that are rooted in Jewish history.

Everyone's Jewish journey is different and many people express Jewishness differently to others. Accepting and respecting differences is as important as understanding what binds us together.

To understand better the incredible and broad diversity of the Jewish community, I interviewed seven Jewish people from around the world – Rachel Riley, Hen Mazzig, Ashager Araro, Isaac de Castro, Elisheva Rishon, Amy Albertson and Eliyahu Lann – to provide a window into their personal experiences of growing up Jewish, as well as how they express Jewish Pride.

It is fine that you or I express pride differently, but what we can and must agree on is that pride – healthy pride that rejects rather than absorbs non-Jewish perceptions of what constitutes a 'good Jew'

– is imperative to the survival and continued thriving of our incredible community.

Perhaps we cannot change the mindsets of antisemitic Jewish members of JVL or INN, and we certainly cannot travel back through time to sway Tiberius, Theobald or the Yevsektsiya. But we can look forward to building a community whose pride is an antidote to the disease of internalised antisemitism, which helps give the non-Jewish antisemitic world its power.

THE INTERVIEWS

As individuals we may base our Jewish Pride on our own unique perspectives, but our pride is also collective. It belongs to us all as a people and it binds us each to the rest of the Jewish community.

This is why I reached out to seven people in my personal community to understand how they embody Jewish Pride, in order to offer a beautiful prism of the diversity of light that each of these people emits through the pride they all have in their Jewishness.

One of the other most important things about a Jewish Pride movement is the celebration of this diversity and my seven interviewees represent just some of that diversity.

Rachel Riley is a British Ashkenazi woman

Hen Mazzig is a gay Mizrahi man from Israel

Ashager Araro is part of the Beta-Yisrael community,
living in Israel

Isaac de Castro is an Ashkenazi and Sephardic man from Panama

Elisheva Rishon is a Black American orthodox woman
with a Sephardic & Ashkenazi background

Eliyahu Lann is an Ashkenazi and Sephardic
trans man living in Australia

Amy Albertson is a Chinese-American Ashkenazi
patrilineal woman living in Israel

Representing so many Jewish identities was of fundamental importance to me when writing this book. While we are all Jews, part of the
same beautiful people, we have amongst us an unbelievable range of
backgrounds, histories and cultures. My perspective is as a gay Ashkenazi British man, so rather than me telling their stories for them, it
was important to give space to others to tell their own stories.

I met each of the seven interviewees over the last two years through
Twitter. Though we met online fighting antisemitism, we became
connected due to our shared values and passion for the Jewish community. Each of the seven is a powerful advocate for our people in their
own right and I am so proud to highlight their voices in this book. Their
stories, while personal to each, represent a family of Jewish stories, each
as important and vital to our pride as a people as any other.

During these interviews I learned, I laughed and most of all, I was
enlightened. I thank the seven interviewees for sharing their stories
not only with me but with the world. Please read them with an open
heart and with a willingness to listen and engage with experiences that
may differ from your own.

Despite the individuality of their experiences, they are undoubtedly and unashamedly filled with collective Jewish Pride.

Chapter 5

RACHEL RILEY

BRITISH MEDIA PERSONALITY Rachel Riley was born in January 1986. She is not only well known for her role on Britain's long-running TV series, *Countdown*, but also for the manner in which she became a very outspoken activist against antisemitism and advocate for the Jewish people during the Labour party antisemitism crisis.

Rachel is an Ashkenazi Jew. Her mother is Jewish and her father is not. Like many other Ashkenazi Jews, Rachel's mother's family lived in the Russian empire but fled at the end of the 19th century during the wave of anti-Jewish pogroms. It is against this backdrop that Rachel's, my own and millions of other families of Ashkenazi Jews fled the Russian empire, in which our ancestors were raised. It is within this Ashkenazi history and culture that we formed our Jewish identities.

One specific Ashkenazi cultural topic that we come back to time and again in this conversation is food, specifically Jewish Ashkenazi food. This played an important part in the way that Rachel connected to her Jewish identity as a child. Every time her family came over, 'we had the Ashkenazi Jewish spread, we had all the goodies,' she tells me. We discuss eating bagels (although we disagree on whether it's bagels or beigels) and our shared love of egg and onion spread, smoked salmon and cream cheese and chicken soup and *kneidlach*. A huge divide in the Jewish world is whether or not you love pickles. Unfortunately, Rachel and I fall on opposing sides of this debate. She is an ardent fan while I find them disgusting.

Rachel tells me that because her Jewish identity was shaped so much by culture, and not by religion, she didn't always feel fully welcome or comfortable in Jewish spaces. 'My Jewish identity was confused,' she suggests. This is not because she did not feel Jewish – she absolutely did: 'As a kid, I knew I was Jewish,' Rachel says. She felt different to her non-Jewish classmates, who, for example, celebrated Easter, yet her Jewishness 'played more of a role in not defining me as Christian'.

While she has always felt 'proud to be Jewish', Rachel did not always feel at home in the Jewish community as other more religious Jewish people tried to impose their narrow definition of what it means to be Jewish on her. 'My family worshipped more at Old Trafford [the Manchester United football club grounds] than they did at *shul*,' she jokes. Rachel didn't speak Hebrew and only really ever went to *shul* on Yom Kippur. 'It was kind of casual,' she recalls.

An interesting explanation that Rachel offers for her family's 'social Jewishness' was the fact that they lived in predominantly Jewish areas – initially East London and then Essex – so didn't have to try 'too hard to be Jewish, as it was kind of all around them'. This reminds me of Israelis I have spoken to who are very relaxed about practising their Jewishness because they live in the Jewish state and their lives are defined by Judaism and Jewishness. Rachel suggests that this cultural Jewishness was a little confusing for her, as she knew she was different to her predominantly non-Jewish classmates, felt very Jewish, but did not specifically observe many Jewish practices. This served to muddle her identity somewhat, she believes. Her Jewishness did not feel 'ingrained, as it had been in previous generations in my family'.

However, antisemitism had an impact on her Jewish identity early on – as it has continued to do in her adult life. 'I remember from a really early age, I knew about the Holocaust,' she says, 'and this was … part of my identity – and it is a part of my identity. Knowing I am Jewish, and knowing what would have happened to you during the Holocaust, is very impactful. Also knowing my family fled pogroms also formed part of my Jewish identity.' The awareness of the threat of Jewish identity being erased has also clearly been important to Rachel.

'My mum's maiden name was Kaye, but it would have been Kolominsky before they changed it to sound "less Jewish",' she says.

I am struck by the similarity in our family's stories. My ancestors also came from the Russian empire. They also fled pogroms and moved to Glasgow's version of the East End of London – the Gorbals. My mother's maiden name was originally Shmulevitz and my grandfather changed it to Samuels, also to sound less Jewish. These similarities are quite unifying and connect us.

While Rachel's confusion about her Jewish identity led to her not always feeling totally comfortable in the Jewish world, she also felt the same in the non-Jewish world. This was based on 'not being Christian and always feeling different and separate when I was at school and they started singing Christmas hymns'. Having also attended a typical British 'non-denominational' school, this is something I can very much relate to. I did, and I still do, feel slightly separate from British culture.

When she attended Oxford University, Rachel, like many Jewish students, sought out and joined JSoc (the Jewish Society), and, along with a friend, attended Jewish-themed events. This engagement with Oxford's JSoc sadly came to an end when, at a cocktail event, she ended up chatting to a woman who made disparaging comments about people with only one Jewish parent. This made Rachel feel deflated – 'like an imposter' – and she never returned to JSoc after the incident.

It is terrible to hear how someone who later became one of the most important public voices in the fight against antisemitism was made to feel this kind of imposter syndrome in the Jewish world. It serves as a reminder of what the cost to our community can be if we drive people away by being unwelcoming. While it is important that membership of our community is inspired by traditional Jewish law (although I believe there is a legitimate discussion to be had on what that law looks like), it is wholly unacceptable that Rachel was made to feel like, what she describes as, 'a bad Jew'. Being an ethno-religion, there are several different ways to express and practice your Jewishness and Judaism. To judge someone for not being Jewish in the same way that you are Jewish is inappropriate. This kind of gatekeeping has no place in an inclusive Jewish Pride movement.

Immediately after university, when Rachel was just 22, she joined the new cast of *Countdown*. This immediately catapulted her to fame in the United Kingdom. For non-British readers, *Countdown* is an iconic British game show involving word and number tasks. Rachel's impressive role is to check the answers of the maths contestants and to solve any questions which the contestants are unable to. While Rachel tells me that she never hid her Jewishness – it is literally in the first line of her 'Early life and early career' section on Wikipedia – she also never made a great play of it.

That is, until 2018, nearly 10 years after Rachel joined *Countdown*.

Our conversation takes a slightly darker turn when we discuss what brought Rachel's Jewishness to the forefront: the Labour party antisemitism crisis.

At this point, Rachel reflects on the fact that during this period, and for about five years previously, she had started to see antisemitism creeping into modern British life. She recounts stories about hearing Israel being demonised and delegitimised and the fact that anyone making any kind of statement regarding Israel, Jews included, felt the need to qualify it in some way with a criticism of the Jewish state. However, Rachel's involvement in the fight against antisemitism really took off in 2018.

After seeing a brief BBC news report about antisemitism in the Labour Party, Rachel began investigating the issue and was stunned to discover the depth of the problem. Moreover, Rachel could not fathom why she wasn't seeing more mainstream reports on it. Combined with the Jewish community's growing desire to challenge Labour to clean up its act – demonstrated in the March 2018 'Enough is Enough' march in central London's Parliament Square – this motivated Rachel to use Twitter to speak out.

At first, she remembers, she simply wanted to spread some positivity about Jews: to show the British people that the reality of Jews had nothing to do with the hard left's perception of them. She recalls a story told by Susie Dent, the words expert on *Countdown*, about the origins of the word 'breadline' (in Britain, being 'on the breadline' means that you are impoverished). The term emerged when the 19th century Jewish yeast manufacturer Charles Louis Fleischmann served bread to the homeless, who in turn waited in line (thus the term breadline). She shared the story on social media, tweeting: 'Who knew "breadline" had such an interesting and lovely word origin?! Well @susie_dent did of course! Bloody Jews again.'[304]

The same day that Rachel heard that story, she also saw shocking posters being displayed in London bearing the words 'Israel is a Racist Endeavour' in response to Labour's adoption of the examples included in the International Holocaust Remembrance Alliance definition of antisemitism. She immediately felt compelled to speak out in defence of British Jews. But when she did, Rachel was, in her words, 'introduced to that leftist world of antisemitism. I didn't even have to go looking for it. When I criticised Corbyn, it came to me. Every time I spoke out there was a tsunami.'

Being such a public figure, much has been written about Rachel's tireless campaigning on behalf of the Jewish people. What began with a tweet that aimed to spread positivity about Jews resulted in her becoming one of the key voices in the British Jewish fight against antisemitism.

Rachel is, however, remarkable in her humility when discussing her role. At first, she recalls, she did not feel equipped with enough knowledge to join the fight and spent months devoting countless hours to learning about both the history of the Jewish people and antisemitism. Rachel wanted to ensure that, when she spoke out, she was doing so with as much knowledge as possible.

Her first major public interview about antisemitism came at the same time as the 10th anniversary of her joining *Countdown* when she joined the fellow Channel 4 presenter Krishnan Guru-Murthy's podcast. What should have been the celebration of an impressive milestone in her professional life was instead mainly focused on Labour's antisemitism, in which she 'poured my heart out to Krishnan'.

As Rachel notes, there are so many other things we would all love to be doing rather than talking about antisemitism, especially as it subjects us to, as she puts it, 'incredible abuse, bonkers stuff'. But antisemitism poses such an enormous threat to the continuation of our people that we are forced to spend our time combating it. That thousands of Jews are forced to spend their time combatting Jew-hatred as opposed to being able to contribute to society in other ways is a tragedy and terrible waste of potential forced on us by the non-Jewish world.

Something that also arises during our discussion is the manner in which Jewish women who raised their voices against antisemitism have been targeted with a specific brand of antisemitism laced with misogyny. While we all share the common experience of receiving abuse for being Jewish, it's crucial to understand how our experiences may differ because of our other identities and which factors play into this. It is also important to note that many of the Jews (and non-Jews) who stood up and raised their heads above the parapets in the fight against Labour antisemitism *were* women – 'the Esthers' as Rachel aptly labels them (the reference comes from the Purim story of the Jewish Queen Esther). We couldn't come up with a definitive answer as to why this might be the case, but agree that these Jewish women are incredibly brave and courageous and our community as a whole has a huge amount to be thankful to them for.

Rachel believes that her experiences in fighting against antisemitism has absolutely strengthened her Jewish identity and her feelings of Jewish Pride. 'To be part of something and fighting alongside my fellow Jews has definitely intensified my feelings of "Jewish Pride",' she argues.

The experience also led her reconsider her Jewish identity. 'I have seen how people treat me when they don't know I am Jewish versus when they see me as "Rachel the Jew",' she suggests. This leads us to discuss the concept of 'passing' and how Jews that look like myself and Rachel can pass as white. Despite this ability, the second our Jewishness is revealed any advantage we may receive for being 'white' can immediately be revoked. In online discussion, particularly those centred on the United States, passing is often described as a privilege and light-skinned Jews are often classed as a 'privileged' group, akin to white people. But when we talk about white people, we don't just mean people with light skin, we are speaking instead about people who are classed as powerful, free from oppression and are often oppressors themselves. This clearly does not reflect the light-skinned Jewish or the wider Jewish experience.

At this point it may be prudent to clarify exactly what Rachel and I are saying. We are *not* saying our skin is not light, and we are *not* saying that we do not benefit from the advantage of being perceived as white. What we are saying is that revealing our Jewishness can often lead to this advantage being rescinded and that all light-skinned Jews continue to face a great threat to our community due to antisemitism.

When I tell Rachel that I do not identify as white but as Jewish, she replies: 'Yes, we have no box! There is no Jewish box on census forms, and to identify as Jewish we have to click the Judaism box in the religion section.' This denial of Jews as a people, combined with the idea that Jews are solely members of a religion, has a long history that is tied to assimilation, but it ultimately erases Jews like Rachel, who is a self-confessed atheist. Rachel's identity, which was strengthened further via the fight against Labour antisemitism is an example of the many ways one can be Jewish. We should never be made to feel bad or ashamed for not living our Jewish life the way others do.

Another surprisingly positive by-product of the awful Labour antisemitism crisis was the fact that most parts of the Jewish community came together as one. Orthodox Jews, Reform Jews and Jews who only feel connected to Jewish ethnicity, history and culture joined and stood together to shout: 'Enough is Enough!' This has certainly strengthened the Jewish community as well as our own Jewish identities. The British Jewish community's response was a sight to behold, deeply inspiring and empowering. British Jews spoke up for themselves and said to their fellow Britons: 'We matter and we will not tolerate this anymore.' It was an amazing example to the rest of the Jewish communities in the Diaspora of what we are capable of when we stand together to fight antisemitism. However, as we have seen throughout history, there was a cost to this incredible show of Jewish strength. 'I don't say this lightly,' Rachel says, 'British Jews are traumatised by what happened.' The Labour antisemitism crisis was a moment of reckoning for the British Jewish community that rocked us to our core and made us realise our position in British society was not as secure as we had first thought.

But while the fight against antisemitism may strengthen Jewish identity, this is not necessarily healthy. 'We can't get around the fact that taking part in something like the "Enough is Enough" campaign will strengthen your attachment to the community,' Rachel argues. 'You come together with people you've never met to fight for a common cause, that is so powerful and unifying.' However, she continues, 'basing your Jewish identity solely on fighting antisemitism is probably not healthy. There is so much to be proud of beyond our resilience. There's our food, culture, contribution to the world, so much!'

Talk naturally returns to food as Rachel and I circle back to talk about our Ashkenazi heritage. While Rachel is now vegan, she says the only non-vegan food she really misses is the Ashkenazi food of her childhood. Despite the fact that many other parts of the Jewish world are disparaging about Ashkenazi food, it is clearly something incredibly important to both of us. It represents home, something that connects Rachel to her Jewish heritage. It also holds something symbolic and representative within it: much of Ashkenazi cuisine was born out of forced poverty, antisemitic legislation banning Jews from various jobs as well as land ownership, and limited access to different types of food from often being ghettoised and forced to live on the outskirts. Yet Ashkenazi Jews still managed to nourish themselves and create a cuisine.

Our conversation then moves on to the strength of all Jewish people, but we take special pride in the incredible resilience of Ashkenazi Jews, our relatives, who, like other Jewish communities, created a beautiful thriving culture under immense pressure. An important aspect of Jewish Pride is not just creating an inclusive Jewish community, but one that encourages all Jewish communities to feel pride in their respective specific histories while fostering a wider sense of Jewish identity.

We close our time together, talking about Maven, Rachel's new beautiful baby daughter. I ask what kind of Jewish identity Rachel hopes that her daughter will have. She responds simply by saying she wants Mave (as Maven is known) to feel 'proud of being Jewish'. 'I want her to feel comfortable in the Jewish community,' Rachel says, 'but, most importantly, I want her to feel totally comfortable with who she is. To never hide her Jewishness'.

It feels apt to end our conversation chatting about Mave, the next generation of Jews, and another strong Jewish woman in the making. Rachel remarks that we have a duty to create a culture of Jewish Pride. We have to teach our young people not just our resilience and amazing survival skills, but also our incredibly rich culture, our traditions and our contribution to the wider world.

Speaking with Rachel is inspiring. She chose to take a journey of Jewish discovery so she could support and advocate for her community in its time of threat – and she did it on her own terms while staying true to herself. She learned that her form of Jewishness is valid, and that is also what she now teaches others.

I end the call with Rachel feeling incredibly proud. Not only is she a truly kind and generous person, but she is also a real symbol of a strong Jewish woman who embodies modern British Jewish pride. Rachel Riley is a maths genius, a British public figure and also a proud Jew.

How wonderful!

Chapter 6

HEN MAZZIG

HEN MAZZIG is a Mizrahi Jewish LGBTQ+ activist. He was born in September 1989 in Petach Tikvah in Israel. His father's family roots lie in the Jewish community of Tunisia and his mother's family were from Iraq. He is a *Sabra*, meaning he was born in Israel, and has always felt completely Jewish as his life was defined through the Jewishness of not just his own family, but his country at large.

As a British Jew who never felt totally at home in the UK – and never felt fully able to participate in British culture – this is quite incredible to me. Hen's life has always been deeply shaped by Jewishness and Judaism. He was off school for Jewish holidays, the weekend was based around Shabbat, kosher food was all around him. 'My Jewish identity growing up was shaped by being an Israeli', he tells me. Despite being born in Israel, which could lead some to being more laissez-faire about Zionism, Hen is an ardent Zionist – but not only because he believes in the concept of a Jewish state and the right of Jews to self-determination. For Hen, it is much more personal. 'Zionism saved my family's lives,' he argues. 'Without Zionism, I would not exist'.

Not only did Zionism bring his mother and father's families together, but it offered them the only place of refuge to flee dire and terrifying persecution in Tunisia and Iraq. While the majority of Hen's family did escape antisemitic oppression in these countries, his great-grandfather was hanged by Arabs in Iraq for being both Jewish and, in their eyes, *their* definition of Zionist. 'My great-grandfather was not a victim of white supremacy. He was not a victim of Nazism, he was a victim of Arab antisemitism,' he explains.

This is an important distinction to make, as forms of antisemitism not perpetrated by white supremacists are often erased by some on the left. They seem unable to comprehend that a group that they view as oppressed by the west – in this case, Arab people and Muslims – could themselves act as oppressors. Hen is a fierce advocate for the entire Jewish community and people, but he places special emphasis on the experience of his family and thousands of other Mizrahi families – 850,000 of whom either fled subjugation and violence in the Middle East and North Africa or were forced out under threat, exile and/or attacks after the creation of the State of Israel.

Despite Hen's story, and that of the wider Mizrahi Jews, being such a major part of the Jewish experience, he speaks of his frustration that antizionists and even the broader Jewish community know so little about the Mizrahi history and experience. 'It's crazy to me that this story of so many hundreds of thousands of Jews is so unknown,' Hen says.

Jews have always held a presence in the Middle East, North Africa and Persia, both before and after they were exiled from Judea by the Romans. Prior to the establishment of Israel, Jews in the Middle East and North African region were oppressed for centuries by their Muslim rulers. They were classed officially as *dhimmis,* which translates literally as a 'protected person'; however, for Jews, the reality was quite different.

In principle, *dhimmitude* allowed Jews (and Christians) to continue practising their respective faiths, but it did not guarantee they would be treated well. As discussed in Chapter 1, the Damascus blood libel that took place in 1840 is just one example of the precarious position that Jews held under these rulers.

In his paper on antisemitism in Muslim communities and Muslim countries, German academic Günther Jikeli argues that 'negative attitudes towards Jews in Muslim countries are the rule, not the exception'. 'In view of new research,' he suggests, 'the arguments that antisemitism is primarily a result of Middle East conflict or of discrimination/colonization seem to be outdated.'[305]

People often argued that the Muslim world was 'better for Jews' than the Christian world. But it is more accurate to say that antisemitism worked differently in different parts of the world. Mizrahi Jews were oppressed, subjugated and faced violent antisemitism as did their Ashkenazi, Sephardic and Beta-Yisrael brothers and sisters. Thus, despite some obvious differences, Hen argues that 'all Jewish communities all over the world have experienced antisemitism and this shared experience should only bring us closer.'

An example of violent antisemitism the Mizrahi community faced – the *Farhud* – is a personal one that Hen tirelessly seeks to raise awareness of. This 1941 Nazi-inspired pogrom took place in the Iraqi capital of Baghdad and saw Arab Muslims perpetrate the brutal and violent murder of an estimated 750 Jewish people, as well as committing numerous rapes, attacks, and, ultimately, the ethnic cleansing of Jews in Iraq. The centuries of *jizya* tax paid by local Jews to be that 'protected class' was clearly worthless.

Hen has spoken about his difficulty in connecting with Holocaust discussions when non-Ashkenazi victims are often not included in the conversation. He stresses the importance of this story: 'People rarely consider the impact of the Holocaust on Mizrahi or even Sephardic Jews, but we were also victims of the Nazis and their allies. The Nazis targeted all Jews. Every Jewish life stolen is a tragedy, whether it was a Jew from Warsaw in Poland, Baghdad in Iraq, or Thessaloniki in Greece.'

The importance of this message cannot be understated. I am a professional Holocaust educator who, thanks to Hen's activism, now makes sure to include facts about the suffering of non-Ashkenazi Jews. Under the Nazi occupation, for instance, 4,000 Tunisian Jews were deported for forced labour, 350 were murdered and 600 to 700 died due to starvation and disease. Such discussions strengthen enormously my students' understanding of the totality of the Holocaust.

The pain of the erasure of the Mizrahi experience is etched onto Hen's face, particularly when he tells me that no Arab country has ever offered any reparations to their former Jewish citizens, much less apologised or made amends for the enormous crimes they committed against them. 'Germany has done so much to apologise, and while it can never be enough, it's more than the Arab countries have ever done,' Hen argues. 'They persecuted us, drove us out and they've gotten away with it.'

Hen argues that Zionism *must* be a central element of any Jewish Pride movement. He proudly served in the Israeli Defence Force (IDF) for five years as a lieutenant in the COGAT (Coordinator of Government Activities in the Territories) unit and worked as an intermediary between the IDF, the Palestinian Authority, the UN and many non-governmental organisations that work in the West Bank. He is extremely proud to be a Jew and to be an Israeli.

When I ask him to explain why he believes Zionism is central to Jewish Pride, he responds:

> Israel has been at the centre of Jewish life for millennia. Whether that was when we had a state of our own or when we were praying towards Jerusalem in the Diaspora, it was all about Jerusalem and Israel, and now when we say 'next year in Jerusalem' at *Pesach*, it's not abstract. It can really happen! And it doesn't mean you have to support every action or policy of the Israeli government – I sure as hell don't – but it means you believe in a Jewish state that allows Jews to feel safe and to take control of their own destiny.

This pride shines through in how Hen talks about Israel, the Jewish community, and why they matter so much for him. His deep feeling of Jewish pride is all the more striking given the bigotry and erasure that Mizrahi people face in the world: in the Middle East and North Africa, Israel and the Jewish Diaspora. As a child, Hen felt intensely connected to his Israeli 'brothers and sisters'. His beautiful tales are of feeling a bond with and no difference between himself – a child of the Middle East – and his Ethiopian Jewish friends or his Ashkenazi friends. Hen remembers: 'We were all Jews living in Israel. We were the physical embodiment of Zionism.' They shared the experience of being immigrants, refugees, or the descendants of immigrants and refugees, who were building a new country where Jews could finally feel safe. They also felt the same real threat of destruction and geno- cide from the very countries that Mizrahi Jews had originally fled.

However, the sense of connection Hen feels has been tested throughout his life when he witnessed how Mizrahi Jews were treated in Israel. As referenced in the introduction, Mizrahi Jews were victims of systemic inequality in Israel. This led to Hen internalising the idea that being Mizrahi was somehow less than being Ashkenazi. When, for instance, as a child he was asked what he wanted to be when he grew up, he said: 'I want to be Ashkenazi.' Hearing this proud advo- cate for the Mizrahi community say he once longed to be Ashkenazi is heartbreaking. Understanding the way Mizrahi people have been treated in Israel historically explains why Hen, as a young Mizrahi boy, would have felt this way.

Hen provided me with the following statistics regarding the status of Mizrahi Jews in Israel, who make up over 50% of the country's Jewish population:

- Students in Israeli universities today: 61% Ashkenazim, 20% Mizrahim, 18% Arab Israelis

- Israeli state attorneys: 10 Ashkenazim, 0 Mizrahim

- Government legal advisors: 11 Ashkenazi, 2 Mizrahim

- Governors of the Bank of Israel: 8 Ashkenazim, 0 Mizrahim

Hen even felt compelled to tell one of his primary teachers that his mother was Ashkenazi in order for her to accept him. Another memory from his primary school days that Hen recounted underlines the cultural prejudice which Mizrahi Jews often experience. When his teacher asked the class what their favourite music was, Hen, being a young child, named the Egyptian singer Umm Kulthum who his family listened to at home. 'I remember that the teacher laughed at me and told me that Umm Kulthum ... wasn't cultured,' Hen says.

Hen's childhood internalised shame that being Ashkenazi was somehow better than being Mizrahi resonates with me. As I previously suggested, seeing no positive depictions of LGBTQ+ people made me feel that being gay was somehow wrong. A lack of representation can damage us in ways we don't even realise.

I am sure we would all agree that Israel should be a place for all Jews. That Jews from around the world have brought with them to Israel their cultural baggage and traumas is a tragedy that requires empathy, education and understanding. As Hen argues: 'All I want to do is help the Jewish community become the best version of itself. Every community has issues but these are not set in stone, we can change.'

Hen explains this specific dynamic by simply saying that the Jews who emigrated to Israel were not immune from the same European prejudices towards people from other parts of the world. He argues that this is not about blaming, or specifically assigning this tendency to, Ashkenazi Jews; he is simply suggesting that all people are capable of these ideas – whether or not they are a persecuted minority themselves. This is a very valuable lesson for us all. He also says that he does not believe that Ashkenazi Jews who absorbed this Eurocentrism think that they are inherently better than their Mizrahi brothers and sisters, rather they have simply internalised the notion impressed upon *them*: that European culture ranks higher and all other forms of culture are less important, as represented by the cruel dismissal of Umm Kulthum as his favourite singer by Hen's teacher. Hen also insists: 'Speaking about the discrimination of Mizrahi Jews should not be done to undermine the history of Ashkenazi Jews,' Hen argues. 'It is not done to defame Ashkenazim nor negate the deep connection of all Jews to the state of Israel. I see Ashkenazi Jews as my brothers and sisters – like family.'

It is important that we can distinguish the experiences of Mizrahi Jews in Israel and issues of Ashkenormativity in the Diaspora. Hen believes that there are Jews in the Diaspora, particularly in America, who don't consider Mizrahi Jews at all when thinking about the Jewish community. He cites as an example the decision in December 2019 by, *The Forward*, a progressive American Jewish news publication, to hire five new writers in order to 'engage a broad, diverse audience'.[306] Hen thinks it is great that *The Forward* wanted to widen the conversation on Jewish issues, but he could not hide his pain that, inexplicably, it did not think it important to include Mizrahi voices in this search for greater diversity and that consequently these were, once again, left out. There are currently over 4 million Mizrahi Jews in the world, who constitute over a quarter of the world's Jewish population, but, time and time again, they are either purposefully ignored or erased through ignorance.

As a Mizrahi Jew, Hen identifies as a 'Jew of colour'. This term originated in the United States and is used to describe Ashkenazi Jews who do not pass as white, or Jews who are specifically Beta-Yisrael, Mizrahi or Sephardic or who have other minority ethnicities for various reasons. Hen explains why he uses this label: 'I don't think any Jew is white, we are a different category, but we can't deny that some Jews do pass as white, which obviously shapes their experience, particularly in the US. The label of [Jew of colour] makes it clear that not only am I not white because I am Jewish, but I don't even pass as white, which of course, particularly in America, changes my lived experience.'

As Hen explains it, Jewish Pride is about empowering Jewish people to celebrate themselves while also offering tools to address important internal issues within the Jewish community. 'No community is perfect,' he reiterates. 'People are people, but we have to recognise our failings and work hard to better ourselves.'

To me, this is also real love – to love in spite of imperfections while working hard to improve. Hen describes his Jewish Pride being centred on the history, culture and resilience of the Jewish people – specifically his Mizrahi community, but also, of course, the wider Jewish community. The history of the diverse Jewish communities, Hen argues, also contains a common thread: 'No matter where they were, no matter what was done to them they kept their Jewish identity.'

Hen's eyes shine with pride when he says this and it is true. It is remarkable that, despite everything we have been through, we are still two proud Jews sitting in different countries with different time zones, discussing how much we love being Jewish. 'One of the ways I express my Jewish Pride is through the work that I do,' Hen explains. 'I want to show young people that – despite what many on the left say – you can be progressive and proudly Jewish and Zionist. I want them to be proud and not ashamed.'

Hen used to feel so ashamed of his identity – first as a Mizrahi Jew in Israel and then later just as a Jew in the non-Jewish world – and this shame damaged him. He wants to prevent this hurt from being inflicted on young Jewish people, to help them understand that they are part of an incredibly resilient and culturally rich community that has so much to offer. Hen talks proudly of how the Jewish community has managed not only to survive, but to thrive, and that, despite our shared experiences of antisemitism, every diverse part of the Jewish community has managed to develop a rich culture. Moreover, Jews have also made enormous and significant contributions to the rest of the world – an amazing feat, we agree, when you consider that there are only 14.7 million Jews in the world.

Hen and I speak in March 2020, during the Covid-19 pandemic, and he talks about his pride in the fact that so many innovations have indeed come from Israel, including a potential cure for the virus. Hen explains Israeli innovation – something of which I am equally proud – and Tel Aviv's status as one the best start-up cities in the world. 'Israelis are very ballsy and it comes from our history and also our current situation,' he suggests. 'Living in a country with borders that are not secure, leads us to take risks and to innovate.' Once again, we come back to the incredible resilience of the Jewish community which, under enormous stress, is really able to make lemonade out of lemons.

Part of Hen's Jewish Pride is his rejection of the antisemitic charges laid against Israel and he is bold in describing them for what they are. He is very clear about how modern antisemitism focuses on Israel and the fact that antizionist Jews who live in the Diaspora are enormously privileged. 'Just because they feel safe wherever they are at that moment,' Hen asks, 'why should that mean that every other Jewish experience – both historical and current – is invalid?'

Hen loves Israel because, despite the difficulties his communities have experienced, it is the Jewish state and has offered hundreds of thousands of Mizrahi Jews (as well as Ashkenazi, Beta-Yisrael and Sephardic Jews) a safe refuge from real and violent Arab antisemitism.

Hen's work of raising awareness about the history of the Mizrahi community, both in Israel and prior to its formation, is vitally important. When I tell him the impact he has had on my own work he says: 'It makes me so proud to be advocating for my community and to teach Jews around the world about the amazing history of Mizrahi Jews.'

Hen is thoughtful when talking about how antisemitism has had an impact on his Jewish Pride, saying that, while it is sad, he cannot get away from the fact that growing up in a country with neighbours which have sworn to destroy you affects how you feel about yourself. Facing these constant threats – and having to join your national army to defend yourself against them – absolutely instils a sense of pride in your community, he argues. Similarly, his experiences at London University's University College in 2016, when hundreds of students turned out to protest against, and managed to disrupt, a speech he was due to give, also led him to consider his Jewish identity in a non-Jewish setting.

Ultimately, both examples of antisemitism were a moment of reckoning for Hen: he could either be afraid and ashamed of who he is or say: 'No, I deserve to be here. I matter just as much as you do.'

When I ask Hen if he thinks antisemitism having an impact on our identity is a bad thing, he replies: 'Maybe, but after 3,000 years of antisemitism do we really think it's going away any time soon?'

This is a profound thought and it is something I myself have wrestled with. But it points to something amazing: the fact that Jews are still here today not just because our community has survived for thousands of years, but because it has survived thousands of years of intense genocidal antisemitism. I try to base my Jewish Pride on internal Jewish qualities – our culture, our contribution to the world, our history – but Hen, like Rachel, has helped me recognise that also finding pride in the *resilience* of the Jewish community in the face of antisemitism is powerful.

As our conversation draws to a close, Hen suggests: 'The Mizrahi community is an integral part of the wider Jewish community. The culture that they have cultivated over thousands of years is rich and beautiful and it should be celebrated just as much as any other part of the Jewish community.'

In response, I ask Hen what about being a Mizrahi Jew makes him most proud. As we are both men who love to eat, our conversation quickly turns to food. 'From my Iraqi side, the food is the most incredible, my favourite is *kubba* [a minced rice and meat patty],' he says.

Hen also tells me that every time a Mizrahi Jew comes to him and tells him that, because of his activism and work, they now feel pride in their heritage, he himself feels a wave of pride. Hen's pride is contagious and his continued love for all parts of the Jewish community, in spite of some of its failures, is inspiring.

His criticisms do not belie resentment or bitterness. 'I love being Jewish, it's who I am and who I have always been and I hope that every Jew – wherever they are from – feels part of a safe and inclusive Jewish community,' Hen says. 'It will take work, but I know we can get there.'

I couldn't have said it better myself.

Chapter 7

ASHAGER ARARO

ASHAGER ARARO was born in December 1990. She is a proud Beta-Yisrael woman. She was born in Ethiopia before her family made *Aliyah* to Israel when she was aged just one. The first thing that Ashager tells me is that being Jewish is her primary identity and she says that she owes this fact very much to her Beta-Yisrael heritage.

Despite the fact that many people, including many Jews, are not familiar with the Beta-Yisrael story, the history of their community is rich and deep, stretching back thousands of years. The origins of the community are unclear; some suggest they are the descendants of the Queen of Sheba and King Solomon or that they are the descendants of Jewish merchants from the region who travelled to Ethiopia thousands of years ago. What is clear and most important, is that a Jewish community existed in Ethiopia for thousands of years. Incredibly, an independent Beta-Yisrael state, the Kingdom of Semien, within the border of modern Ethiopia, was established in the 4th century.

Whether we are familiar with the story of the Beta-Yisrael community or not, it is remarkable that, for a period, Jews in Ethiopia were the masters of their own destiny, ruling their own autonomous Jewish state.

This autonomous Jewish state was established in response to attempts to convert Jews in Ethiopia to Christianity. Thus, despite being so isolated, the experience of the Beta-Yisrael community echoes the persecution experienced by other Diasporic Jewish communities. It is remarkable that every single Jewish community, regardless of where they lived, faced similar oppression.

For over a thousand years after its establishment, there were successive wars between the Ethiopian Jewish state and its Christian neighbours. These wars continued under successive Jewish monarchs – including an independent Queen Regent, Queen Judith – for hundreds of years until the Kingdom was annexed in 1627 when Beta-Yisrael autonomy was ended forever.

Following this defeat, the Jews were once again at the mercy of Christianity and victims of Christian antisemitism, much like their Ashkenazi and Sephardic brothers and sisters. They were sold into slavery, had their lands confiscated and the practice and study of Judaism were forbidden, with Jews the victims of forced conversion.

Following the Kingdom Semien's final defeat, the position of the Beta-Yisrael community reflected elements of that of the Ashkenazi, Mizrahi and Sephardi. They suffered forced conversions as well as legal discrimination. Under this antisemitic forced conversion effort, Jews were told that if they refused to become Christians, they would lose the right to own land. This, Ashager tells me, 'was incredibly coercive as Ethiopia was an agricultural society, so being refused the right to own land takes away all chance of earning a livelihood and sustaining yourself and your family'.

Emperor Yeshaq's command – 'He who is baptized in the Christian religion may inherit the land of his father, otherwise let him be a *Falāsī*'[307] – left a poisonous legacy. Following this, the Jewish community in Ethiopia were known by the derogatory term of *Falasha* or the *Falashmura* meaning 'outsider'. Ashager's own grandfather was a victim of Ethiopian antisemitism and the 'othering' of the Beta-Yisrael community. After repeatedly asking, she found out that he had been murdered. 'They murdered him. They murdered him because he was a Jew,' her mother finally told her.

Hearing Ashager tell me about the history of the Beta-Yisrael community and their autonomous Jewish state is extraordinary. It truly demonstrates Jewish determination – particularly that of the

Beta-Yisrael community – to fight to maintain their Jewishness, regardless of external pressures.

Ashager believes this has a contemporary resonance. 'We must echo this determination today when our community is still threatened by so many,' she argues. It is a deeply inspiring lesson for Jewish people today who are trying to define Jewish identity through our own internal conversations, as opposed to allowing outside influences to determine our experiences and who we are. Regardless of whether we are Jews in Israel or the Diaspora, we must be masters of our own destiny.

Tragically, as the Beta-Yisrael tradition is an oral tradition, much of their history was lost during this period. However, a letter written by a Beta-Yisrael man in 1890 offers important clues as to their plight. 'Formerly we were very numerous; formerly there were 200 synagogues, now only 30 remain,' he wrote. 'In the time of the Dervishes [Sudanese-Mahadist invaders], a frightful number of people died from famine ... We are in great misery. Our books have been destroyed; the Dervishes burnt them by fire. We have no longer any schools; they are destroyed.'[308]

Despite the intense antisemitism they endured at the hands of their Christian neighbours, the Beta-Yisrael community continued to be proudly Jewish and to practice Judaism. While it is important to always recognise the similarities between all Jewish communities and their experiences, it is equally important to honour that which makes us different.

In the same manner that there are differences in the way Ashkenazi, Sephardic and Mizrahi Jews practice and express their Jewishness, there are also variations in the way Beta-Yisrael Jews practice and express their Jewishness. 'The Beta-Yisrael community is purely Torah-based, we didn't have the Talmud,' Ashager suggests. 'Our religious and community leaders are not called rabbis; we call them "*kes*". We did not celebrate Chanukah or Purim, as those events took place after we received the Torah and we have our own festivals, such as

Sigd.' Sigd falls on the 29th of Cheshvan, exactly 50 days after Yom Kippur. Sigd, which recognises the accepting of the Torah, means 'prostration' in Ge'ez, an ancient Ethiopian liturgical language and is a state holiday in Israel.

Ashager explains more about how seeing herself primarily as being Jewish 'comes directly from my Beta-Yisrael identity'. As the Ethiopian community was cut off from the rest of the Jewish world, they saw themselves as the last Jews and dedicated their entire community's existence to keeping Judaism and Jewishness alive. Ashager says: 'They had to preserve Judaism, otherwise they believed it would die.'

This belief, Ashager tells me, is what she sees as, 'the biggest difference between the Beta-Yisrael community and other Jewish Diasporic communities'. Most other parts of the Jewish Diaspora tried to assimilate to be accepted, while, in the face of antisemitism, the Beta-Yisrael community became even more staunchly Jewish, 'even going so far as creating their own villages, where just Jews could enter'.

This phenomenal resilience in the face of very real and powerful oppression is a beautiful testimony to the strength of Jewish spirit. The suffering of the Beta-Yisrael continued well into the 20th century. Following the Italian invasion of Abyssinia (the old name for Ethiopia) in 1935, the Jews were treated with more hostility. Racial laws implemented in Italy by the fascists also targeted the Beta-Yisrael community and the practice of Judaism was forbidden. This fact, which is not widely known, again demonstrates the totality of the Holocaust.

Following the end of the second world war and the establishment of the State of Israel, many in the Beta-Yisrael community hoped to make *Aliyah* to help build the new Jewish state but they were denied permission to leave by Emperor Haile Selassie. While small pockets of Jews did manage to sneak illegally from Ethiopia to Israel, mass migration did not take place until the 1980s. The well-documented famines that decimated Ethiopia, as well as civil war and the hostility of successive new governments towards the Jews, led Israel to deploy one of the most incredible rescue missions in the history of mankind. Like thousands of other Beta-Yisrael, Ashager's family had to make the incredibly arduous journey – in which thousands perished – from Ethiopia to Sudan, from where they were airlifted to Israel. This amazing feat has become a kind of Jewish folklore, showing how Israel will ensure that all Jews, regardless of where they are from, can depend on the Jewish state for support.

During Operations Moses, Joshua and Solomon in Ethiopia, over 20,000 Beta-Yisrael were flown to safety in Israel. The story of this relatively small number of Jewish people is also the story of all Jewish people: we are the Beta-Yisrael and they are us. Regardless of where we are from, what languages we speak or even the holidays we observe, we are one Jewish people who all have a connection to the land of Israel, our indigenous homeland. We have a responsibility to teach about both the diversity of the Jewish world as well as our shared experiences.

The Beta-Yisrael history of preserving Judaism and Jewishness at all costs has instilled in Ashager an innate sense of Jewish Pride. Her Jewishness and her pride in it governs her entire life, she suggests, and it drives her actions. She keeps kosher, she observes the Jewish holidays. 'I am actively Jewish,' she declares. This is something Ashager is very passionate about. Discussing how we instil pride in the younger generation, she argues that we have to be actively Jewish: 'You can't pass down a tradition of fear if we want people to be proudly Jewish. They have to understand our history and where we came from – which means telling all Jewish stories, including the Beta-Yisrael one – but also our cultural or religious practices.'

I very much agree with Ashager's sentiment. I was lucky that my parents brought me up observing Shabbat and the Jewish holidays and they kept a kosher home. I went out on a Friday night for the first time, without my family when I was 22. My relationship with my Jewishness was expressed through these acts and, because of this, it still is. I cook Jewish food and I observe Jewish holidays. I listen to Jewish music and I always say *kaddish* on my father's *yahrzeit* (the anniversary of his passing).

For Ashager, Jewish Pride is vital for the continuation of our community. 'Young people need to feel pride in being Jewish,' she argues. 'They need to feel it in their souls so they never give it up, but they have to have something – beyond antisemitism – to feel connected to.' Listening to her talk about the importance of history and a connection to our cultural practices fills me with pride. She is right: we have so much to be proud of, far beyond the fact we have survived so much. Yes, that is remarkable and should absolutely be celebrated. But we must celebrate just as much how we have thrived. Over thousands of years, we have created beautiful and distinct cultures which is amazing.

Ashager tells me that pride based around our history and culture is also important; if we don't spread awareness about it, we will allow the external world to define us. If we don't understand the importance of our laws, our cultural practices and our own history, then we believe the non-Jewish world's perceptions of us, and, in extreme cases, this can internalise antisemitism.

A video that Ashager made last year on reclaiming Zionism made this very point. In it, she says: 'Zionism is the ongoing rebellion against hundreds of years of a power structure that assigned Jews "a proper place" in society.' Hearing Ashager discuss her Zionism is incredibly powerful. It is very easy for advantaged Jews in the Diaspora to attack Israel or even define themselves as antizionist, but that position is deeply troubling. Israel has literally been a place of refuge for Jews from all over the world. Jews – whether from Tunisia, Iraq, the Soviet Union, France, or Ethiopia – have all found protection in Israel when they became unsafe in their countries of birth.

'It's very easy for a Jew who has never really felt threatened to hate Israel,' Ashager explains, 'but without Israel, we wouldn't exist.' Whether or not you agree with the actions or policies of the Israeli government, to deny the right of a Jewish state to exist is dangerously antisemitic and ultimately condemns millions of Jews to their deaths.

Ashager believes that 'we must reject antisemitic perceptions of what it means to be Jewish and we must define our own identity.' As I have stated repeatedly, we are Jews and we alone should define our identities and our values. If we allow something like Zionism – which is so fundamental to the Jewish experience – to be stolen from us and warped into something evil, then we have failed to take hold of our own destiny as Jews.

I am writing up my interview with Ashager during *Pesach* 2020 and this alone is very symbolic. *Pesach* is about recalling the slavery of the Jews in Egypt and our 40 years of wandering before reaching Eretz Yisrael, the land of Israel. The parallels to the Beta-Yisrael story – and that of Ashager – are uncanny. It is moving to hear her say that we need to 'throw the chains off the non-Jewish perceptions of the Jewish people' – and she is right. We need to throw off the chains, reclaim Zionism and determine our own identities without feeling forced to shed or distort our Jewishness to make us more palatable to the non-Jewish world.

Our conversation about Jewish Pride eventually moves on to modern-day Israel and to the current situation of the Beta-Yisrael in Israel. Listening to Ashager speak about her love for Israel is very poignant, but she is very clear that this love for her homeland, and her strong Zionism, does not stop her from criticising the Jewish state – and it is precisely this love that is behind any criticism she has of Israeli policy or aspects of its society. She deeply wants Israel to grow, improve and be the best it can be.

As of 2018, there are 148,700 Beta-Yisrael living in Israel. During our conversation, Ashager describes how 'Beta-Yisrael people, when they first moved to Israel en masse, because of questions over their Jewishness, were forced to convert to "ensure their Jewishness".' She tells me of the racism they experience, including the police brutality they face and the fact that they suffer from the highest poverty rate among the Jewish Israelis. During the summer of 2020, Beta-Yisrael, and their allies, joined global demonstrations to protest anti-black racism.

Another issue faced by the Beta-Yisrael community is the fact that, despite surviving for so long, they find themselves assimilating into another culture and losing part of their own identity. Ashager says she did not necessarily feel this way because she moved to Israel when she was so young, but friends of hers who grew up in Ethiopia feel a sense of bitterness that they have had to blend into Israel as opposed to Israel recognising the diversity of their experience. She tells me of a friend who wants to get married by a *kes* – a Beta-Yisrael religious, communal and cultural figure – but because *kessim* aren't recognised as rabbis by Israeli law, the marriage won't be legal. This is obviously frustrating for the Beta-Yisrael community, who have preserved their traditions and culture for so long. But, as Ashager says, 'Israel isn't perfect and it has room to improve but I still firmly believe in the concept of a Jewish state and I will fight to defend it.'

This passion for defending Israel led Ashager to work for Stand With Us, an international organisation which advocates for Israel on campuses all over the world. University campuses are a hotbed of antisemitic antizionist activity, so its work is vital. Ashager visited South Africa a number of times for Stand With Us and was shocked to find it one of the most antisemitic places she had visited. In a video that went viral, she was confronted by a group who screamed abuse in her face and told her that they support the genocidal Hamas terrorists.

One of the most common antisemitic accusations thrown at Israel is that it is a white colonialist state. This argument ignores the existence of Jews like Ashager and Hen and incorrectly frames Ashkenazi Jews as white Europeans, when they were only in Europe because they were exiled from their indigenous homeland through ethnic cleansing and genocide.

The argument that Israel is a racist imperialist state does not hold when levied at Ashager and, as she recognises, this has made her an important advocate for the Jewish state. 'The amazing thing is when they throw these accusations at me, there is no logical way they can stick. Obviously, they don't stick when they're thrown at any Jews, but when I stand there – a proud Black Jewish woman – they are not in a position to explain racism, imperialism or colonialism to me.'

Ashager has devoted her professional life to advocating for all Jews, the Jewish state and her Beta-Yisrael community. She asserts that *this* is an important part of having Jewish pride: 'For me, pride is about raising my voice up. Not being afraid of being told that I am wrong because I believe in my community and I believe in our right to advocate for ourselves.'

Jewish people are often shamed into silence. We are often frightened to express our views because we know from experience how we are frequently perceived. Ashager rejects this fear. She does not dismiss the realities of antisemitism and she is well aware of the importance of physical safety, but she defiantly argues: 'I will not be quiet because the non-Jewish world tells me to be quiet. I will not stop advocating for the Jewish community, and specifically the Beta-Yisrael community, just because it makes people uncomfortable.'

As she told me at the beginning of our conversation, being a proud Jew is her primary identity and she takes her role as an educator and advocate very seriously. She is the co-founder of Battae in Tel Aviv. Battae is, in its own words, 'the Ethiopian Israeli Heritage Center, which serves as a place for people to explore and appreciate the story of Ethiopian Jews in Israel.'

One of the reasons that Ashager helped establish Battae is to teach the rest of the Jewish community about the Beta-Yisrael experience. 'We truly believe that by connecting people, giving them a historical background, having one-on-one experiences with them, we are able to change our society and mend social divisions,' Ashager wrote of Battae's work. In its first three weeks, it had over 600 visitors who came to learn about the incredible Jewish story of the Beta-Yisrael community.

Ashager's work is a sight to behold. She is a shining advocate for both the Beta-Yisrael and the wider Jewish community. She embodies Jewish Pride.

Speaking to Ashager is really exciting. She is both courageous and committed and will not allow her identity as a proud Jew to be defined by the non-Jewish world. 'I feel so lucky to be Jewish, to belong to such an amazing community, with such an amazing history,' she tells me.

I couldn't agree more. We are lucky to be Jewish. Not only because of our beautiful, resilient and diverse community, but also because we have such powerful advocates like Ashager working hard to educate future generations about what it means to be a Jew. Like the generations of Beta-Yisrael leaders before her, Ashager is ensuring the continuation of a proud Jewish people for generations to come.

Chapter 8

ISAAC DE CASTRO

ISAAC DE CASTRO was born in October 1997. His heritage is both Sephardic and Ashkenazi. While he was born in Miami, he has lived all his life in Panama, before returning to the US to attend Cornell College in New York state. On both sides, he is a descendant of Jews who fled persecution. On his mother's side, Isaac's family lived in Lithuania and Romania. On his father's side, it can be traced back to Spain in the 15th century.

Isaac's namesake is Isaac de Castro Tartas, who was burned at the stake for refusing to renounce Judaism when he was Isaac's age. His last words were to recite the *Shema*. He cried out: '*She-ma yisrael, adonai eloheinu, adonai echad*' ('Hear O' Israel, the Lord is our God, the Lord is One'). Following the Spanish Inquisition in 1492, Isaac's family fled to Portugal. But within five years, they were then faced with the 1497 Portuguese Inquisition. After a period of living as crypto-Jewish (Jews who outwardly lived as Catholics, but maintained their Jewishness secretly) doctors, Isaac's family moved around Europe, seeking safety. For periods they lived in Amsterdam, Hamburg and London. From Europe, the family moved to the Caribbean, specifically to Curacao and the Virgin Islands. From there, in the late 1800s, Isaac's father's family moved to Panama. Isaac's grandmother on his father's side was the child of a Mizrahi Jew from Syria and a Sephardic Jew who fled to the Ottoman Empire following the Inquisition.

One of the main reasons I wanted to speak with Isaac for this book was his passion for Sephardic history. This is a beautiful, and sometimes tragic, story that is not often discussed in wider Jewish circles. Despite there being some confusion regarding the term, Isaac defines Sephardic Jews as Jews who, following our exile from Judea, settled in the Iberian Peninsula before exile and the Inquisitions led many of them to flee to other countries.

While Jews were eventually expelled from Spain and Portugal in 1492 and 1497 respectively, the process to destroy these Jewish communities had begun much earlier. In Spain, the 1391 pogroms saw Jews murdered in over 70 regions and kingdoms such as Seville, Castile, Aragon and Valencia. These events may have taken place over 600 years ago, but they are still a very relevant and important part of Jewish histories. People often think that the Spanish and Portuguese Inquisitions just led to forced conversion and expulsions (as if that weren't awful enough), but they were so much more than that. Jewish people were regularly burned at the stake, tortured and savaged by their neighbours en masse. By the Middle Ages, Jews had lived in Spain since their expulsion from Judea by the Romans. However, their clear deep-rooted connection to the place where they lived did not spare them from both religious and racial antisemitism.

Isaac recounted the story of his trip to Spain in 2019, which was pivotal to his understanding of the pain of the Inquisition. He visited the country to finalise the process, and sign the papers, for his Spanish citizenship, which he was eligible for because of his Sephardic heritage. During this trip, he made a pilgrimage to Toledo so he could better understand the history of what happened to the Jews of Spain. He tells me when he visited two synagogues, Sinagoga del Transito and Santa María La Blanca, both extraordinarily beautiful but subsequently turned into churches.

Most traces of Jewish life in Spain were totally destroyed and all evidence that a huge and important Jewish community ever lived there was erased. Santa María La Blanca, the second oldest synagogue in Europe, is still owned by the Catholic church, so Isaac had to pay to enter. He tells me Spanish Jews have recently asked for it back, but there has been no response. In Santa María La Blanca, Isaac says, he saw the history of the Inquisition 'presented in a very folklore-y way and the "Golden Age" of Spain was emphasised [and] how good Spain was for the Jews, which was odd being in a place that represented the cultural genocide of the Inquisition'.

It was so painful for Isaac that, he tells me, 'I kept having to choke back my tears. I was looking at the very real destruction of my people. This wasn't just a story from history. It was my people's and my family's story. When I got back to my hotel room, preparing to fly back to America, I just cried. The waves of pain for my ancestors washed over me.'

Isaac, an architecture student, explains: 'As someone who is particularly interested in the art and power of buildings, it was devastating to me to be standing in a building that was once a symbol of Jewish pride and was now a symbol of our destruction.' On this day, Isaac realised that what was done to the Iberian Jews was genocide. 'That is not something we talk about enough and that has to change,' he argues. 'Many Jews see the concept of never forgetting as solely in reference to the Holocaust, but the Inquisition has to be remembered too.'

Throughout our conversation, Isaac makes the point over and over again of how important it is for all Jews to feel connected to each other's history. 'Jews are Jews regardless of whether we are Ashkenazi, Sephardic, Mizrahi, Beta-Yisrael or other and we all share the same history and experiences and we should recognise that as such,' he suggests. 'I felt the same pain when I was learning on-site about the Spanish Inquisition as I did when learning about the Holocaust in eastern Europe.'

Following the orgy of violence of 1391, hundreds of thousands of Jews across Spain converted – under coercion and duress – to Christianity. Massacres and forced conversions continued sporadically for the next 100 years until January 1492, when the story of the Spanish (and, five years later, Portuguese) Jews took another tragic and terrifying turn with the Alhambra Decree (also known as the Edict of Expulsion). The decree, issued by Queen Isabella I of Castile and King Ferdinand II of Aragon, ordered the expulsion of practising Jews from Castile and Aragon and its territories and possessions by 31 July 1492. The Jews were given six months to pack and leave their country of birth – in which most had over millennia of deep connections and history – and all they had ever known. The expulsion of Jews from European countries was not just limited to Spain. Several other states, including England, had already expelled their Jews by this point. Over 200,000 Spanish Jews converted to Catholicism because of the Alhambra Decree and the various pogroms. Following the 1492 edict, between 40,000 to 100,000 Jews were expelled. This is clearly a monumental and pivotal moment, not just in Sephardic history, but the history of all Jews. It is horrific to think that an entire Jewish community was destroyed and dispersed in this way.

The Spanish Inquisition has become part of Jewish history, but it was an immensely violent act and the Jews who experienced it must have been terrified. It is vital that we humanise these historical figures because, as Isaac says, 'this is an important part of Jewish history and although it happened nearly 600 years ago, Jews everywhere should connect to it, just as they do to our more recent histories or even our biblical stories.'

This devastating story is the backdrop to Isaac's life; it is why his family left the Iberian subcontinent and why they spent years travelling between different European countries and why they eventually settled in Panama. But, Isaac notes, Sephardic Jews proved extraordinarily resilient. 'An amazing thing about the Sephardic community – who have been exiled twice – is that they managed to maintain a truly beautiful culture, which still exists to this day,' he suggests.

Isaac is immensely proud of being Jewish, and, despite being a descendant of Ashkenazi and Sephardic Jews, he feels connected to all Jewish peoples and stories. This is something I very much relate to. Growing up I knew that I was Ashkenazi but I felt, above all, Jewish; this was my identity and I have always, as Isaac does, felt connected to all other Jewish stories and sub-ethnic groups. Like others I interviewed, Isaac is particularly proud that Jews have not just survived – itself miraculous given the unbelievable adversity we have faced – but have thrived.

'Jewish culture – whether you are Ashkenazi, Beta-Yisrael, Mizrahi or Sephardic – is beautiful and rich with incredible histories and that to me is amazing; that we survived *and* we created these cultures gives me so much pride,' Isaac argues. He feels lucky to be Jewish, a feeling that has only intensified since he started his journey to learn about Jewish history, something we are both particularly passionate about. Understanding where we came from, what we have endured and how we overcame our immense challenges has been a huge factor in the deepening of Isaac's already strong Jewish identity.

Isaac believes that a Jewish Pride movement needs to be rooted in an appreciation of our history. 'How can we possibly be proud of ourselves as Jews,' he asks, 'if we don't know our history?' As someone who has studied history for most of my adult life, this speaks to me deeply. Our history is our context, it explains why we do what we do and is a vital part of Jewish Pride.

Isaac and I both agree that it is impossible to have a real, sustaining and healthy Jewish Pride without understanding our incredible Jewish story. A Jewish Pride movement which was not rooted in our collective history would be shallow and based on misplaced emphasis. It is also vital for maintaining connections between our diverse Jewish communities. Understanding the similarities of our experiences can break down barriers that exist between our communities and help foster a wider sense of Jewish Pride. But none of this is possible without first understanding our history. It is something that unites each of the amazing people featured in this book: they have all sought to understand our wider Jewish history, as well as their own sub-ethnic Jewish historical experiences.

Isaac is the personification of this wider Jewish pride. He feels deeply connected to both his Ashkenazi and Sephardic heritage and represents them in how he lives his life as a Jew – and Isaac also feels immense pride in the experience of the Mizrahi community as well as the Beta-Yisrael community. 'It's very easy to split off and define ourselves solely as "Ashkenazi" or "Mizrahi" or "Beta-Yisrael" any other sub-ethnic Jewish group, and while it is important to understand the specifics of each experience and culture, we can't lose sight of the fact that we are one Jewish people,' he argues.

Isaac's motivational call for a unified Jewish community inspires me – an Ashkenazi Jew – to ask him more about his Sephardic heritage. An important part of creating and maintaining a unified Jewish community is exploring and understanding the experiences of other Jewish communities. I was raised with Ashkenazi traditions but I want to understand Isaac's Sephardic experience better, so I can deepen my own connection to Sephardic culture.

Isaac tells me he is thrilled when non-Sephardic Jews engage in Sephardic culture. 'My cousin – who is fully Ashkenazi – messaged me last week and told me about the Ladino music he is listening to,' he says. 'He was able to tell me about Ladino songs that I had never even heard of and last Shabbat my grandmother – who is also Ashkenazi – was singing Ladino songs while making *blintzes*, it was so beautiful!'

Ladino is a Judeo-Spanish language that developed in the Iberian Peninsula similarly to the specific Jewish languages of Judeo-German (the Yiddish of the Ashkenazim) and Judeo-Arabic, spoken by Mizrahi Jews. These diverse Jewish Diasporic languages in a way represent all Jewish people. We may have slightly different experiences, but we are all unified by Hebrew and our connection to the wider Jewish community.

Ladino grew out of old Spanish but was developed further by the
Sephardic Jews in exile in the 15th century and was spoken by diasporic Sephardic Jews throughout the Mediterranean, in what is now
Turkey and the Balkans. A rich culture of music, poetry and story-
telling emerged from Sephardic Jews in Ladino. While the numbers
of Ladino speakers are declining, Isaac is learning it to help ensure
its survival. At this point, he tells me to go to YouTube to listen to
a Ladino song called *Sien Drahmas Al Dia*, which translates as 'One
Hundred Drachmas A Day'. It is powerfully beautiful. In fact, I
encourage you to pause your reading to listen to it. The song is also
haunting and, while I don't speak Ladino or even Spanish, I connect
with its stunning melody and my understanding that this is an expression of Jewish culture.

Tragically, Ladino, like so much of Jewish culture, was almost
totally destroyed by the Holocaust. The majority of the Sephardic
Jewish centres of Europe – the Netherlands, France, Greece and
Yugoslavia – were targeted by the Nazis and their allies. An esti-
mated 66,000 Jewish Yugoslavians and 60,000 Jewish Greeks were
murdered as their culture was devastated. The fate of Thessaloniki's
Jews is a particularly tragic story in the history of Ladino and Sephar-
dic culture in general. Prior to the Shoah, Thessaloniki had the largest
Jewish population in Greece with about 50,000 Jews residing there.
This Jewish community was over 500 years old, but in just two years
(1941-1943) it was completely shattered, with 45,000 Jews deported to
Auschwitz-Birkenau and gassed on arrival. The story of the Jews of
Thessaloniki offers an important lesson when considering the impact
of the Holocaust. The Shoah was not just a destruction of 6 million
Jewish souls, but also of their culture, which had taken hundreds of
years to establish.

The experience of the Sephardic Jews during the Holocaust is
representative of the shared experience of all Jewish people. Ashkenazi Jews, Sephardic Jews and Mizrahi Jews were all targeted and

persecuted by the Nazis directly. While it is obviously important to learn their specific stories so we can properly understand the experiences of different communities, it is vital that we not lose sight of the shared impact suffered by all Jews – such as how the Yiddish and Ladino cultures of Ashkenazi and Sephardic Jews were almost totally destroyed.

This underlines why a Jewish Pride movement must be inclusive; not just one of different types of Jews, but of diverse Jewish histories. We must tell the stories of all Jews to strengthen the wider Jewish community. The stories of Ashkenazi Jews, Beta-Yisrael, Mizrahi Jews and Sephardic Jews are all of our stories and it's our duty to learn them. As Isaac says: 'We have to learn our history, otherwise what are we basing our Jewish pride on?'

There are only 14.7 million Jews in the world – our population has not yet recovered to pre-Holocaust levels. Definitively splitting off into sub-ethnic communities surely would not be a viable or sustainable decision. Isaac tells me that he refers to himself as a 'Jewish mutt' and says that he hopes there will be more joining together of cultures. With the establishment of the State of Israel, this is now a real possibility. Like Isaac, my niece and nephews are mixed Ashkenazi and Mizrahi. I hope they grow up learning about both parts, and feeling connected to both aspects, of their identity while simultaneously being defined by their general Jewishness.

The concept of Jewish identity is a complex one. As Isaac suggests: 'Modern conversation on it has been greatly influenced by American norms, which don't necessarily fit our community, so it's like forcing a square peg into a round hole.'

Isaac is not white passing and as such has often been classed as a 'Jew of colour'. However, unlike Hen who addressed this in Chapter 6, this is not a term that Isaac feels particularly comfortable with: 'By definition, if I am a Jew of colour, then my light-skinned family members are "white Jews" and I don't believe such a thing exists. Their ancestry and their experience are *not* of white people. Saying this, I, of course, would never dictate to someone how they should identify, but for me, it is not something I feel comfortable with.'

On this issue, Isaac suggests: 'The term "white Jew" is also often used as a synonym for "Ashkenazi", however many Ashkenazi Jews do not pass as white and there are Jews of Mizrahi, Black or Sephardic descent who do, so are they white Jews or does their membership of these sub-ethnic groups still allow them to be classed as a Jew of colour?' It's also true that there are differences between the experiences of non-white passing Jews, so we must ask, how a term like, 'Jew of colour' encapsulates and represents that nuance?

Isaac suggests: 'The whole conversation seems to be based on an American model of understanding identity, which does not fit the Jewish community.' He stresses: 'Not using these non-Jewish ideas isn't about ignoring injustice in the Jewish world – we can and must address these – but, in my opinion, they are not helped by borrowing these terms from a specific American context.'

In terms of how we differentiate between some of the clear distinctions between the Jewish sub-ethnic groups, Isaac simply says: 'Why not just be specific? If you are a Sephardic Jew, then you are a Sephardic Jew, a Black-Ashkenazi Jew is a Black-Ashkenazi Jew. The catch-all term for all non-white-passing Jews is not necessary as we have terms to describe us already without importing a binary term from the non-Jewish world.'

This solution would help explain the differences that absolutely exist between our experiences, while not passing comment on other Jewish communities – in the way in which, Isaac believes, 'Jew of colour' implies that some Jews are necessarily white.

Whether you agree or not with Isaac does not really matter. To be one community, we do not need to only have one perspective. However, what does matter, is respecting people who have expressed a preference as to how they would like to be identified. 'We have

to honour, respect and love each part of the Jewish community,'
Isaac argues. 'That obviously means righting our wrongs and really
considering how we want to move forward as an inclusive community, with pride.'

At this point, we circle back to Isaac's Jewish Pride. He reiterates
that his pride is centred on our history: 'Pride has to be based on
knowledge and action. We have to understand that we have an incredibly rich and vibrant history that has shaped our present. We simply
can't express Jewish P*ride without first exploring our history.*'

Isaac also believes that Jewish Pride should involve Jews unashamedly standing up for themselves. This is why, in July 2020, he
co-founded the Instagram page @JewishOnCampus to provide a
platform for Jewish students to share their experiences of antisemitism at university and to stand together against Jew-hatred. Within a
month of establishing the page, @JewishOnCampus has over twenty
thousand followers, a sure sign that Isaac's unapologetic stance
inspires and empowers other Jewish students to fight antisemitism.

As Isaac's journey shows, Jewish Pride is an active process. We
must not assume that, just because we are Jews, we automatically
understand our history. Like anything in Jewish life, we must actively
seek out knowledge. As Isaac says, this process will actually help us
feel more connected to the Jewish people as a whole, not just our
sub-communities: 'You will find something in the enormously rich
tapestry of Jewish history you feel connected to regardless which
group it "belongs to" and you will also realise the innumerable shared
experiences all Jewish groups have.' Seeking out knowledge, discussing and arguing about it with our friends, is itself steeped in Jewish
culture. This culture of debating, arguing, disagreeing and discussing
– acknowledging the importance of dissent and disagreement – is a
vital part of Jewish life and our worldview.

Isaac's conscious effort to seek out knowledge and embark on a
journey to explore his identity on a deeper level is hugely inspiring, as

is his dedication to highlight and combat antisemitism. It is wonderful that he is able to honour both his Sephardic and Ashkenazi heritage, while simultaneously maintaining and fostering his deep connection to the entire Jewish people. It is beautiful to watch a young Jewish person who is driven by a desire to understand our history in order to gain a deeper understanding of who and where we are now as a people – and it is promising for our Jewish future.

Chapter 9

ELISHEVA RISHON

ELISHEVA RISHON is a Black Orthodox Jewish American woman. Her mother, who is Black and has Sephardic roots, was born Jewish and her father converted to Judaism before Elisheva's birth. Straight off the bat, Elisheva brings up the anti-Black racism that she has experienced: 'My Jewishness is often called into question so it's important to state that, despite what some people ignorantly argue because I am also a Black woman, that I am Halachically Jewish.'

Her father converted to Judaism through Chabad in New York's Crown Heights; an area that has once again hit the headlines due to recent antisemitic attacks. When I ask Elisheva about the impact on her of this antisemitism, and the tensions between the Black and Jewish communities, she says she is unsurprised. 'Listen, I am a child of the Crown Heights riots [a 1991 race riot which saw Orthodox Jews being attacked by local Black youths after a Black child, Gavin Cato, was run over and killed by a Hassidic Rabbi's driver] and the issues that sparked those were never resolved,' she responds. 'It's just so disappointing that minority communities can't come together to fight their common threats, instead of turning on each other.'

Elisheva was brought up in the Orthodox communities of Crown Heights and Flatbush (Midwood) and her family was very observant. 'We went to *shul* every Shabbat and all the *chagim* [Jewish holidays],' she explains. 'It was not an option not to go. This was our whole life'.

Her father was a seasonal *hazan* [cantor] at the *shuls* they attended. 'It would fill me with pride when he would take part in those services,'

Elisheva recalls, 'because it was the rare time I would get a look of approval from someone in the shul. 'Cause no one could do it like he did.'

Elisheva says of her Jewishness and Judaism today: 'I am a religious and culturally modern Orthodox woman because, for me, I feel the best place for Jews to be in this day and age is present and visible in the modern world. I think this is key in the battle against antisemitism.' Much of Elisheva's activism comes from wanting to be a role model for young Jews everywhere and this features heavily in her work.

Elisheva's Jewish identity is directly connected to her religious background and practices. 'The Orthodox world does not separate religious practices from daily life,' she suggests. 'They are intertwined permanently.' It is clear that, despite some of her experiences, Elisheva still adores the Orthodox way of life. 'I love the feel of the Orthodox sense of community, Shabbatons, the *Yeshivish* talk we speak that no one else gets, the fashion style, the fact that Jewish geography is super easy.' Elisheva's love of the Jewish community is palpable and uplifting.

But this love of Judaism and Jewishness has sadly been tested by the anti-Black racism she has experienced. 'Since the day I was born I have grown up around other members of the Jewish community telling me I can't possibly be Jewish just because I am Black,' she says. To fit in, Elisheva tried to make herself even more 'worthy' of acceptance by being 'extra *shomer negiah* [abiding by *Halacha*], wearing black more than I had to, being super-duper pro-Israel 24/7, showing more *kavanah* [devotion] and dedication in kissing a *mezuzah* when no one else would just to prove how "Jewish" I was.'

That a member of our community would ever be made to feel like this is heartbreaking. No one should have to try so hard to be accepted. They should simply be accepted for who they are. Elisheva's story demonstrates just how much work we still have to do to realise our dream of having an inclusive Jewish Pride movement that, as Hen said, 'celebrates our diversity instead of allowing it to divide us'. Tragically, Elisheva describes her situation as 'like being in a toxic relationship. To love a community that doesn't love you back, the way that you want to be loved'.

As Elisheva and I discuss her experiences, we are aware of the potential backlash to her story. That people will not really read and hear what she is saying, but merely react to emotional triggers. Elisheva is *not* saying that all Jews are racist towards Black people. She is *not* demonising Jewish people. She is *not* trying to feed antisemitism. She loves being Jewish and she loves the Jewish community. Elisheva recognises that prejudice exists in every community. No group, regardless of whether they're a minority or not, is immune to the virus of hate and bigotry. It exists in the LGBTQ+, Muslim, white, Black, Asian, Latin and Jewish communities alike. Elisheva is opening up to reveal her lived experience with us – and, for that, we should be grateful. We can learn from her story and we should approach this difficult and painful subject with an open heart and a willingness to understand and hear what Elisheva is saying.

One of the most inspirational things about Elisheva is her resilience, which is fed by her Jewish Pride. 'I feel and express my Jewish Pride through makeup and fashion,' she says. This is something I absolutely relate to – I always try to match my kippah to what I am wearing and make it a part of my outfit. It is always a sign of pride when people express their identities through their passions and interests and the way Elisheva has woven this into her Jewishness is a beautiful expression of herself. She tells me about the decision she made to learn how to do makeup well when she realised after a search for her skin tone in the orthodox 'Shabbos makeup' foundations that none of the Jewish brands carried her skin tone. By teaching herself how to do makeup and showcasing her looks she wants to show the world that Black women do love to wear makeup and also bring attention to that fact that Orthodox Jewish 'Shabbos makeup' does not carry foundation shades for all Jewish women.

Representation is a huge part of Elisheva's activism. She wants to show the world that people like her exist and that their stories are valid and an important part of the Jewish experience. She says she took her love of makeup a step further during Hanukkah 2019 when she did creative and beautiful makeup looks for every night of the holiday. 'I saw Christmas makeup looks being done over a two-week period but no one was doing it in the Jewish world,' she suggests. 'So, I did it to inspire Jewish make-up artists next year to take it on.' I can only imagine how powerful it was for young Jews to see Elisheva representing Judaism in such an exciting way.

Long before I sat down to interview her, I noticed how Elisheva blended being an Orthodox woman with expressing her fashion and style. She says that people often tell her: 'Elisheva, I had no idea you could look religious and stylish at the same time!'

Elisheva is a real role model as a proud representative of the Jewish community. She has taken her Jewish Pride a step further in creating a brand, 'Eli7Designs', that expresses Jewish Pride through fashion. Elisheva is committed to making diversity and inclusivity a major part of Jewish Pride – a notion that has come up time and time again in these interviews and is clearly something many of us feel passionately about.

'The greatest reward,' Elisheva says, 'is how interactive my customers are, telling me how wearing my *koach* [strength] shirt made them feel strong, how having the 'Malka' (queen) bag makes them feel good, or how happy their 'Blewish' (Black and Jewish) daughter or spouse feels when they wear my 'Black, Jewish and fabulous' hoodie. Making people feel empowered and good is why I do this.'

Having people like Elisheva, who work hard to build a strong and proud Jewish community, is crucial. She wants to make the world a better place and 'make the Jewish community a more inviting and welcoming place for the next generation'. What a wonderful sentiment.

Elisheva's insights into a modern Jewish Pride movement are shaped by her experiences living in the United States. She recounts something she has heard her mother say, time and time again: 'Some American Jewish people have gotten comfortable in America and have begun prizing being American on top of everything else – even being Jewish – and that means they internalise all things American, good and bad, which is why I personally feel we have issues such as sexism and racism in the American Jewish community.'

Elisheva's sense of Jewish Pride, ironically, grew out of feeling excluded by her community. But it is inspiring how she has taken this experience and, instead of resigning herself to, or internalising, it, has instead chosen to transform it. Feeling pride merely because you are part of a collective is not necessarily the best recipe for a healthy sustained pride movement. First and foremost, pride has to come from within, whether it's Jewish or Black or both. Pride is personal and everyone's pride looks different. For example, Elisheva expresses her Jewish Pride through her makeup and fashion as this works for her.

What can happen when we open up ourselves to internal pride is that we can use our personal relationship with Jewish Pride to inspire others, so that those who haven't necessarily taken their own journey of discovering their identity will be inspired by yours to explore their own sense of pride and express it for themselves. We must always remember that pride is contagious!

Elisheva and I strongly agree that building Jewish Pride means having a strong, united, inclusive and diverse community. Part of that, she argues, is 'understanding the experiences of Orthodox Jews. We are often targeted by other parts of the Jewish community because of our values.'

I have always admired Elisheva's ability to talk about difficult issues in the Jewish community without passing judgement on specific groups. This is something that seems particularly important given that Orthodox Jews are so often the victims of violent antisemitic attacks. She says categorically that this is not an Ashkenazi problem. She has experienced anti-Black racism from Mizrahi Jews and Sephardic Jews as well. Despite her clarity, people unfairly accuse her of being anti-Ashkenazi or anti-Orthodox. She is proudly Ashkenazi, Orthodox and Black and appreciates and loves both parts of herself. She loves the Jewish community but that love will not allow her to stay silent on issues that we need to address.

Some people have accused her of being *chillul hashem*, an act that brings shame on the Jewish people. This is absolutely not the case. Elisheva's love for the Jewish community is what pushes her to speak about her experiences; like Hen and Ashager, she does not do so to demonise or punish, but to raise awareness of her lived experience so the community can address these issues. A shining example of Jewish Pride if ever I saw one.

When describing the antisemitism she has faced, Elisheva details the hate she receives from white supremacists, who loathe her for being *both* Black and Jewish. This is something I can relate to as a gay Jew. Growing up people would often tell me: 'the Nazis would really have hated you.' She tells me that she also has to deal with antisemitism from the Black community, including from the Black Hebrew Israelites, a group of Black Americans who incorrectly claim that they are the descendants of the Israelites and as such are the 'real Jews'. Groups like this only remind her of how strong antisemitism is and how much Jewish people need to come together if we are to deal with it.

Elisheva believes that being at the intersection of Black and Jewish allows her to feel proud of both of these incredible communities. Some of her descendants came to America fleeing antisemitism, while others were brought on slave ships. Both communities have survived under the most intense persecution and that gives Elisheva a huge amount of strength. She rejects any idea of competition over which community has suffered more – a frequent game which only serves to damage both. She is passionate about recognising all experiences and will not be dragged into any sort of 'oppression Olympics'. But avoiding this has become more and more difficult with the growth of light-skinned Jewish people being described as 'white' or 'privileged'. As Elisheva says, such labelling 'disregards and erases the violent antisemitism that all Jews have always faced – and continue to face to this day'.

We discuss the fact that American norms, such as specific understandings of prejudice, are being both absorbed by, and imposed upon, the Jewish community. Towards the end of our conversation, Elisheva points out that, at no point during it, has she used the words 'white Jew'. Instead, she says, if she was going to discuss light-skinned Jews she would describe us as 'white-presenting' or 'white-passing'. This is because she feels passionate about recognising the deadly antisemitism *all* Jews face from white supremacists on a daily basis, and will never try to play it down to amplify any racism she experiences.

To me, this is really moving. Someone who has so often struggled with feeling unseen by her community continuously makes an effort to make sure other Jews also feel represented and their experiences are not erased. Elisheva is an example to all people on how to discuss prejudice. Both experiences are as valid as the other and both communities should be working together to fight the common enemy of white supremacy.

Elisheva is concerned with how polarised people have become, displaying an inability to show nuance and care about two different things at the same time. 'I believe it is possible to address racism in the Jewish community and still be a proud Jew,' she argues. 'Just as it's possible to call out antisemitism in the Black community, while still being proudly Black.' She continues: 'Being Black and Jewish, I see how each group can treat each other [at times] and I call it out whenever I can because I see what is happening … [the] misconceptions, miscommunications and hatred between both communities. I see that we should be bonding together but we don't and it kills me. I feel that America set us up to hate each other with red lining designed to pit minorities against each other.'

Elisheva also sees a similar pattern reflected in the Israeli-Palestinian conflict. 'I believe that being a Zionist means that you can also care about the Palestinians and Arab-Israelis in that conflict and *also* care about Jewish Israelis,' she says, 'because demonising an entire people for who they are is never going to solve any conflict.' I couldn't agree more with her thoughts on this: such binary thinking stops us from discussing important issues with love. Even in our Jewish Pride movement, we will not be able to agree on everything.

The best thing to do is to ensure that, when we disagree, we always listen, believe each other's truths, and speak with respect – just as Elisheva does.

When I ask her what she wishes the rest of the Jewish world knew about the Black Jewish experience, Elisheva's response is fascinating. 'A lot of Black Jewish people in American Jewish communities who are born Jewish usually have Ashkenazi or Sephardic heritage,' she says. 'And recently, some even have Mizrahi heritage. Most of us, however, are not recognized for our Jewish ancestry because if we present as Black, we are treated as Black and referred to as Black, as opposed to people understanding our genuine ethnic heritage.'

She goes on to explain: 'For example, what do people say when they talk about [the rapper] Drake? I have often heard them say: "Drake's mother is Jewish. She is Ashkenazi Jewish." That's the wrong answer, though. His mother is Jewish, so he is Jewish by all streams of Judaism. So, instead, people should be saying: "Drake is a Black Ashkenazi Jew". But they don't because the fact that he is Black makes them feel that his mother's heritage is separate from his heritage. It really disturbs me because every Jewish law says this is not how it is done.'

It is clear from talking to Elisheva that the Jewish world is not immune to prejudice. As she herself argues, this does not mean that the Jewish community is not a beautiful one with so much to offer. It means that our community – like *all* communities – has issues we need to work on. This is not *chillul hashem*. This is looking closely at our community with love and an understanding that, as human beings, we are not perfect and we have work to do. That is what Jewish

Pride is really about. Rather than hating on or aggressively criticising members of the Jewish community who are 'problematic', we can take pride in coming together to create a community and movement based on inclusivity. Whether you are a Black Jew or a gay Jew or any other type of Jew, you should be welcomed into our community and made to feel comfortable. The greatest disservice we could do to our community is to avoid talking about these issues and pretend they do not exist, thereby letting our fellow Jews suffer in silence.

Elisheva understands well how a culture of silence works. 'There were years where I would not speak on it and ignore racist situations just to avoid being called a *chillul hashem*,' she says 'Because at my core, all I ever wanted was to be accepted.'

Thank God that Elisheva now does speak out about these issues – it is the only way we can ever hope to realise a Jewish community that is a safe space for *all* Jews.

As our interview comes to a close, I realise that I feel a close connection with Elisheva. We both occupy dual minority identities and have experienced prejudice from both communities. That is not an easy thing to cope with. It can have a harsh impact on your mental health. But, despite the issues we have had with it, I also share with Elisheva a love of the Jewish community and a desire to make it and the world better. We are dedicated to owning our Jewish Pride in ways that work for us and we attempt to inspire and empower the wider Jewish community, despite the challenges we have each faced.

On her Eli7Designs website, Elisheva writes: 'Being Born a Black Dark-Skinned American Orthodox Jewish Girl, these 5 parts of my identity were constantly a source of controversy for many. But I have learned that every single part of my identity is beautiful and unique.'

There is no doubt in my mind that our beautiful and diverse community is enriched by Elisheva Rishon because of how she embodies this sentiment.

Chapter 10

ELIYAHU LANN

ELIYAHU LANN was born in Watford in Britain in April 2001. He is the fourth child of seven, and, by his own admission, a 'classic middle child'. His mother's family, though the descendants of Sephardic Jews, were totally assimilated and secular, while his father's family were originally Russian Haredi Jews. Eliyahu is a transgender Jewish man, an advocate for the Jewish LGBTQ+ community, and aims to show the world through his work that it is possible to be 'a proud transgender member of the Jewish community'.

Eliyahu first came to understand what being transgender meant when he was 10 years old, so, like many LGBTQ+ Jews (myself included), his Jewish identity was the primary identity that was formed first. When you belong to the LGBTQ+ community and another minority group (like the Jewish community, for example), your LGBTQ+ identity is always formed against the backdrop of another fairly established identity, as we often come to our LGBTQ+ identities later. This means that for many Jewish LGBTQ+ people, like Eliyahu and myself, being Jewish comes first and is our primary identity.

His parents' divorce marked a key moment in the development of Eliyahu's Jewish identity. 'This is when a big split happened, I moved between two worlds,' he recalls. 'My mum's side of the family was incredibly secular but then my dad's side, my grandparents, were originally Haredi, so in many ways, I was moving between two polar opposite Jewish identities.' He tells me that his grandmother, who sadly passed away when he was still young, used to make traditional

Jewish food like chicken soup. 'Being Jewish was a part of my cultural identity,' he says. 'I knew that we were different'.

His Jewish life changed drastically when his mother remarried and the family moved to the state of South Australia in 2012. They settled in a fairly remote area that, if not quite the outback, was certainly not the metropolitan city of Adelaide. Still not yet a teenager, Eliyahu found himself to be incredibly isolated. 'I was raised in a place with no LGBTQ+ people, certainly no trans people and no Jews,' he explains. 'I was the first of everything, which is intense.'

People often forget that being Jewish or LGBTQ+ really means you are members of a minority group – not just in terms of oppression, but in terms of numbers. Being the only Jewish or LGBTQ+ person in your community can be both very isolating and highly pressurised; you become the sole representative of your community, without other Jews or LGBTQ+ people to teach you or support you.

This is something we must consider when forming our Jewish Pride movement. We often, and sometimes understandably, focus our attention on the centres of Jewish life, but we must not forget that not all Jews live in London, New York or Israel and every Jew, regardless of where they live, is a member of our community and deserves to be supported as such. It is also important that we do not allow non-Jewish concepts from specific places to dominate the global Jewish conversation. No one Jewish experience matters more than the others and we must understand that when we engage in dialogue on the global Jewish community.

This is why I included an Australian Jew in these seven interviews. Despite the fact that there are roughly 113,000 Jews living there, due to Australia's geographical location, the county's Jewish population is often not discussed when we talk about the global Jewish community. For example, when researching this interview, I learned about the experience of the Australian treasurer (or finance minister), Josh Frydenberg who is also the son of a Holocaust survivor. Eliyahu tells me that during the May 2019 general election, posters of Frydenberg, who is also deputy leader of the governing Liberal party, were defaced with Hitler moustaches. He has also been the victim of a 'birther' campaign, which argued that, through his mother, a Hungarian Holocaust survivor, the minister held dual Hungarian-Australian citizenship and was thus ineligible to sit as an MP. After a long legal battle, Australia's Highest Court unanimously dismissed the claims. In its unanimous judgment, it noted the 'catastrophe, anti-Jewish violence and terror' which his mother's family escaped and suggested the 'niceties of proof of the production or issue of documents ... can be put aside when one recognises the realities of 1949' when they arrived in Australia.

Frydenberg has also spoken up about antisemitism in Australia, where Jewish children in primary schools are being tormented because of their Jewishness. In 2019, research suggests, there was a 30% rise in 'serious'[309] antisemitism in Australia. As Jews everywhere experienced, Covid-19 has exacerbated the situation. As Julie Nathan, research director of the Executive Council of Australian Jewry and co-convenor of the Australian Hate Crime Network, suggested: 'Australian racists online have been posting comments and sharing various images, presumably originating from overseas, portraying the coronavirus as a "Jew", as well as accusing "the Jews" of creating and spreading the virus, and expressing the wish that all Jews die from the virus.'[310]

Antisemitism exists everywhere. It is thus important that all Jewish people and all Jewish communities feel not only a part of our global community but also feel the reach of Jewish Pride. We cannot overlook or ignore specific Jewish communities vulnerable not just to antisemitism, but also to the shame that it so often brings.

Having grown up experiencing and taking part in Jewish culture through his grandparents, Eliyahu found himself the only Jewish person in his school, where he faced intense antisemitism. It was also during this traumatic time that Eliyahu realised he was transgender. When I asked him what this was like, he told me that, before he real- ised, he used to lock himself in the bathroom and cry: 'I didn't know what was going on, I didn't understand what was going on with me. I didn't know who I was. When I was a pre-teen I used to rough-house and play sports, but, as you get older, you are taught to follow the gender binary more strictly and I didn't understand or like it.'

Thankfully, Eliyahu had access to the internet and, when he was 12 years old, he came across a video by British transgender You- Tuber Alex Bertie. This was the first time Eliyahu was exposed to being transgender. 'It resonated with me and I connected to it, but I also didn't want it because the ramifications are enormous,' he suggests. 'It was incredibly confronting and scary. I saw someone who had mental health issues because he was transgender and he was suffering and I didn't want that. I was 12 years old. It was a lot.'

In December 2014, Leelah Alcorn, a young transgender woman who Eliyahu knew online, took her life. This tragedy occurs all too often in the transgender community. Research shows that transgender people are twice as likely to think about and attempt suicide [311] than the rest of the LGBTQ+ community, who are, in turn, four times more likely to attempt suicide than their heterosexual counterparts. During this period of his life, Eliyahu's mental health was poor and he was self-harming. Leelah's death led Eliyahu to realise that, if he didn't come out, he might also attempt suicide.

In 2015, Eliyahu officially transitioned at school. But being the first transgender person in his school, his teachers didn't know how to handle this situation nor how to meet Eliyahu's needs. The school had little idea what it was doing and asked him very invasive questions. This is a common experience for transgender people, where cisgender (non-transgender) people ask very personal and intimate questions, which they would never ask another cisgender person. This is not appropriate, especially since Eliyahu was still a child. Yet, the school's behaviour also forced Eliyahu to take on a leadership role while he was still a teenager.

Eliyahu's experience helps explain why, at such a young age, he has become an important Jewish voice on Twitter – because he has been forced to lead. 'I didn't have a choice then when I was helping my school understand transgender and Jewish issues and I still feel like I don't have a choice,' he believes.

He came out to his parents because, as a minor, his school needed their permission to change his name. He told his parents in March, a month before his birthday, so 'they could write my real name on my birthday presents and card'. Initially, he says, his mum struggled to understand what was happening but eventually she accepted it. His dad also did not accept it at first, which led to a break-down in their relationship for a year. Thankfully, they now have a great relationship again.

While Eliyahu was coping with coming out and pioneering transgender rights in his school and community, he also had to cope with the trauma of constant antisemitism. In fact, he says, 'for the most part, the bullying I experienced was as a Jew, not as a transgender person. They accepted me for being transgender, but they didn't accept me for being a Jew'.

Swastikas were constantly graffitied on school walls, on desks and in the bathrooms. He was told 'to burn in the ovens' and faced images of Hitler with the words 'what he did was right'. Eliyahu says that he couldn't get through a single day without seeing multiple reminders of the genocide committed against his people. This is something that people, both Jews and non-Jews, don't really appreciate. Antisemitism based on the Holocaust, and even just depictions of the Holocaust itself, are incredibly triggering and traumatic. It is a constant reminder of the horror and loss that we experienced and it has an impact on our mental health.

During the interview, Eliyahu and I discuss nightmares of the Holocaust we have had (other Jewish friends have shared this too).

Non-Jews do not understand the weight of this because of how the Holocaust is taught. They are taught about it from a non-Jewish perspective, where the Jews are framed as passive victims with little explanation of how this genocide continues to affect us. 'Two-thirds of our people in Europe were murdered. Yiddish and Ladino were destroyed,' says Eliyahu. 'Of course, we have intergenerational trauma and it's real and it impacts us.'

Eliyahu remembers at school seeing Indigenous Australian students allowed to leave the class during lessons on the colonisation of Australia. Without being told, he realised that during lessons on the Holocaust, as a Jewish student, he deserved this right too. I find this so remarkable because, due to the way the left often prioritises certain forms of prejudice over others, Jewish people, as has been discussed, are not seen as a legitimate minority.

This, of course, is not true, but this idea clouds people's perceptions of Jewish victimhood. But Eliyahu knew instinctively that this is wrong and that his experiences were just as valid as anyone else's. This is a lesson for all of us. We can never allow anyone to tell us that our experiences are less important than those of others. We must reject the attempt to erect a hierarchy of minority pain and demand the same acknowledgement and support that others are given.

During his gap year before going to university, Eliyahu moved back to the UK. He spent all his time in London researching and learning about his family and his Jewish heritage. This is where, for the first time, his transgender and Jewish identities intersected.

Eliyahu tells me that there were two synagogues near his father's house; one was Liberal and the other was Orthodox. Due to his upbringing with his grandparents, he says 'he felt more comfortable' in the Orthodox synagogue, but he feared how, being transgender, he would be received there, so he chose to go to the Liberal synagogue.

This is one of the major ways that being LGBTQ+ impacts our Jewishness. It literally dictates how we express and practice it.

As Eliyahu shows, it affects our decisions on which synagogues to attend and which communities to be a member of. This is a tragedy. LGBTQ+ Jews are entitled to belong to the community they feel best fits with how they want to practice their Judaism. They should not feel precluded from joining Orthodox synagogues.

Of course, we should recognise the progress that Orthodox Judaism has made regarding LGBTQ+ issues. Eliyahu references the LGBTQ+ guide that the British chief rabbi, Ephraim Mirvis, issued to Jewish schools in 2018. This was a landmark moment when the Orthodox community understood the responsibility it has to LGBTQ+ Jews. However, as with so much else, there is still a lot of progress to be made. Sadly, Jews like Eliyahu may still not necessarily feel comfortable in an Orthodox environment.

Nonetheless, Eliyahu experienced LGBTQ+phobia in the Liberal synagogue. He says that people were obsessed with labelling him and trying to work out his identity and would try to 'catch him out'. He was even told by someone: 'Oh, I met your partner last week.' This was an attempt to see which pronouns – him, her or they – Eliyahu would use in response. The trick failed: Eliyahu didn't have a partner at the time. This demonstrates that all Jewish communities still have to make a lot of progress regarding LGBTQ+ Jews. Eliyahu, Hen and myself are all passionate activists for the Jewish community *and* we are all proud members of the LGBTQ+ community. We deserve to feel safe and comfortable in the wider Jewish community.

During Eliyahu's gap year in the UK, he was also the victim of a violent antisemitic attack. He tells me:

In 2019, I was walking home from Synagogue, the Erev Shabbat Evening Service – it was about a 45-minute walk home through a forest – and I was physically attacked. As I lay on the ground I thought: *'Though they lived in Britain during the Holocaust, my family changed their name from Weinstein to Wynn to sound less*

Jewish.' … And here I was, in 2019, getting a beating in a forest for the same things they were beaten for … existing as a Jew. They called me 'Zionist' [and] a 'kike', threw my kippah into the trees, and kicked me until I couldn't move. I realised that no one else was there. No one would come to save me. No one would even care. And I would have to pick myself up alone, like Jews always do.

When Eliyahu says he was beaten for 'existing as a Jew', it reminds me of something Mr Beris, a Romanian Holocaust survivor, told me in 2012. He sat next to me recalling the crimes Romania committed against its own Jews and said: 'My fault, my crime, was that I was born a Jew.' Eliyahu's harrowing story is a reminder to everyone that violent antisemitism that targets Jewish people still exists. It is not a thing of the past. It is just as traumatic as it always has been throughout our history.

After his gap year, Eliyahu began a media and communications degree at La Trobe University back in Victoria, Australia, where he sadly experienced yet more antisemitism. In 2016, a white supremacist group known as Antipodean Resistance at Eliyahu's university put up posters that called to 'legalise the execution of Jews'[312]. It is shocking and absolutely unacceptable that Jewish students still have to endure this kind of deep intense racism.

In 2020, Eliyahu's university, Socialist Alternative, a Marxist group, held events denying Soviet Union's ethnic cleansing of Jews and discussing the 'true history of the Russian Revolution'. As a descendent of Russian Jews, Eliyahu was deeply upset by the erasure of his family's terrible experiences of antisemitism. Eliyahu is now reflecting on what he faced at school. It is only since joining Twitter and seeing other Jewish people's reaction to his experiences, that he realised how traumatic they had been. This is something I can relate to. I only processed the intense antisemitism I experienced at university about seven years after I had left. The tragedy of prejudice is when those who experience it don't even feel it because it is such a part of their everyday lives.

As we talk about antisemitism, our conversations turn to Jewish Pride. 'Despite the antisemitism I have faced, I am unapologetically Jewish,' he responds when I ask about how he expresses it.

Eliyahu's use of the word 'unapologetically' is really important. Jews are often asked to apologise for so many aspects of our identity in order for the non-Jewish world to even consider accepting us. We are asked to accept that antisemitism is less harmful or important than other forms of prejudice. 'We should never apologise for being Jewish,' Eliyahu says. 'We should never be made to feel less important than any other group of people and we are just as deserving ... [of] allyship as any other minority group'.

Like me, Eliyahu wears a kippah every day and a Magen David necklace as he says that these outward expressions of Jewishness are important: 'They let the world know who I am, without me even having to say it – which I don't mind doing! I am showing the world that I am a proud Jew and I don't care what they think about that.'

I love this. It is healing to hear someone as young as Eliyahu rejecting the shame of antisemitism. It shows us that we have the power to reject the non-Jewish world's view of what it means to be a Jew and that we do not have to let this dictate how we feel about ourselves. It gives us permission to be proudly Jewish.

Eliyahu is a role model for all Jews of all ages, beliefs, backgrounds, genders and corners of the earth. He has been a pioneer in standing up for both of his communities at an incredibly young age. Not only has he accepted the heavy responsibility for standing up for LGBTQ+ people and Jews, but he has embraced it with dignity: 'I want to shout it from the roof-tops that I am Jewish, I love it, and I would never change it.'

When I ask him what he specifically loves about it he says: 'Everything! I love our resilience, our traditions, our community, our history and bodies.'

When I ask what he means by 'our bodies', he responds: 'I mean our physical bodies. Our hair, our body-shapes, our noses, everything! We have to reject Eurocentric beauty standards that tell people that do not fit them that they are ugly.'

He is right, Jews are so often shamed for our appearance and many of us have tried to conform to European and western notions of beauty. But all Jews are beautiful and should feel this as Eliyahu does.

Eliyahu's pride, much like mine, is about rejecting the non-Jewish world's ideas of what it means to be a Jew, and about seeing value and worth in the Jewish world – even when non-Jews do not. He is a proud transgender Jewish man determined to shape his own identity based on a healthy perception of himself. He is able to combat antisemitism, express his Jewish Pride and to still advocate for other communities without compromising himself.

Eliyahu knows that Jewish people are just as important as any other community and he is deeply committed to defending the Jewish world and helping it progress. He is a brave warrior who is unapologetically Jewish. There are countless Jewish progressives who could learn a thing or two from Eliyahu's deep Jewish Pride. It is incredibly heartwarming to know that, with young leaders as committed and inspiring as Eliyahu, the Jewish community is in safe hands for generations to come. We are so incredibly lucky that Eliyahu is Jewish.

Chapter 11

AMY ALBERTSON

AMY ALBERTSON was born in Sacramento California in May 1991. She is the daughter of a Chinese-American woman and an Ashkenazi Jewish man. Amy is the descendant of immigrants and both sets of her ancestors emigrated to the United States during the 20th century, fleeing persecution and seeking new opportunities. She speaks fondly about her atheist Jewish grandmother who lived in Brooklyn and her secular father, and how they were responsible for her Jewishness growing up. She explains that, as a child, her Jewish experiences were all rooted in culture and were devoid of any religious practice. This makes Amy's Jewish journey an amazing and inspirational one.

Amy says that *Pesach* was her favourite holiday growing up and she felt connected to it, even though her family didn't own a *Haggadah* (she says she didn't even know what one was until college). It's clear listening to Amy that, while she was not exposed to a strong grounding in Jewish traditions or cultures, she was drawn to them. As a child, she doesn't remember having a particularly strong Jewish identity, which she partially attributes to growing up in a predominantly mixed neighbourhood as well as her father's secular identity. 'He grew up in a secular environment and then, when he became a teenager, he really strayed away from identifying as Jewish because he didn't like how it made him feel different,' Amy says of her father. 'He didn't want to point himself out as different.' I can understand this and it's a really sad testament to how antisemitism affects individual Jews and how comfortable they feel connecting to Judaism and Jewishness.

But Amy's stories about her cultural relationship with being Jewish, and her father's experiences, seem quite typical of many people from the United States I have spoken to. While her Jewish journey is peppered with different Jewish experiences – from *Pesach* to Kabbalat Shabbat – she only realised their significance later in life when she began exploring Jewish culture in a deeper and more meaningful way.

Growing up in a community of mixed children and not identifying so strongly with her Jewish heritage, Amy did not experience antisemitism until she was at middle school. It came at a school dance during an argument with a friend. 'A friend of my friend came up and started interrupting us and I was really mad and I said, "excuse me, I am trying to talk to him" and the friend started looking at me and laughing and saying "aren't you Jewish?",' she recalls. 'I didn't understand why he was laughing but I knew it was wrong and I knew I didn't like it.'

This experience rings true to me and many of my friends who have faced antisemitism but haven't necessarily been armed with the knowledge or vocabulary to explain why it is offensive. Amy's reaction – 'I remember being so shocked and confused' – is not an uncommon one. Her experiences of antisemitism are interesting as they reinforce the notion that antisemites don't care if your mother or father is Jewish. We are all the same to them.

As all of her local private secondary schools were Catholic, Amy chose to attend the more academically rigorous Christian Brothers High School. This is where she received religious education and, amazingly, this is where Amy first began to learn about Judaism. She praises her teachers for teaching her about Judaism in a 'fairly open and liberal way' and says: 'This is where I began to learn about Judaism the religion, as opposed to Jewish culture.'

At this time, Amy felt spirituality growing inside of her. She remembers that, during one of her classes, she had to do a project on Judaism and, while she was researching *Pesach*, another group (of non-Jewish) students was examining *kashrut* (Jewish dietary laws). When Amy spoke up about being Jewish, a girl from that group responded: 'What do you mean you're Jewish? Do you keep kosher?' When Amy said that she didn't, the girl said: 'Well, then you're not Jewish.' 'It just made me so angry,' Amy says. 'It made me feel so threatened. It's not right for someone else – especially a non-Jew – to try and define my identity for me.'

Sadly, this type of gatekeeping has been a constant throughout Amy's life, whether it is non-Jewish people telling her what constitutes a Jew or Jewish people who reject patrilineal Jews telling her she is not a Jew. At the heart of this specific discussion lies the *Halacha* (Jewish law), which dictates that if your biological mother is Jewish, then you are Jewish. Patrilineal Jews are those whose fathers are Jewish but not their mothers. It is awful that, while she experiences antisemitism like all other Jews, there are those who would deny her Jewishness, which leaves Amy in a very vulnerable and isolated position. It also reminds me that Jews, no matter where they are and what they look like, experience antisemitism. This factor alone unifies our experiences, regardless of our path to Judaism and Jewishness.

As a response to this erasure and antisemitism, when she was 17 years old, Amy asked her grandmother for a Magen David necklace. Emotions overcome her as she describes to me the first time she wanted everyone to know that she was Jewish. It was quite a statement to make for someone who grew up without a strong Jewish identity. But it's a testament to this innate connection to being Jewish which she felt that, despite attempts by some to deny her Jewishness and her own lack of knowledge about Jewishness and Judaism, Amy felt proudly Jewish – and wanted the world to know it. I understand the desire to show the world that you are proudly Jewish, which is why I wear a kippah every day.

Amy's Jewish journey continued when she went to Portland State University in Oregon. Nervous to go to Hillel, a global Jewish campus organisation, because she was afraid of being rejected for being a patrilineal Jew, Amy met another Jewish girl and they decided to go together. Listening to Amy's story, it seems like this Shabbat dinner changed the course of her life. The people she met at this dinner became her closest friends and thankfully she always felt accepted and supported. 'This was a blessing and a curse,' Amy says. 'My community was so open to me but it has made it more challenging when I venture out into other Jewish communities, because of how I am treated.'

Amy became the vice-president of Hillel and, in her second year at university, a Jewish Agency *shaliach* (or outreach officer), Amos, was sent to her university. For the first time, Amy was exposed to programmes about Israel. Sadly, as it often the case, such programmes often face antizionist protests and disruption. Amy remembers her confusion when a protest was held against the screening of a film, *Israel Inside*, by Jerusalem U. 'At this point, I didn't understand the politics at all,' she says. 'Israel was a Jewish country, that's all I really knew. I didn't know it was controversial to believe in Israel, especially because there were Muslim countries and Christian countries. I didn't understand why the Jewish state was controversial.'

It is so refreshing to hear the questions that ran through Amy's mind at this time and it highlights even more clearly how totally irrational the obsessive hatred of Israel, as a Jewish state, really is. 'At this point, I was so confused and mad,' Amy remembers, 'I didn't understand what was going on.' After this, Amy knew she had to learn more and sought out as much knowledge as she could gather about Israel and its conflict with the Palestinians.

She tells me that, at that point, Hillel didn't want to 'touch the conflict', as it was deemed 'too controversial'. But even though she didn't have a huge amount of knowledge, Amy wasn't happy with that stance of silence on Israel. This is where her natural leadership shines through and also her innate connection to her Jewish heritage, which she likens to 'some unexplainable magnetic pull, or fire burning inside of me'. 'I attribute this to my Jewish soul being connected to the Jewish people,' she suggests.

It is disheartening that anyone could doubt Amy's Jewishness when she has been – and continues to be – such a powerful advocate for our community. 'We were the Jews on campus and no one was going to accurately represent Israel, so we had to,' Amy recalls. 'The Palestinian supporters were trying to define the Israel that we were representing so we had to define it ourselves.'

People attempting to define Amy's identity for her has been a sad and unnecessary constant throughout her life. But Amy found her voice and co-founded a movement called CHAI (Cultural and Historical Association for Israel) that would support Israel on campus by putting on Jewish and Israeli cultural events. At this point, Amy tells me, she 'became the face of the Jewish population on campus.'

Again, it's worth reflecting on the fact that, despite her enormous Jewish Pride – one based on activism to support Israel and the Jewish community – there are still those who would deny Amy's Jewishness. Underlining the absurdity of her situation, Amy tells me that her 'entire adult life has been spent advocating for the Jewish people, while they simultaneously tell me I am not a part of them'. I can't think of a better advocate than Amy.

This quote reminds me of Hen and Elisheva. Like them, Amy has experienced rejection and discrimination at the hands of the Jewish community. But their Jewish Pride and real love allows them to overcome this and continue to fight for a better Jewish community. Their strength and pride cannot be underestimated. How does Amy cope with this rejection? 'The thing I have to remember is that this is bigger than us,' she replies. We are so lucky to have such amazing advocates who fight for our community and they make me feel so proud to be Jewish.

Amy ran CHAI for the last two years of her university career and during this time she also began working with the head of education for one the local Conservative synagogues. Amy met with a number of different rabbis, including Rabbi Zuckerberg, who encouraged her to learn and explore Judaism. It is important to remember that, while Amy felt a deep connection to Jewishness and Judaism, she made an inspirational choice to learn and study. It is safe to say that many people who never have their Jewishness doubted know far less about our heritage and religion than Amy does.

At this point, our conversation turns briefly to the topic of conversion to Orthodox Judaism and how people have accused her of 'not wanting to convert or not caring about Judaism because her family are secular'. Amy responds: 'It's not true, I have studied and explored so much of it.' But why should Amy even feel the need to convert? 'I ultimately realised that I don't want to,' she says. 'I am Jewish and I feel Jewish and if people – whose reasons I don't find to be legitimate – disagree, then that's their problem. I can't convert for them.'

As with all things, understanding the relevant history is essential to fully understand Jewish laws. Historically, as evidenced through the Torah's emphasis on the patrilineal heritage of its subjects, Judaism was not matrilineal. That law only seems to have emerged after the expulsion from Judea. Many Jewish kings and forefathers married non-Jewish women and their descendants were still considered to be Jewish. Moses married Zipporah, the daughter of a high priest of Midian. During the Roman conquests and colonisation of the Jewish state, rape – as it always has been – was used as a tool of war and many children were born to Roman fathers. As a response, to ensure the survival of the Jewish people, Judaism became matrilineal.

Neither Amy nor I are arguing for removing all rules that govern who is, and who is not, considered Jewish. There should absolutely be laws that dictate this question and we understand that the *Halacha* won't change. Moreover, while Amy obviously disagrees with the idea of defining Judaism solely as matrilineal, she still talks about her respect for all Jews regardless of their views. However, it is also important to understand this issue from its proper authentic historical context. Amy isn't asking for rules to be changed for everyone, she is just asking for our community to find a way to work towards creating an inclusive Jewish world.

For me, this is invaluable. Jewish Pride is about the creation of an inclusive Jewish community; one that honours our diversity but also seeks to amplify that which connects us and our similarities, as opposed to only looking at our differences. This is also, as Amy points out, not just an issue with regards to patrilineal Jews. 'Not being accepting or kind to each other is the division within the Jewish community, regardless of who it targets,' she argues. 'Even from the Haredi to Modern Orthodox. I hear Modern Orthodox Jews say things about Reform Jews and vice versa. I want to say to them: "You guys, put that aside. Ok, you pray this way, I pray that way. Some don't pray at all and Jews have always been like that and it doesn't mean you're a better Jew".' It is ludicrous for us – a community that faces such intense levels of hate around the world – to spend so much time arguing with, and excluding, our own.

After years of campaigning for the Jewish state on campus, Amy finally visited Israel, the land she had learned so much about, by going on a trip organised by the educational organisation Birthright. Soon after coming back to the United States, Amy returned to Israel to take part in a five-month Masa Israel internship programme. After this immersion, Amy decided to make *Aaliyah*, which in some ways feels like the natural next step of her journey. However, it was not without its challenges. Although the civil law of the Right of

Return allows Amy to make *Aaliyah*, the Rabbinate, which governs Judaism, would not recognise her as Jewish.

Amy was counselled in this by Amos, her *Shaliach* friend. She was told that she would not be considered Jewish, her children wouldn't be considered Jewish and she would not be able to get legally married in Israel. Only Orthodox Jewish weddings are legally recognised in Israel. 'In Israel, the line between religious tradition and culture is very blurry,' explains Amy, 'and even secular Jews won't date non-Halachic Jews, or they will date you but not marry you. That's hard when you feel in your soul that you are Jewish.' Despite the challenges she knew lay ahead, in January 2015, Amy made the decision to make *Aliyah*. Once again, Amy showed just how committed she is to campaigning, and working, for the Jewish community.

Amy says that her Jewish life and Jewish identity is very much intertwined with Israel, so like Hen, Amy says that Zionism is a major part of her Jewish Pride. 'My Jewish identity and Israeli identity are very much connected to one another and are very intertwined,' she argues. Amy is also refreshingly honest when it comes to how difficult living in Israel can be. Despite it being the Jewish state, Israel has its own distinct culture which does not necessarily feel immediately comfortable to Jews from the Diaspora. Like many other Jews, Amy says, she did not 'make *Aliyah* for an easier life, I made it for an ideological life'. Amy says that she would define herself now more specifically as an Israeli Jew, rather than just a Jew. 'I don't feel as comfortable amongst a group of American Jews as I do with Israelis, I guess it's just a cultural thing. I am an Israeli now,' Amy suggests.

To continue her advocacy in the digital world, and to reach people outside her immediate circle, Amy created an Instagram page, @theasianisraeli, in 2018. This digital platform allowed Amy to share her story and experiences with others and to continue educating people, something she is incredibly passionate about. Over the past two years, she has created an online community (of which I am a part) where she regularly connects with people like her that she never even knew were out there. Amy's Instagram page has allowed thousands of people to feel appreciated, respected and seen. Amy's community demonstrates the desperate need we have for a pluralistic and inclusive Jewish Pride movement.

Amy believes Jewish Pride must be about much more than the fight against antisemitism. 'The Jewish community experiencing so much incredible adversity is a blessing and a curse as a lot of Jewish Pride does come out of that, and it absolutely helps galvanise us,' she argues. 'But to me, when I think of a Jewish Pride movement, it really has to be about positive action and expression, not about victimhood. The only way the State of Israel was born was because we made it happen. The pioneers went and they moved to Israel and built the state.' Amy continues: 'Basing Jewish identity on antisemitism or the Holocaust is really emotionally screwed up. We have to be based on empowerment and we have to be actively Jewish – in whatever way that means.'

This sentiment is incredibly inspiring and one I agree with very much. As Amy demonstrates herself, there are different ways to be Jewish. Everyone will demonstrate their Jewishness slightly differently and this is perfectly valid, as long as they feel pride in our Jewishness. We are a tiny community of only 14.7 million people and, if we do not commit to maintaining it, it will eventually be absorbed by other cultures and disappear. As Amy says, we need action. 'I love to light Shabbat candles, not because I am particularly observant, but because it is what Jews do on a Friday night,' she suggests. 'It makes me feel connected to not only our heritage and traditions, but also the millions of other Jews lighting Shabbat candles at the same time.'

This is the beauty of Jewishness and Judaism being an ethnoreligion – there are so many practices that are part of both our culture and religion. Jews can do the same action, but for different reasons, and these are all totally legitimate. When I say *kaddish* for my father or at the Nazi death camps across Europe, I did it not to sanctify God's name, but to honour Jews by saying a prayer that Jews have said for thousands of years. And this is still beautiful and valid.

Amy and I are speaking during the 2020 Covid-19 outbreak and, for the first time, we begin talking about her experiences as a Chinese-Jewish woman. This period has been particularly hard for Amy as it has revealed and reinforced (although, importantly, not caused) a huge amount of racism towards people from Asia and also, to another extent, Jews. Being at the intersection of these two identities has not been easy for Amy and it certainly is particularly tough now. Interestingly, and this is something I have observed living in Hong Kong, there are some huge similarities between the Chinese and Jewish cultures. We both put a huge emphasis on family, education, food and tradition. It's wonderful that Amy has been able to find commonalities between her two identities. It's really important and not always easy, and it's something I, as a gay Jew, often search for myself.

To put it simply, Amy is an inspiration. She has a value system that she has chosen to live her life by. She has been an incredible advocate for the Jewish community, despite experiencing discrimination because she is both a patrilineal Jew and a Chinese-American Jewish woman. A path that began in Sacramento in California has taken Amy to Israel and she has become a major advocate for the Jewish community. Her Jewish Pride is tangible. 'The Jewish people are amazing, look at what a tiny community we are but look at the impact we have had on the world,' she suggests. 'And, no, this isn't about conspiracies – this is about our incredible and selfless contributions even when the rest of the world rejects us.'

Hearing Amy speak about the Jewish community in this way, makes me realise she could also be speaking about herself. She has made a hugely positive impact in very difficult circumstances. By being so visible on social media and in her work, she makes a real difference – helping people around the world feel seen and valued. The Jewish community is privileged to count Amy as one of its members. I left this conversation feeling proud of our people and our heritage, and so excited about our potential.

Chapter 12

JEWISH PRIDE

BREAKING THE CYCLE

Jewish people have been in a dysfunctional relationship with the non-Jewish world for over 2,000 years. To be accepted, we have tried, over and over again, to change who we are.

In our thousands of years of history, has this sacrifice ever worked?

No.

Every time we change ourselves to be accepted, we look at the non-Jewish world with hope. We think that maybe this time, they will accept us and embrace us, yet they continue to reject us and shame us.

This cycle has to stop.

The way to stop this abusive, destructive and exhausting cycle is to turn to ourselves for that acceptance and love.

Our journey is not about fighting antisemitism. That is the non-Jewish world's journey.

The Jewish journey is one of self-discovery, self-acceptance and self-love – in the name of collective pride.

Turn inwards, learn our history, understand our diverse experiences, and connect to our collective Jewishness in order to define our own identity – rather than basing that identity on the latest fantastical image that the non-Jewish world is trying to impose on us.

This is where our journey of Jewish Pride begins.

JEWISH PRIDE: A GUIDE

Let us chart how far we have come together. We have categorised antisemitism and seen the common threads that bind all examples of anti-Jewish racism throughout history. We have explored the role that anti-Judaism played in the foundations of western society and why antisemitism has persisted throughout history. We have seen Jewish identity change in an attempt to circumvent antisemitism and we have examined the stories of Jews who have absorbed the Jew-hate that swirls around them in the 'cloud of antisemitism'. By Chapter 5, we began thinking about the idea of Jewish Pride and we listened to the stories of seven incredible Jewish people from around the world. They shared with us their Jewish identity and experiences and how and why they feel pride in their Jewishness.

Now our collective journey towards Jewish Pride and the rebuilding of our people begins.

For my Jewish readers, a question: Where do you feel shame in your Jewishness, what helps you reject that shame and what can make you truly feel Jewish Pride?

And for my non-Jewish readers: Where have you allowed the non-Jewish world to form your image of Jewish people – and how can you take what you have learned from this book and dismantle the shameful structures of antisemitism?

I said in Chapter 1 that this is not a book about fighting antisemitism, because that is not something Jews are able to do on a large scale, nor is it actually our responsibility. The non-Jewish world must engage in a very public reckoning regarding its antisemitism. Jews can facilitate this. We can engage in dialogue and help provide testimony and context, but that is the extent to which we are able to help dismantle institutional antisemitism.

I began this book by explaining how important LGBTQ+ Pride has been for me as an individual, and my community at large. At one point in my life, I felt that my sexuality was not something to be proud of. I was deeply ashamed of it and tried to hide. I do not feel that way anymore. I am very proud of being gay and I would not change it for the world. I love the resilience of the LGBTQ+ community, I love our culture and what we have contributed to the world. It is part of the reason I am who I am. The concept of pride in the LGBTQ+ community saved my life. It gave me the confidence to proudly identify as a gay man and to openly express this part of my identity. It stopped me feeling shame and it helped me form a community.

Regardless of how some antisemites view it, Jewish Pride is not about 'Jewish supremacy'. It is not about Jewish people thinking that they are better than non-Jews. It is simply about educating, inspiring and empowering Jews to feel pride in our Jewish identity. Although antisemites will always try to portray Jews taking control of their own destiny as Jewish supremacy, we can rest assured that this accusation is rooted in their hate, not our motives.

In 2019, Linda Sarsour, the former leader of the Women's March, admonished progressive Zionists at an American Muslims for Palestine meeting (AMP is the organisation we encountered in Chapter 4 that If Not Now partnered with). At this meeting, Sarsour accused Israel of being based on Jewish supremacy: 'Ask them this, how can you be against white supremacy in America and the idea of being in a state based on race and class, but then you support a state like Israel that is based on supremacy, that is built on the idea that Jews are supreme to everyone else.'[313]

Israel is not based on Jewish supremacy. The creation of the modern Jewish state of Israel was a progressive act of decolonisation that attempted to right the wrongs committed against the Jewish people for 2,000 years. Sarsour is wrong and is using a common tactic often deployed by the American progressive left, whereby Israel (and light-skinned Jews) are equated with white supremacy. This delusional accusation ignores the fact that Jewish people are one of the primary targets of white supremacy. This idea is ultimately rooted in an antisemitic conspiracy fantasy, where Jews are depicted as believing we are fundamentally better, and therefore more deserving of resources, than non-Jews.

The founding of the Jewish state and the creation of a global Jewish Pride movement were not, and are not, rooted in supremacy. They were about the rejection of what Isaac Deutscher, the famed Jewish socialist writer, referred to as 'the marks of indignity; all the stigmata of shame'.[314] They are rooted in the rejection of shame that antisemitism tries to impose on us. They are rooted in Jewish people deciding not to warp or change our identities to be accepted by the non-Jewish world. They are rooted in the Jewish world wanting to engage with non-Jews – as equals. If my expressions of LGBTQ+ Pride are deemed acceptable, then I can see no legitimate reason as to why my feelings of Jewish Pride wouldn't be equally embraced. After all, is pride not a progressive value? Aren't empowering and inspiring minority groups to feel pride in their identities not encouraged by those on the left?

ACTIVE AND CONTINUOUS WORK

It is crucial to recognise at the outset that sustainable and intergenerational Jewish Pride does not happen without continuous work. It is not something that one just feels unless one decides to pursue it, and it is also not something that occurs overnight. Years of antisemitic shaming take a long time to process and fully reject. It is also not something that one can base on just one facet of Jewishness. There is so much beauty in our peoplehood so our pride must be a multifaceted representation of this complexity.

In my life, I have had to work toward feeling pride in my gay identity. I had to decide to read gay history, seek out gay role models and explore the gay community before I even began to feel pride. As minorities, we are bombarded with negative representations of our identities; rejecting these takes work. But the journey to pride is a beautiful one that leads us to understand ourselves and our communities on a much deeper level. It must be a path that we actively decide to take. As the Chinese proverb states: 'A journey of a thousand miles begins with a single step.'[315] But only you can decide to take that first step.

The rest of this chapter is dedicated to what I believe are some of the most important aspects of a Jewish Pride movement – one that educates, inspires and empowers all Jewish people to embrace their Jewishness and reject the shame of antisemitism.

WHO ARE THE JEWS?

Chapter 1 of this book includes a section titled: 'Who are the Jews?' At that point, I was simply trying to establish a definition of Jews that would enable us to understand the people whose history and identity would be at the centre of this book. Returning to that question is essential for those embarking on a journey into Jewish Pride.

My answer to this is rooted in historical authenticity. If we refer back to history, the Jewish people were a *nation*, an *ethnicity* and a *religion*. A civilization. A people. To really understand Jewishness, we cannot exclude any of these integral parts of our identity. However, as a result of attempts to circumvent antisemitism many Jews today, especially in the west, only understand their Jewishness through the lens of religion. Not only does this actively exclude atheist Jews, but it isn't an identity rooted in a complete and authentic understanding of what it means to be a Jew. The Jewish people have survived for thousands of years. But we will not survive for thousands more if we do not accurately understand and represent ourselves.

The ramifications of misunderstanding Jewish identity have a major impact on us. They can also damage our relationship to other Jews, including imposing our own experiences onto them. For example, understanding Jewish identity solely through a religious lens can be used, and is used, to delegitimise Zionism because our nationhood, and the Jewish people's relationship to the land of Israel, is misunderstood. If we are not a people, then we are just a disparate set of individuals bound by a shared faith, which can be discarded. This is not who we are. We are *Am Yisrael*, the *people* of Israel.

The Jewish people warping our identity to be accepted by the non-Jewish world is tragic enough. But that warping has resulted in too many generations of Jews misunderstanding what it *really* means to be Jewish. We must not change ourselves to be accepted, we must embrace who we are – who we *truly* are – based on Jewish history, Jewish tradition and Jewish experiences. When understanding modern Jewish identity, we must see it through the prism of all of its authentic components and reject internal and external misconceptions.

Important Jewish philosophers in our recent past have also grappled with these issues. Mordechai Kaplan, the founder of Reconstructionist Judaism, argued in the 1930s for American Jews 'to reconstruct their lives on the cultural foundation of a historical peoplehood'.[316] Kaplan's seminal text 1934, *Judaism as a Civilization*, lays out the argument that being Jewish is more than just a religion, and it can, and must, include the notion of Jewish ethnicity and peoplehood.

If we misunderstand who we are, then a Jewish Pride movement will be based on false, narrow and ahistorical definitions. This misunderstanding will also threaten our future survival as a people. As Kaplan argued: 'Jews should learn Judaism's essential character so that they might know what to do with it in times of stress.'[317]

I would like to build on this by suggesting that understanding who Jews are is not only important in times of stress – it is always important. We have to properly educate ourselves on who we are as a people. How can we truly feel pride in our identities if they are not rooted in our actual experience? How can we expect the non-Jewish world to understand who we are if we do not understand ourselves?

A more rounded understanding of Jewish identity is necessary when we define who we are – and who we are not. This allows us to create boundaries when interacting with the non-Jewish world, especially when facing, identifying and rejecting their perceptions of who we are. I teach my students to explore and understand who they are so they can go into the world with confidence and not let others define them. We as individuals, and as a collective, must also do this work with ourselves and each other.

A full understanding of Jewish identity can also help us overcome specific issues facing our people today. Amy's experience of having a Jewish father and a non-Jewish mother has meant that her identity has been erased by *Halachic* Judaism. I recognise the importance of *Halacha* in guiding, preserving and continuing Jewish identity – as well as the fact that millions of Jews around the world observe it. But we cannot disregard other facets of our authentic collective historical experience. The Torah is clearly based on the patrilineal line. Historically, children born from Jewish fathers and non-Jewish mothers were considered members of the Jewish people. Therefore, when considering modern perspectives on Jewish identity, we have to fully explore its historical manifestations, which included patrilineal Jews.

It is also crucial to recognise that Jews by choice – individuals who have converted to Judaism – are included and welcomed as part of the Jewish people. Although they convert through the religious part of our identity specifically, they also take on the wider sense of Jewish peoplehood through this process. They join the Jewish civilisation. Their Jewishness must never be doubted or questioned.

As Kaplan argued about Jewishness in 1934: 'It has functioned as a civilization through its career, and it is only in that capacity that it can function in the future.'[318] Patrilineal Jews may not be *Halachically* Jewish according to Orthodox Judaism, but they are undoubtedly members of the Jewish people, nation, ethnicity and civilisation.

Ultimately, they are still part of the diverse and authentic facets of Jewish identity.

Clearly, we are not done with these conversations, but if we approach them from a historical *and* modern perspective, we can reach an enlightened understanding of the authentic nature of Jewishness.

ONE PEOPLE WITH A MULTITUDE OF EXPERIENCES

To rebuild a Jewish people that is whole and unified, we have to understand and embrace the specific and unique experiences of various Jewish communities and individuals throughout the world. My seven interviewees were purposefully and carefully selected because they each represent various facets within the Jewish community. Each of the seven has had a different Jewish life, in different parts of the world, yet each of their experiences is as valid as the next and are essential for the rebuilding of the Jewish people in pride.

Hen is a Mizrahi Jewish man who advocates for the Mizrahi community, educating non-Mizrahi Jews around the world about their story. My multiple conversations with Hen have been enlightening and have given me a more complete understanding of Jewish identity. In turn, I use this knowledge of the Mizrahi experience to give my students a fuller understanding of Jewishness.

Both of my siblings married Mizrahi Jews and my nephews and niece belong to both the Mizrahi and Ashkenazi communities. We can embody this concept ourselves by listening to, and actively, telling diverse Jewish stories – this is how we instil a sense of pride in both our uniqueness and our commonalities for ourselves and our Jewish children. Hen's story, a Mizrahi story, reflects all of our stories and it's crucial we recognise this.

Similarly, Elisheva, a Black-Jewish Orthodox woman, advocates tirelessly for her Black, Jewish and Orthodox communities. She raises her voice to show that Jewish people like her exist and are a valued part of our community. Hers is a specific and unique experience and one that many Jewish people might not immediately recognise. But Elisheva's is a Jewish experience and therefore, like other Jewish stories, it is an integral part of our wider Jewish experience. She is a proud member of our people and she should always be made to feel that she belongs simply because she *does* belong.

Our people have always included members from different tribes, and though we come together as one, we should recognise and celebrate our individual communities. We should not allow non-Jewish, shallow ideas of what makes a Jew define our own ideas of Jewishness. By defining our own identities, we make space for a multitude of experiences that come together to make up a whole: the Jewish people.

As we have seen through these and the other interviews, there is not just one way to express Jewishness or to be Jewish. Each of these people identifies as proudly Jewish but expresses this in a variety of ways.

In advance of our conversation, Isaac sent me some Ladino music to listen to. I knew vaguely about Ladino, and how it was almost totally destroyed by the Shoah, but experiencing this beautiful music, and learning about the stories that accompanied these songs, made me feel so much closer and more connected to the Sephardic experience as a whole. Even though the melodies sounded slightly different to what I was used to, and even though I couldn't understand the language I was hearing, reading the translations of these songs moved me.

These were Jewish stories – told in a different melody and in a different language than I am familiar with – but they were unmistakably Jewish. Hearing Ladino music, and learning more about the Ladino language, made me feel more connected to my other Jewish brothers and sisters because I understood more about their specific experience. Moreover, while they may be different to mine in some ways, I was able to see how much this binds us together. Jewish Pride isn't just about celebrating and honouring all Jewish stories and histories, it is, as Ashager stated in her interview, about embracing each other's cultures to strengthen our bond with each other. Ashager's work on Battae, the Beta-Yisrael cultural centre in Tel-Aviv, aims to educate other Jews about the Beta-Yisrael community, in part so that they can feel connected to it. While my recent ancestors were Ashkenazi Jews, researching this book, and learning more about Beta-Yisrael, Mizrahi, Sephardic and other Jewish communities, has made me feel closer to the Jewish people as a whole. After all, from all the corners of our world, we still mark Shabbat together.

INTERCOMMUNAL PRIDE

For the Jewish people to unify our entire community in pride, we must address the issues and inequalities that exist among our people. However, we must never believe that our Jewishness is the source of these inequalities; rather, pride in our Jewishness is what helps overcome them. It is about recognising, as with *all* people, that prejudice and ignorance exist amongst the Jewish community – and believing we are capable of working through this.

Discussing these issues is vital and very Jewish. It is not, as some have accused Elisheva, *chillul hashem*. Such accusations are nonsensical deflections. Elisheva's efforts to raise awareness of anti-Black racism in the Jewish community only come from a place of pride and belief that the Jewish people, as a whole, can do better.

In the past, when I experienced homophobia from Jews, I often felt conflicted as to whether I should discuss it in case it increased antisemitism. However, I realised that I had a *responsibility* to discuss it. Non-LGBTQ+ members of the Jewish people may not be aware of the homophobia in some parts of our community and if I do not inform them, then how can I expect or even hope they will work with me to combat it?

While minority members of the Jewish community have a responsibility to speak out, there is also a responsibility that lies with the parts of the community to which we are speaking. As all Jews have experienced in the non-Jewish world, it can be difficult to advocate for our minority community, and it can be made even more challenging when others refuse to listen to, or hear, what is being said.

The words of the Talmud *'Kol Yisrael Aravim Zeh Bazeh'* ('All Israel Is Responsible for One Another')[319] make very clear the responsibility that Jews have to each other. Right now, we have a responsibility to ensure that every single Jewish person feels respected and included amongst our people. To exclude Jewish people because they are Black, gay or patrilineal, to demonise Orthodox Jews or Reform Jews or Ashkenazi Jews, or to erase the experiences of Mizrahi, Sephardic Jews or Beta-Yisrael, is to fail in our responsibility to the Jewish people, to the people of Israel, to which we all belong.

Jewish people know the pain of prejudice better than many others – so, we should work to create a home for all Jews. Antisemitism does not care whether someone is a patrilineal Jew or a Black Jew or a gay Jew. To them, a Jew is a Jew, regardless of our differences and nuances. Yet accepting ourselves as one people does not mean that we should see ourselves as a monolith. We are not. As we know, we are a collective of many Jewish stories. As such, we have a responsibility to ensure that our community can be a place of safety, security and celebration for all Jewish people.

Ultimately, Jewish people are just people. We are no better and no worse. And that means we, too, suffer from the plague of prejudice. However, we are capable of confronting these issues. And we should take pride in this capability.

THE IMPORTANCE AND CHALLENGES
OF JEWISH SOCIAL JUSTICE

As we have explored, there are Jews who adopt Jewish concepts such as *Tikkun Olam* as a call to social action. There is nothing wrong with finding such a meaning in this concept, as long as the authentic roots of *Tikkun Olam* are understood – and as long as the concept is not taken out of context to say Jewish identity is *solely* based on supporting others.

There is also nothing wrong with Jews advocating for other communities; in fact, I believe that we should. Especially as there are many Jews and their families at the intersection of plural identities. To support me, you also have to support the LGBTQ+ aspect of my identity.

However, with regards to social justice issues, in recent years, I have seen rhetoric that argues that Jews have a 'moral responsibility' to help other communities. Again, to be clear, I do think that Jews *absolutely* should support other groups. However, the idea of a moral Jewish responsibility can be dangerous and creates a binary where 'good Jews' are social justice activists and 'bad Jews' are not. As this is a human issue, not a Jewish one, the truth is more complex and nuanced than that.

Jews have been, and continue to be, targeted, abused and murdered. Shaming Jews into a moral binary based on their social justice work, especially while we are trying to cope with and process our own trauma, is unfair and insensitive.

Part of Jewish Pride is believing that we are worthy of the same respect, support and allyship as other communities. We are allowed to – and we must – advocate for ourselves. Each community's experience matters just as much as any other, and we must never be shamed into silence.

In the summer of 2020, during the global Black Lives Matter protests, I was devastated to see this cycle of antisemitism emerging once again. Antisemitism was apparent in vandalism of synagogues, and in the spreading of traditional anti-Jewish slurs and conspiracy fantasies. It emanated from a variety of sources including celebrities with enormous social media platforms spreading antisemitic rhetoric. Jews who stood up against this antisemitism were told: 'This was not the time.' But those urging silence were wrong. Jewish people have the right to point out and condemn antisemitic threats and rhetoric whenever and wherever they see it. We can support other communities and movements, while simultaneously supporting our own, and we should be suspicious of anyone who says otherwise.

It is also worth noting that Jews who advocate for wider social justice, and who use Jewish values to promote their advocacy, should do so with caution. Social-justice minded Jews should be aware that, historically, Jews who have stood with other communities, have sometimes been targeted by these same communities they supported.

Albert Memmi wrote about his experience of this very phenomenon during the fight for Tunisian independence following the second world war. 'How could I, who applauded so wildly the struggle for freedom of other peoples, have refused to help the Tunisians in whose midst I had lived since birth and who, in so many ways, were my own people?' he wrote. 'Thus, having ceased to be a universalist, I gradually became ... a Tunisian nationalist.'[320]

However, despite progressive Tunisian Jews campaigning for independence, independent Tunisia swiftly, systemically and physically turned against its Jews. Memmi reflected on this traumatic experience, suggesting: 'The ground we had thought to be so solid, was swept from under our feet.'[321] Tunisia's progressive Jews ignored the conservative and antisemitic elements to the independence movement, and threw themselves into the struggle to decolonise Tunisia. This brought them into conflict with others who did not believe that the new Tunisian state would include Jews.

However, the 'Jews of the ghettos', as Memmi referred to them, were proven right. 'And – why not say it? – the ghetto was right. The intellectuals were self-deceived, blinded by their ethical aspirations,' he argued.[322] Due to a fervour for their version of social justice, these progressive Jews forgot their Jewishness. But the rulers of the new Tunisia did not forget. Despite their support, the Jews were expelled. The Tunisian experience is a lesson for all Jews today.

If we are to be a people of socially aware individuals, then we must also embody Jewish-centred social justice. The notion that Jews do not need support or allyship is rooted in a conspiracy fantasy, the misidentification of light-skinned Jews as white, and tropes about Jewish power and privilege. We should never be shamed into feeling guilty for focusing our attention on combating antisemitism and supporting the Jewish community. We are able to do this *and* support other communities.

Based on his experiences in Tunisia, Memmi was correct in arguing: 'No historic duty toward other men should prevent our paying particular attention to our special difficulties.'[323]

SURVIVING *AND* THRIVING

The notion of 'Jewish resilience' is based on our historical ability to overcome and survive antisemitism – and many of us rightfully take great pride in this. Numerous empires and powers – the Babylonians, the Greeks, the Ottomans, the Christian church, the Nazis and the Soviets – have all tried to destroy us. But where are they? They have either totally disappeared from the face of the earth or they exist in a state of deeply diminished power. We are still here, thousands of years later, building a Jewish Pride movement.

We often take this fact for granted. We joke that Jewish *chagim* (festivals) often boil down to three things: 'They tried to kill, we survived, let's eat!' But if we stop and consider how remarkable this is, it is astounding.

However, our survival is not the only thing to celebrate. We have also found ways to thrive. Yiddish, Ladino and the multiple Judeo-Arabic languages and the beautiful cultures that accompany them, demonstrate Jewish cultures that have thrived even when we have been forced into exile. Jewish development did not stop after our expulsion from our homeland. Our traditions, our customs and our perspectives continued to evolve and change despite multiple attempts by the non-Jewish world to stamp out Jewish life. Not only have we refused to be erased; we have instead often become more determined to live and thrive with passion and a deep commitment to our people. These attempts to wipe us out were often a catalyst for a Jewish resolve to create and build.

As an Ashkenazi Jew whose family lived for a period in eastern Europe, I am immensely proud of Ashkenazi Jewish culture. I love Ashkenazi food, I love *klezmer* music and I love the stories of the *shtetls*. Despite being oppressed for generations, like other Jewish groups, these Ashkenazi Jews not only maintained a continuous connection to their homeland – and thus to the rest of the Jewish people – but, despite their difficult circumstances, they built a thriving and rich culture of their own.

I remember visiting Warsaw and seeing the vast remnants of Yiddish theatre, newspapers and culture. When I looked at what they had created, I felt honoured to be a descendant of these Jews. Like all Jewish cultures, Yiddish culture, though itself an expression of Ashkenazi civilization, helped maintain a unified Ashkenazi Jewish identity, at a time when Jews were being pressured to acculturate. What Jews achieved under the most extreme situations is staggering. Yiddish culture – like *all* Jewish cultures – was formed like diamonds under immense pressure from the non-Jewish world. We must recognise and value this fact.

Sadly, as we have seen, when Jews feel comfortable and complacent, we are quick to adopt non-Jewish cultures, rather than cultivate our own. The determination of our forefathers and mothers to create vibrant Jewish communities is something we should not take for granted. It should inspire us going forward, to continue crafting thriving and rich Jewish cultures regardless of what the non-Jewish world throws at us.

JEWISH RESISTANCE

For thousands of years, Jewish people have stood up to, and struggled against, antisemitism. Our history is filled with pivotal moments where we fought for our right to exist as Jews. To cite just a few examples of military resistance in our early history: the Maccabean revolt against the Greek rulers of Judea lasted from 167 BCE to 160 BCE; the first Jewish-Roman war ended in 70 CE when Tiberius Julius Alexander helped destroy the Second Temple; and the Bar Kokhba revolt saw a three-year war waged by the Jews to reclaim Jerusalem and Judea from the Romans.

And we don't have to look to examples from 2,000 years ago. Jewish military resistance continued during the Shoah when Jewish partisans – most famously in the 1943 Warsaw ghetto uprising – fought back against the Nazis and their allies. While some of these acts of resistance were not successful, the point is that *we fought back*. We did not roll over and submit to the non-Jewish world. This is a characterisation created to undermine us. We have always fought to preserve the Jewish people.

More recently, the British and American Jewish communities took to the streets to make their voices heard in 2019 as they protested against antisemitism in their respective countries. Watching this from afar, in Hong Kong, I felt so proud of these two Jewish communities. They were not going to allow the non-Jewish world to attempt to harm them without fighting back.

All of the people I interviewed in this book also resist antisemitism by raising their voices to defend the Jewish people. Rachel, Hen, Ashager, Isaac, Elisheva, Eliyahu, Amy and Rafaella have used their platforms to campaign for the Jewish people and resist antisemitism, each one demonstrating Jewish strength and resilience.

Britain's former chief rabbi, Lord Sacks, echoed this spirit of Jewish resistance when he began a speech in the House of Lords with the words: 'My Lords, it pains me to speak about antisemitism, the world's oldest hatred. But I cannot keep silent.'[324] He is right. We cannot, and we should not, keep silent.

Though I have repeatedly said that combatting antisemitism is primarily a non-Jewish task, Jewish people should still stand up against these avalanches of Jew-hate through telling our stories, refusing to be silent and loudly and proudly standing up for ourselves. We have to believe that Jewish people matter just as much as any other group, and that we have every right to protest when we are not being treated equally. We should not wait for the non-Jewish world to notice antisemitism or for it to include us in discussions on minority rights. We should demand that they do and it should be a deal breaker if they do not.

In Britain, Jews are legally classed as an ethnic minority under race relations legislation and are officially included under the banner of BAME (Black, Asian, Minority Ethnic). Yet during discussions about ethnic minorities in the UK during Covid-19, Jews are never mentioned. This is extraordinary when we consider that, despite making up only 0.3% of Britain's population, reports in April 2020 indicated that Jews made up 2.1% of the country's initial Covid-19 fatalities.[325]

In response, Eliyahu wrote an article for the *Jewish Journal* in May 2020 to raise awareness of the dangerous exclusion of Jewish people from discussions on ethnic minority deaths. His article is an act of resistance. He refused to wait until the non-Jewish world took notice. He decided to take action himself to raise awareness of the impact of Covid-19 on British Jewish people.

Of course, the context today is different from many of those that came before us, but the basic motivation remains the same. Throughout history, our acts of resistance have shared the same intent and passion: to defend the Jewish people. Most conversations on Jewish resilience simply celebrate that we have survived. But the reality is we survived, not by accident, but because we fought back against antisemitic oppression. We defended being Jewish – sometimes at the highest of costs – and the reality is, we survive to this day because our ancestors resisted antisemitism and defended the Jewish people.

Their commitment to the Jewish people compels me to action. We have been handed the baton of Jewishness. It is our responsibility to ensure that the Jewish community is nurtured, maintained and defended. Jewish resistance works to make sure that our community continues to survive for generations to come. And this unwavering dedication to our Jewishness empowers me and gives me strength.

UNBROKEN THREADS: MEMORY

The key to maintaining a continuous peoplehood is rooted in understanding and honouring our history, which tells the story of us moving forward and evolving while never letting go of the threads that bind us to our past and to each other.

As Jews today, we are connected to countless generations of Jews that came before us. What are most of our *chagim* about? Purim is about escaping genocide at the hands of Haman; Hanukkah is about the victory of Judah Maccabee over the ruling Greeks; and *Pesach* is about the Exodus from Egypt. Whether you believe that God delivered the Jews out of Egypt or not, these essential stories are all rooted in history and mark pivotal moments in Jewish history.

An important question I ask myself is: how do we live in modern societies while maintaining our links to the past? My answers lie in Jewish memory.

We can take for granted the connection we have to our history because honouring, and learning about the past is just what we do as Jews. However, if we take a step back we realise how remarkable our ability to remember and connect is. The Maccabean revolt, a true Jewish rebellion, took place in ancient Judea in 167 to 160 BCE. That was over 2,100 years ago. Yet every year my family and I faithfully light our Chanukah candles, just as millions of other Jewish families do around the world. This phenomenally enduring tradition feeds Jewish memory and celebrates our resilience, meaning that Jews will forever commemorate and remember this historical milestone – and be inspired by it today in fostering the Jewish people.

Commitment to our history, to memory, has motivated Jewish people in maintaining our traditions and identity even under the most horrifying circumstances. Jews during the Holocaust continued to celebrate Chanukah and Shabbat. In the Theresienstadt ghetto, a Jewish prisoner stole a block of wood and carved a beautiful Chanukiah so that imprisoned Jews could honour the 'festival of lights'. These more recent stories are empowering and show the history that binds to each other. We simply cannot pass on Jewish Pride if we do not teach, understand, and pass on our history.

Historical knowledge is vital for the continuation of a Jewish people but this also requires work. Rachel provides a wonderful example. In our interview, she recognised that when she first encountered antisemitism online, she didn't have the knowledge to speak out against it. But what Rachel did next is an inspiration to us all: she set out to learn. She spent months researching antisemitism so she could use her platform effectively to defend Jewishness. Not everyone wants to be an activist, and not everyone needs to be an expert on Jewish history, but having a basic understanding of our history is an important part of maintaining and strengthening the Jewish people.

The question I keep coming back to is: how can we find Pride in being Jewish if we do not understand what being Jewish is? As discussed earlier, understanding means authentic definitions of both Jewishness *and* our history – where we came from and the impact that has had on our culture and people.

Ultimately, we put our entire civilization in danger if we do not teach and learn our history. That may sound dramatic but ask yourself: how can we get teenagers today to feel pride in being Jewish if they don't understand how special it is that they are Jewish to begin with? If we teach our history, we will allow future generations of Jews to both feel connected to, and to understand, the experiences of our past, while our community continues to evolve. In a paper on Jewish religious, ethnic and national identities, the Israeli academic Daniel J Elazar wrote: 'We can now see throughout the Jewish world, including Israel, that it takes almost no time for a civilization to be disrupted by lack of proper education of its new generations.'[326]

Having survived for thousands of years, we cannot allow our ancient civilisation to now be endangered by letting go of our historical memory. Memory preserves us as a people. It can only be passed down through generations if we properly educate ourselves and our children about our experience, and gather and hold on to the threads that connect us to our past.

UNBROKEN THREADS: JEWISH ACTION

Inextricably linked to Jewish memory is Jewish action. To be Jewish and to celebrate Jewish Pride, we must not only feel Jewish but we must be *actively* Jewish. Only then can we create a culture of tangible empowerment that we are able to pass on to future generations. We cannot simply pass on feelings if they are not anchored by something more substantial. Whether we call our action 'ritual' or 'practice' and whether it is rooted in God, our peoplehood or both we must find a way to be actively Jewish.

When writing this book, I reflected a lot on my own Jewish life. I was lucky to be raised in a very Jewish home with two parents who were deeply committed to being Jewish. As a family, we observed the holidays and every Friday night we sat down together to celebrate Shabbat. I slept over at my childhood best friend's house often on Shabbat for years and with his family, we ate *seudah shlishit* (a third meal customarily eaten by Jews on Shabbat), we made *Havdalah* (the ceremony to mark the end of Shabbat) and we observed the Shabbat laws. We attended a Jewish primary school where we learned about Jewish history and heritage and laws. Every Shabbat, I accompanied my mother and father to synagogue. After I returned from a gap year in Israel, I worked for the Jewish community both in Scotland and in the rest of the UK.

My upbringing was very Jewish. We never celebrated Christmas or Easter and I had my first Easter egg when I was 31 years old. We were still a British family, we lived in Glasgow in Scotland, and I attended a non-Jewish secondary school. We didn't segregate ourselves but my parents worked hard to build a strong Jewish identity in their children. On reflection, it clearly worked: I am writing a book about Jewish Pride, both my siblings made *Aliyah* and my brother served in the Israeli army for almost 10 years.

Upon reflecting on how to maintain our links to previous generations, the thing that I kept coming back to was action; a sentiment also expressed by Ashager and Amy. My Jewish life has been one of action. My parents made the conscious choice to create a Jewish family that lived a Jewish life; one full of connection to our past and based on the tangible action in our lives. When I think of expressing my Jewish identity, I think about watching my mother light the Shabbat candles or going to my father's best friend's family for *Pesach* and Rosh Hashanah. These incredibly meaningful memories are all linked to action.

The beauty of Judaism and Jewishness – being both a multi-denominational religion and a multi-ethnic and international people – is that there are multiple ways to be Jewish. For example, I do not consider myself to be an observant Jew but I wear a kippah every day, say *kaddish* for my late father and mark Shabbat and other Jewish festivals. Do I personally do these things to honour God? No, I don't; I don't even know if I believe in God. I do them because this is what Jews do, this is how we express our Jewishness, and this is how we connect to our past, to each other and to being actively Jewish. Saying *kaddish* for my father – just as he did for his father and my grandfather did for his father – means I am part of an unbroken chain of Jewish peoplehood, memory and commemoration. In my opinion, it does not matter that I am not saying *kaddish* to sanctify God's name. The act itself makes it worthy and legitimate.

Jewish action can also be a form of spiritual resistance, as has been true throughout our history. Through these acts we maintained our humanity and Jewishness in the face of dehumanisation and attempts to destroy us. For example, the *conversos* in Spain and Latin America continued to secretly light Shabbat candles, despite being forcibly converted to Christianity and despite the threat of discovery and punishment. Beta-Yisrael practiced Judaism for centuries despite being legally discriminated against. Mizrahi Jews continued to lead active Jewish lives despite being legally classed as *dhimmis*. And, during the Shoah, Jews continued to recite Jewish prayers or have Jewish weddings despite the terrible danger that put them in. Jews from the past deciding to be actively and proudly Jewish in a world that discouraged or forbid it is incredibly brave and inspiring, and is an important lesson for all of us today.

Whether it is as a form of spiritual resistance or an expression of Jewish peoplehood or religion, Jewish action can help sustain a strong Jewish identity. This is crucial and is deeply rooted in the concept of Jewish Pride. This is not just a feeling; an undefinable airy concept. No, it is something that we must embody in a tangible way, that leads to a sustained, sustainable and substantial feeling of Jewish Pride.

JEWISH SUCCESSES AND CONTRIBUTIONS

Because antisemitism often 'punches up' – framing Jews as being wealthy, powerful and privileged – I have often witnessed Jewish people feeling timid about celebrating our successes, fearing that this will be used against us. Yet it is crucial that we stop enabling antisemitism and reject it. Instead, we must celebrate and honour our successes as any other marginalised community does.

Jewish people are, as I have suggested, a tiny national, ethno-religious minority whose population numbers 14.7 million people worldwide and we have been a major focus of global persecution for over thousands of years. That any Jew has managed to achieve success while facing demonisation, legal discrimination, pogroms, ethnic cleansing, genocide and expulsions – multiple times through-out history – is remarkable.

We rarely celebrate this, because to do so, some fear, would be to confirm the idea that Jews are obsessed with money, power and even a belief in our supremacy. To counter this, we must redefine our successes in our proper historical context, not in the eyes of our antisemitic neighbours.

A much-touted example of Jewish success is the fact that, despite our minority status, of the 935 Nobel prizes awarded, Jewish people have won roughly 20% of them. For a community that makes up 0.2% of the world's population, this is an astounding achievement. And why shouldn't we celebrate it? It is the non-Jewish world's problem if it wants to take this fact to feed its conspiracy fantasies – not ours.

Many of you will have known this statistic about Nobel prize, but did you know that the inventor of the flexible straw, Joseph B Friedman, was Jewish? Or that Robert Adler, the man who invented the remote control was as well? How about Emma Lazarus, who wrote the words 'Give me your tired, your poor, your huddled masses yearning to be free'[327] that are famously inscribed onto the Statue of Liberty?

There are countless remarkable people from all over the world that we could hold up as examples of Jewish successes and contributions. I am particularly fascinated by Hedy Lamarr. Hedy Lamarr, an Austrian-Jewish émigré who moved to America to continue her acting career in Hollywood. While acting in Austria, she was described as 'the most beautiful woman in Europe'[328] by the film and theatre director Max Reinhardt. But, as well as being a beautiful movie star, Lamarr was also an inventor.

Already an experienced inventor, and feeling compelled to help the Allies during the war, she realised that torpedoes would have greater success if they were radio-guided in a way which allowed the signal to hop frequencies, so it could not be jammed. In August 1942, she received a patent for a 'frequency hopping, spread-spectrum communication system'.[329] Lamarr and her partner, composer George Antheil, donated it to the US military and it eventually became the basis for modern Wi-Fi and Bluetooth technology. Lamarr did not earn a penny for her patented contributions and was only recognised decades later after an enormous concerted effort.

Sadly, Lamarr experienced misogyny and antisemitism. What is also interesting, though, is that she did not celebrate, or even publicly recognise, her Jewishness; the antisemitism she experienced in Austria had clearly left a deep scar. However, that shaming continued in the US. She was told by the film producer Louis B. Mayer that audiences 'wouldn't fantasize about a Jew'.[330] Lamarr even encouraged her mother to convert to Catholicism in 1938. In a letter uncovered by Alexandra Dean, the director of *Bombshell*, a film about her life, Lamarr wrote to her mother: 'Please do this for me, because I don't want to be identified as a Jew in Hollywood.'[331]

It is beyond tragic that antisemitism forced Lamarr to hide and deny her Jewishness, but we as a community can still embrace her and be proud of her incredible achievements as a Jewish woman. I assure you that the vast majority of people who use the internet today aren't aware that the Wi-Fi that connects them to it was invented based on the work of a Jewish woman.

Another contribution that Jews have made to the non-Jewish world is their work in a range of social justice movements. It is well known that Jewish people helped found the NAACP and were heavily involved in the black civil rights movement in the 1960s. Many Jewish communities and organisations from around the world also stood with the black community in 2020 as it protested against systemic racism.

However, the major contribution that Jewish people have made to the LGBTQ+ rights movement since its inception in 19th century Germany is much less well known. Magnus Hirschfeld, the famed physician and sexologist, was a German Jew who founded the Scientific-Humanitarian Committee, the first LGBTQ+ rights organisation in the world. Having been repeatedly targeted and attacked by the Nazis – who, on coming to power, destroyed his Institute of Sexual Knowledge and burned its books – Hirschfeld left Germany and went into exile.

The Jewish contribution to the modern LGBTQ+ rights movement continued as the struggle moved to the United States. To learn more about this, I contacted my friend, journalist Peter Fox, another gay Jew, to learn more about how American Jews fought hard to secure LGBTQ+ rights. During our conversation, Peter told me that one of the things that 'made me feel comfortable in my gay skin when I was 18 or 19 years old, was realising that the American LGBTQ+ rights movement has a shared history with the Jewish community'.

Peter told me that some of his major heroes in the LGBTQ+ rights movement were Jews, such as Harvey Milk. Harvey Milk was a gay Jewish civil rights activist who was the first LGBTQ+ person ever elected to office in the United States. His grandfather, Morris Milk (previously Mausche Milch) founded the Congregation Sons of Israel in New York. Lillian Faderman, author of the 2018 biography of Milk, *Harvey Milk: His Lives and Death,* said of his Jewishness: 'It was so important to his identity. There were all sorts of sentimental ways that his Jewish identity was important.'[332] Walter Caplan, a Jewish friend of Harvey's who hosted him for Seder every year, stated: 'He didn't deny in any way his Judaism, and it was actually a cornerstone of who he was and everything that he did.'[333]

Harvey's campaign manager, Anne Kronenberg, was also an LGBTQ+ Jew who eventually co-founded The Harvey Milk Foundation. Peter tells me that it wasn't just Harvey Milk whose Jewishness and gayness helped him accept his own sexuality. He cites Evan Wolfson, a gay Jew, who wrote his 1983 Harvard Law thesis on same-sex marriage. Evan went on to found Freedom to Marry in 2001, which, in the words of its website, 'built and shaped the national strategy and leveraged the work of many to win the freedom for same-sex couples to marry nationwide'.[334]

Yet celebrating our contributions to the world should not be the sole base for accepting our value as a people, much more our humanity. We matter because we matter, not because of how much we help others. However, that we – a people who have experienced so much oppression and prejudice – can see beyond this to understand the importance of advocating for other communities that we may, or may not, belong to, is profoundly important.

While antisemites accuse Jews of controlling the world, the fact of the matter remains: we are a tiny minority community that has achieved amazing things. We should be inspired by, and proud of, this fact. Jewish children throughout the world should be taught about Jewish successes, like Ruth Bader Ginsberg, the first Jewish woman to sit on the supreme court, not as a way to make them feel superior to non-Jews, but to allow them to see that they are part of a millennia-old community that has worked hard while placing value on knowledge and education – and that they themselves can achieve anything they put their minds to.

There have been periods when Jewish communities have responded to the trauma of antisemitism or its aftermath by encouraging Jews to keep their heads down. Our response in future, however, must be based on the idea of an educated, empowered and inspired Jewish people. A people who feel pride in their Jewishness and who are unafraid of celebrating ourselves and our achievements – and who do so with our heads held high.

JEWISH SELF-IDENTIFICATION

Reclaiming identity is essential to building a Jewish Pride movement. However, beyond this we need to take back Jewish concepts that the non-Jewish world has appropriated, such as Zionism.

As we have seen, the meaning of Zionism has been hijacked from the Jewish people and redefined as something evil. This warped definition of Zionism is a bastardisation of what Zionism is really all about. But Jewish Pride isn't just about reclaiming Zionism. It is also being crystal clear that Jews, and Jews alone, get to define Jewish concepts.

Jews have been connected to the land that is now Israel through religion, language, culture, history, archaeology and ethnicity for thousands of years. Since we were expelled from it in the first century CE Jews have never forgotten our connections to our indigenous homeland. Sephardic Jews even inscribed their longing for a return to their indigenous land on their synagogues. In the Córdoba Synagogue, it states: 'This minor sanctuary has been refurbished by Yitzchak Mahab, son of the wealthy Ephraim, in the year 5075; may God remove curses from our nation and speedily rebuild Jerusalem.'[335]

Centuries later, in 1862, Abba Zaga, a *kahen* (priest) and leader of Ethiopian Jewry, attempted to lead an ultimately unsuccessful mass *Aliyah*. This attempt predates the first wave of *Aliyah* from the Russian empire. In a letter to Jerusalem, Zaga wrote: 'They command us to separate ourselves from the Christians, to immigrate to your land, to Jerusalem, to join our brethren, and to offer sacrifices to God, the God of Israel, in the Holy Land.'[336]

Later in the 19th century, Theodore Herzl, the father of modern Zionism, was spurred to action by attending the Dreyfus Trial in

France. He saw a Jew, in Enlightened post-revolutionary France, being framed for treachery and abused as a Jew, not as a traitor. This led him to realise that Jews, regardless of where we live, could not be safe, and thus modern Zionism was born. During a time of intense violent antisemitism, especially in the Russian empire, Herzl campaigned tirelessly for a much-needed Jewish state. In 1896 he wrote *Der Juden-staat* (*The Jewish State*), arguing in it: 'The Jewish question persists wherever Jews live in appreciable numbers. Wherever it does not exist, it is brought in together with Jewish immigrants. We are naturally drawn into those places where we are not persecuted, and our appearance there gives rise to persecution.'[337] Ultimately, no matter what Jews did, or where Jews went, they have always continued to face antisemitic persecution.

Sadly, history proved Herzl right. Just 45 years after the publication of *Der Judenstaat*, the Nazis began exterminating Jews in Europe. In the interim period, Jews were murdered en masse throughout the Russian empire and its successor state, the Soviet Union. This is the context of the creation of modern Zionism.

Antizionists often portray Zionism as a form of colonialism. They argue that Jews are white Europeans who invaded a Middle Eastern country and expelled its indigenous people. This is not the case. Even Ashkenazi Jews, who are most often said to be ethnically European, are indigenous to Israel. Jews have always existed in the Middle East and North Africa, and in what is now Israel – as well as Palestine and Jordan. Jews are indigenous to that land – and the majority only left because they were expelled through ethnic cleansing and genocide.

The indigeneity of the Jews to the land of Israel has not and will not change, and sadly neither has the need for a refuge for Jews. After the establishment of the State of Israel in 1948, Ashkenazi and Sephardic Holocaust survivors, as well 850,00 Mizrahi and Sephardic Jews from the Middle East and North Africa, found refuge in Israel. If Israel had not existed where would these Jews have gone?

More recently, Ashkenazi Jews from the Soviet Union found safety in Israel and Beta-Yisrael were rescued and brought to Israel to escape persecution in Ethiopia. After having to trek to Sudan – a journey during which many were murdered, beaten and raped – over 20,000 Jews were brought to Israel thanks to Operations Moses, Joshua and Solomon in 1984, 1985 and 1991, respectively. In Ethiopia, they were treated as second-class citizens and endured forced conversions. Immediately after 1948, many Ethiopian Jews expressed desires to make *Aliyah* but were barred from doing so by Emperor Haile Selassie. These were the Jews rescued by Israel in the 1980s and 1990s. Where would they have gone if Israel had not existed because of the modern Zionist movement?

Despite this, the progressive world has made antizionism a pillar of how it defines itself – yet theirs is not a legitimate political position criticising government policy. Antizionism is nothing more than the attempt to deprive Jews of a right to self-determination. To criticise Israel as you would any other country is not antizionism. But to demand Israel's destruction is to remove Jewish self-determination in our indigenous homeland – and in a region that has not only demanded Jews conform to being second-class citizens but has also actively engaged in the often violent ethnic cleansing of Jews.

Antizionism is antisemitism in its content – it rests on the idea of a 'Zionist conspiracy' – and it continues the pattern of justifying antisemitism with 'legitimate proof'. The reality is, many people would not identify antizionism as a form of antisemitism because it not only targets a sovereign state that is locked in a seemingly never-ending conflict with a much smaller and seemingly more vulnerable group of people but also because they simply do not understand antisemitism.

Due to a lack of education about both the conflict and Jewish history, most people are not armed with the knowledge to understand the connection between antizionist rhetoric and historical antisemitism. They exist in a cycle of antisemitism: they've lived most of their lives in antisemitic societies that subtly or not-so-subtly feed the 'cloud of antisemitism'; they are then subjected to a diet of intense criticism of Israel, upon which there is a disproportionate focus; and these then reinforce and 'justify' antizionism. They simply *feel* Israel is a legitimate target without *knowing* much about it.

This poison can, as we have seen, infect young Jews too. Jews who grew up after the second intifada, and never witnessed the failure of the Oslo agreements, are particularly vulnerable to this portrayal of Israel as solely responsible for the continuing conflict with the Palestinians. Couple this with the revisionist account of how Israel is represented on campuses by the progressive left, and it is little wonder why Jewish youth may internalise this antisemitism as a form of shame. We have a duty to our young people to reclaim Zionism, so young Jews can be proud – even if critical – of the Jewish state and reject the antisemitic perceptions of Zionism the non-Jewish world has created.

In a 2019 video, Ashager reinforced the need to reclaim Zionism from antizionists. 'Jews stood up as a collective, built a movement and said that is enough,' she argued in it. Zionism is not the support for one Israeli government or another, it is the support of an idea, so when you are proudly saying you are antizionist, what you are actually saying is I want to go back in time to a place in history when Jews didn't have self-determination.'[338]

Ashager is absolutely right: we need to plainly define Zionism *ourselves* and we must be crystal clear on what it really means to be an antizionist. It is not a progressive position. It represents a deeply antisemitic worldview.

Zionism is a Jewish concept that aims to allow Jews to take control of their own destiny, for the first time in 2,000 years after our expulsion from Judea. Jews alone get to define this, along with all Jewish concepts. This does not mean that we as Jews have to agree on all Jewish values or concepts – after all, I believe in the diversity of our community. However, these conversations should be internal, rooted in historical fact, and Jewish Pride rather than shame. We should never base our understandings of what it means to be a Jew, nor Jewish concepts that aim to maintain us as a people, on the non-Jewish world's often antisemitic ideas of what it means to be Jewish. That is erasure of ourselves and our pride.

JEWISH BEAUTY

A crucial aspect of creating a Jewish Pride movement is embracing and celebrating the beauty that exists in the Jewish community. This can manifest itself in celebrating the beauty of our customs and practices, but also honouring the beauty that exists in our people. Due to Jewish shared ancestry with roots in the Levant, the modern Middle East, there are Jewish people – including many Ashkenazi Jews – who do not conform to Eurocentric beauty standards. This, coupled with one thousand years of the racial libel, has resulted in Jewish people being shamed for their physical appearance. We are presented as a monolith and the beauty which exists in our community is destroyed.

This shaming has led many Jewish people to reject and change their appearance in fear of looking like antisemitic stereotypes of a Jew. I used to feel huge amounts of shame for this reason. I used to dye my hair blonde, and I wanted to get a nose-job. At school, when told that I 'looked Jewish', I remember feeling as if I had been insulted.

As I got older, I began to consider why I hated my nose so much, and I began to process and reject the shame of antisemitism. I realised that the cocktail of Eurocentric beauty standards and the racial libel has had a devastating impact on the self-esteem of Jewish individuals, and this is something we must understand so we can unpack and ultimately guard against.

A Jewish Pride movement that celebrates beauty in the Jewish community does not say there is one specific way to be or look Jewish.

We know that is not the case. We are a diverse people and we must celebrate every facet of that reality.

We must also spend time understanding how the shame of antisemitism has impacted the lives of Jewish people. Jews have been shamed for our physical appearance for a thousand years and it's crucial for our collective and individual self-image that we reject the shame of Eurocentric beauty standards and the racial libel.

We must build a people that feel proud of how they look, however they look. Ultimately, we must foster a people who feel beautiful both inside and out, and who are able to reject antisemitic stereotyping and societal expectations of their appearance.

THE BEAUTY OF JEWISH CUSTOMS

Celebrating Jewish beauty can also focus on the beauty of our traditions and customs. When my father passed away, it was one of the times that I realised how lucky I was to be Jewish. Through Jewish traditions and practices, my family and I were given an irreplaceable guide on how to deal with this incredibly painful time in our lives. Bereaved non-Jewish friends have told me that they felt lost during their period of mourning and they didn't know how to process their grief. Being Jewish meant that I was given structure to mourn my father.

My father, Malcolm, passed away on 4 February 2017. He was buried three days later. I remember non-Jewish friends commenting on how quickly his funeral was arranged and how difficult that must have been. Truth be told, I found it easier. My father had been ill for several years and, when it became clear that he was not going to recover, the thought of his funeral filled me with dread. For me, the fact that he was buried so soon after he passed made his funeral easier; I was still in such a state of shock that I couldn't take it all in. However, the structure of Jewish mourning then gave me the opportunity to begin dealing with my father's passing.

The night of his funeral, and for the following three nights, we sat *shiva* and held prayers at our home. We covered mirrors and took down photos of my father. As per the instructions for the *shloshim* (the 30-day period following burial), I didn't shave and I said *kaddish* every day. After 30 days, I remember getting a haircut. I felt lighter and more like myself again.

I could feel this way because I had honoured my father and followed the structure of Jewish mourning and this made those 30 days easier. I was beginning to feel ready to re-enter normal life. Obviously, when someone you love passes away, you mourn them for more than just 30 days. Jewish mourning rituals continue for a year and then every year, on my father's *yahrzeit* (the Jewish anniversary of his passing), I light a *yahrzeit* candle and I say *kaddish*. The structure that being Jewish gave me to mourn and remember my father has made dealing with his loss so much easier. I genuinely don't know what I would have done without it.

Jewish rituals and practices are beautiful to experience while helping us deal with and process life cycles. When I speak to Jewish friends who are parents, they say that Jewish rituals helped them cope with the first few days of being new parents. When their son was born, they knew they had to arrange his *brit milah* (circumcision), which gave them focus in a time of huge upheaval. Our rituals also help connect us in a very tangible and real way to past and future generations. I know that *kaddish* has been said to mourn the Jewish dead for millennia and honouring my father in this very same way makes me incredibly proud. I am not a religious person, but I didn't need to be to benefit from and appreciate Jewish customs. They are a profound and powerful part of our peoplehood that makes me so grateful to be Jewish.

JEWISH PRIDE

Jewish Pride is a work in progress. It is not something that we – as individuals or as a collective – can fully internalise overnight. It is something we must decide to work towards and it is entirely reasonable if we are not there yet. We are a tiny ethno-religious minority that has faced intense antisemitism for thousands of years and we are all dealing with a number of different traumas. We experience inter-generational trauma, collective trauma and individual trauma arising from current events. All of these have an impact on our Jewish identities and can make us feel ashamed. This is a huge amount to process, but a process we must begin.

This book was never about fighting antisemitism. This book is about *our* people. It is about turning inwards and working together to reject the shame of antisemitism. All while creating a proud Jewish community defining its own identity on its own terms. Based on its own history, values and experiences.

It is natural for us as individuals or diverse Jewish communities to express our Jewishness and our Jewish Pride differently. The seven people I chose to interview represent just some of the diversity of the Jewish people and, though their expressions of Jewishness may differ from yours, their Jewish Pride can be an empowering inspiration to the whole Jewish world.

I am aware that each of the individual sections in this chapter could have been entire books of their own, there is so much beautiful detail in Jewishness, so much to be proud of and so much to celebrate. Many of you reading this may say: 'What about this other aspect of the Jewish community' And you would be right, this list was far from exhaustive.

The truth is, there are countless reasons to be proud of being Jewish. In this chapter, I selected just *some* of the reasons that Jews can embody a strong sense of pride that will ignite the same in other Jewish people. Yet the possibilities are endless.

Love our cultures and our traditions. Love our humour. Love our food. Love our diversity. Love our emphasis on learning and dialogue. Love our people. And, most of all, love our commitment to the continuation of Jewish life.

I feel so incredibly proud to stand with you all as we embark on a journey together to create a Jewish Pride movement.

A movement rooted in understanding Jewish history.

A movement that inspires countless generations of Jews to reject the shame of antisemitism and non-Jewish impositions of what it means to be a Jew.

A movement that empowers each and every Jew to define our own Jewish identity without having to warp this Jewishness to be accepted by the non-Jewish world.

A movement where Jewishness is a source of pride – and never one of shame.

And that, my *mishpacha*, my family, is how we rebuild our people. *Am Yisrael Chai.*

The People of Israel Live.

Proudly.

THE AUTHOR　　　　　RACHEL　　　　　HEN

ASHAGER  ISAAC

ELISHEVA　　　　　ELIYAHU　　　　　AMY

NOTES

1   'Star of David Pride flags unwelcome at DC Dyke March', 8 June 2019. Available at: https://antisemitism.org.il/en/147846/

2   David Hirsh, 'The Corbyn left: The politics of position and the politics of reason', *Fathom*, Autumn 2015. Available at: https://fathomjournal.org/the-corbyn-left-the-politics-of-position-and-the-politics-of-reason/

3   'Tel Aviv – A city with Pride', 2 June 2018. Available at: https://www.tel-aviv.gov.il/

4   Palestinian Campaign for the Academic and Cultural Boycott of Israel (PACBI), 'No to Eurovision Pinkwashing. More than 100 LGBTQ+ groups call for boycott of song contest in Israel', BDS Movement, 29 January 2019. Available at: https://bdsmovement.net/news/no-eurovision-pinkwashing-more-100-lgbtq-groups-call-for-boycott-song-contest-israel

5   James D. Fearon, 'What is identity (as we now use the word)?', Unpublished manuscript, 3 November 1999. Available at: https://web.stanford.edu/group/fearon-research/cgi-bin/wordpress/wp-content/uploads/2013/10/What-is-Identity-as-we-now-use-the-word-.pdf, (hereafter James D. Fearon, 'What is identity (as we now use the word?')

6   James D. Fearon, 'What is identity (as we now use the word)?'

7   Jonathan Sacks, *Future Tense: A Vision for Jews and Judaism in the Global Culture* (London: Hodder & Stoughton, 2010)

8   Michael Lerner, 'The white issue: "Jews are not white"', *Village Voice*, 18 May 1993. Available at: https://www.villagevoice.com/2019/07/25/the-white-issue-jews-are-not-white/, (hereafter Michael Lerner, 'The white issue: "Jews are not white"')

9   'White pride', Anti-Defamation League. Available at: https://www.adl.org/resources/glossary-terms/white-pride

10 'Pride', Stonewall. Available at: https://www.stonewall.org.uk/our-work/campaigns/pride

11 James D. Fearon, 'What is identity (as we now use the word)?'

12 Desiree Guerrero, Study: LGBTQ+ Youth are Four Times More Likely to Attempt Suicide, *Out Magazine*, 11 February 2020. Available at: https://www.out.com/health/2020/2/11/study-lgbtq-youth-are-four-times-more-likely-attempt-suicide

13 Helen Thomson, 'Study of Holocaust survivors finds trauma passed on to children's genes', *The Guardian*, 21 August 2015. Available at: https://www.theguardian.com/science/2015/aug/21/study-of-holocaust-survivors-finds-trauma-passed-on-to-childrens-genes

14 Howard Lovy, 'Rabbi examines trauma passed down through generations', PublishersWeekly.com, 8 April 2019. Available at: https://www.publishersweekly.com/pw/by-topic/industry-news/religion/article/79702-rabbi-examines-trauma-passed-down-through-generations.html.

15 Ben M. Freeman, 'Erasive Antisemitism — Naming a Subcategory of Antisemitism', *Medium*, 20 September 2020. Available at: https://medium.com/@benmfreeman/erasive-antisemitism-cc71bf7259bb

16 Daniel Philpott, *Just and Unjust Peace: An Ethic of Political Reconciliation* (New York: Oxford University Press, 2015)

17　Charles Krauthammer, 'At last, Zion', *Washington Examiner*, 11 May 1998. Available at: https://www.washingtonexaminer.com/weekly-standard/at-last-zion

18　Gil Atzmon et al., 'Abraham's children in the Genome Era: Major Jewish diaspora populations comprise distinct genetic clusters with shared Middle Eastern ancestry', *The American Journal of Human Genetics* 86, no. 6 (June 3, 2010): pp. 850-859, https://doi.org/10.1016/j.ajhg.2010.04.015, (hereafter Gil Atzmon et al., 'Abraham's children in the Genome Era: Major Jewish diaspora populations comprise distinct genetic clusters with shared Middle Eastern ancestry')

19　'Demographics of Judaism', Berkley Center for Religion, Peace and World Affairs, 2020. Available at: https://berkleycenter.georgetown.edu/essays/demographics-of-judaism.

20　David Jay Derovan et al., *The Passover Haggadah* (Los Angeles: Jewish Community Enrichment Press, 1978)

21　The Conspiracy Libel, Twitter Post, 27 September 2020. Available at: https://twitter.com/ConspiracyLibel/status/1309909779373076483

22　Gal Beckerman, *When They Come for Us, We'll Be Gone* (Boston, Mariner Books, 2012)

23　Jeffrey Goldberg, 'Is it time for the Jews to leave Europe?', *The Atlantic*, April 2015. Available at: https://www.theatlantic.com/magazine/archive/2015/04/is-it-time-for-the-jews-to-leave-europe/386279/.

24　Kevin Klose, 'Soviet Jews see growth in anti-semitism: Soviet Jews are fearful of rising anti-semitism', *The Washington Post*, 15 July 1979. Available at: https://www.washingtonpost.com/archive/politics/1979/07/15/soviet-jews-see-growth-in-anti-semitismsoviet-jews-are-fearful-of-rising-anti-semitism/9d822731-c7cc-4d1f-9af7-7fb13827410d/.

25　Philip Spencer, 'The shame of antisemitism on the left has a long, malign history', *The Guardian* 1 April 2018, Available at: https://www.theguardian.com/comment isfree/2018/apr/01/shame-of-anitsemitism-on-left-has-long-malign-history

26　'Working Definition of Antisemitism'. IHRA, Available at: https://www.holocaus-tremembrance.com/working-definition-antisemitism

27　Anthony Julius, *Trials of the Diaspora* (Oxford: Oxford University Press, 2012)

28　Walter Laqueur, *The Changing Face of Antisemitism: From Ancient Times to the Present Day* (Oxford: Oxford University Press, 2006)

29　'Leviticus 17:12-13'. Available at: https://www.biblegateway.com/passage/?search=Leviticus+17%3A12-13.

30　David Patterson, *Anti-Semitism and its Metaphysical Origins* (Cambridge: Cambridge University Press, 2015)

31　Matthias Von Hellfeld, 'Christianity becomes the religion of the Roman Empire – February 27, 380', DW.com. Available at: https://www.dw.com/en/christianity-becomes-the-religion-of-the-roman-empire-february-27-380/a-4602728.

32　Martin I. Lockshin, 'Who killed Jesus?', My Jewish Learning, Available at: https://www.myjewishlearning.com/article/who-killed-jesus/

33　'Matthew 26:57-75'. Available at: http://bible.oremus.org/?passage=Matthew+26%3A57-75

34　Martin Gilbert, *In Ishmael's House: A History of Jews in Muslim Lands* (New Haven, CT: Yale University Press, 2011)

35　Eli Kavon, 'Maimonides on Jewish humiliation under Islamic rule', *The Jerusalem Post*, 23 March 2020. Available at: https://www.jpost.com/Opinion/Maimonides-on-Jewish-humiliation-under-Islamic-rule-622050, (hereafter Eli Kavon, 'Maimonides on Jewish humiliation under Islamic rule')

36 Eli Kavon, 'Maimonides on Jewish humiliation under Islamic rule'

37 Matti Friedman, 'Mizrahi nation', *Mosaic*, June 2014. Available at: https://mosaic-magazine.com/essay/uncategorized/2014/06/mizrahi-nation/.

38 'Arab/Muslim anti-semitism: The Damascus blood libel', Jewish Virtual Library. Available at: https://www.jewishvirtuallibrary.org/the-damascus-blood-libel

39 Jan P. Oller, *Gods, Guns, & Fear* (USA AuthorHouse, 2008)

40 Albert S. Lindemann, 'Lindemann on Frankel, "The Damascus Affair: 'Ritual murder,' Politics, and the Jews in 1840"', Humanities and Social Sciences Online, 1997. Available at: https://networks.h-net.org/node/2645/reviews/4123/lindemann-frankel-damascus-affair-ritual-murder-politics-and-jews-1840, (hereafter Albert S. Lindemann, 'Lindemann on Frankel, "The Damascus Affair: 'Ritual Murder,' Politics, and the Jews in 1840"')

41 Albert S. Lindemann, 'Lindemann on Frankel, "The Damascus Affair: 'Ritual Murder,' Politics, and the Jews in 1840"'

42 Natan Sharansky, '3D Test of Anti-Semitism: Demonization, Double Standards, Delegitimization', *Jerusalem Center for Public Affairs*, 2004. Available at: https://www.jcpa.org/phas/phas-sharansky-f04.htm

43 Daniel Sugarman, 'Belgian trade union official falsely accuses Israel of 'murdering Palestinian children for their organs', *Jewish Chronicle*, 22 October 2018. Available at: https://www.thejc.com/news/world/robrecht-vanderbeeken-belgian-trade-union-official-modern-day-blood-libel-claims-1.471296

44 'Occupying Israel pharmaceutical firms test medicines on Palestinian prisoners', Popular Conference for Palestinians Abroad, 2020. Available at: https://eng.palabroad.org/post/view/54441

45 Paul Vallely, 'Dickens' greatest villain: The faces of Fagin', *The Independent*, 7 October 2005. Available at: https://www.independent.co.uk/arts-entertainment/films/features/dickens-greatest-villain-the-faces-of-fagin-317786.html

46 'Money is the God of the Jews', German Propaganda Archive. Available at: https://research.calvin.edu/german-propaganda-archive/story15.htm

47 'Deuteronomy 23:20'. Available at: https://biblehub.com/deuteronomy/23-20.htm.

48 Christopher Tuckwood, 'From real friend to imagined foe: The Medieval roots of anti-semitism as a precondition for the Holocaust', *Genocide Studies and Prevention* 5, no. 1 2010. Available at: https://doi.org/10.3138/gsp.5.1.89

49 Natalie Zemon Davis, 'The life of a Court Jew', *Tablet*, 24 March 2020. Available at: https://www.tabletmag.com/sections/arts-letters/articles/natalie-zemon-davis-court-jews.

50 'Report reveals dramatic rise in poverty in Jewish community', UJA, 6 June 2013. Available at: https://www.ujafedny.org/news/new-report-reveals-dramatic-rise-in-poverty-in-jewish-community/, (hereafter 'Report reveals dramatic rise in poverty in Jewish community')

51 'Report reveals dramatic rise in poverty in Jewish community'

52 Shlomo Swirski, Etty Konor-Attias, and Aviv Lieberman, 'Israel: A Social Report 2018', Adva Center, 31 March 2019. Available at: https://adva.org/en/socialreport2018/.

53 Ilanit Chernick, 'A quarter of Israel's Holocaust survivors living in poverty', *The Jerusalem Post*, 1 May 2019. Available at: https://www.jpost.com/diaspora/quarter-of-israels-holocaust-survivors-living-in-poverty-588381

54 Aleks Phillips, 'The Office actor shares post saying 'rich Jews play the antisemitism card to protect themselves', *The Jewish Chronicle*, 16 December 2019. Available at: https://www.thejc.com/news/uk/actor-from-the-office-shares-post-saying-rich-jews-play-the-antisemitism-card-to-protect-themselves-1.494372

55 Natasha Mozgovaya, 'Poll: 31% of Europeans blame Jews for global financial crisis', *Haaretz*, 10 February 2009. Available at: https://www.haaretz.com/1.5073513

56 Kim Willsher, 'Brutal murder was anti-semitic crime, says Sarkozy', *The Guardian*, 22 February 2006. Available at: https://www.theguardian.com/world/2006/feb/22/france.mainsection.

57 Gary Allan Tisor, *The Untold Story* (USA: Xlibris Corporation, 2012)

58 'Anti-semitism: A hoax of hate', ADL. Available at: https://www.adl.org/resources/backgrounders/a-hoax-of-hate-the-protocols-of-the-learned-elders-of-zion

59 'Coronavirus and the plague of antisemitism of hate', Community Security Trust, 2020, Available at: https://cst.org.uk/data/file/d/9/Coronavirus%20and%20the%20plague%20of%20antisemitism.1586276450.pdf

60 Izabella Tabarovsky, 'Soviet anti-Zionism and contemporary left antisemitism', *Fathom*, May 2019: Available at: http://fathomjournal.org/soviet-anti-zionism-and-contemporary-left-antisemitism/.

61 'Anti-semitism: Anti-semitism in the Egyptian media', Jewish Virtual Library. Available at: https://www.jewishvirtuallibrary.org/anti-semitism-in-the-egyptian-press.

62 John Strawnson, 'Jeremy Corbyn and Hamas: No longer friends, but still brother', *Jewish News*, 22 August 2018. Available at: https://blogs.timesofisrael.com/jeremy-corbyn-and-hamas-no-longer-friends-but-still-brothers/

63 Raphael Israeli (tran.), 'The charter of Allah: The platform of the Islamic Resistance Movement (Hamas)', Federation Of American Scientists (Harry Truman Research Institute The Hebrew University). Available at: https://fas.org/irp/world/para/docs/880818.htm

64 'The key questions Jeremy Corbyn must answer', *The Jewish Chronicle*, 12 August 2015. Available at: https://www.thejc.com/news/uk/the-key-questions-jeremy-corbyn-must-answer-1.68097

65 Jeremy Corbyn responds to the JC's seven questions, *The Jewish Chronicle*, 19 August 2015. Available at: https://www.thejc.com/news/uk/jeremy-corbyn-responds-to-the-jc-s-seven-questions-1.68184

66 Mear One, Facebook post, 2 October 2012. Available at: https://m.facebook.com/290156246477/photos/a.290349386477.157415.290156246477/10151054305501478/

67 Rob Merrick, 'Jeremy Corbyn forced to backtrack over apparent support for antisemitic mural after Labour MP's protest', *The Independent*, 23 March 2018. Available at: https://www.independent.co.uk/news/uk/politics/jeremy-corbyn-anti-semitic-mural-mear-one-luciana-berger-east-end-a8271111.html

68 'UK delegation to the International Holocaust Remembrance Alliance issues statement condemning tampering with the International Definition of Antisemitism', Campaign Against Antisemitism, 7 August 2018. Available at: https://antisemitism.uk/uk-delegation-to-the-international-holocaust-remembrance-alliance-issues-statement-condemning-tampering-with-the-international-definition-of-antisemitism/

69 Robert Philpot, 'Corbyn Loathes Israel, and Labour's new anti-Semitism rules won't change that', *Times of Israel*, 6 September 2018. Available at: https://www.timesofisrael.com/corbyn-loathes-israel-and-labours-new-anti-semitism-rules-wont-change-that/

70 https://www.thejc.com/news/uk/anger-as-diane-abbott-repeatedly-describes-labour-s-antisemitism-crisis-as-a-smear-campaign-1.461743

71 About Us, Labour Against the Witch hunt, available at: http://www.labouragainst-thewitchhunt.org/about/

72 Rowena Mason, 'MPs should have no say over who leads Labour, argues shadow minister', *The Guardian*, 28 August 2017. Available at: https://www.theguard-ian.com/politics/2017/aug/28/make-labour-leadership-rules-more-democratic-urges-shadow-minister

73 Lee Harpin, 'Bombshell tape shows Jeremy Corbyn ally blamed "Jewish Trump fantatics" for inventing Labour antisemitism', *The Jewish Chronicle*, 30 July 2018. Available at: https://www.thejc.com/news/uk/bombshell-recording-proves-corbyn-ally-blamed-jewish-trump-fantatics-for-false-antisemitism-clai-1.467802

74 'Engines of hate: The online networks behind the Labour party's antisemitism crisis', Community Security Trust, 4 August 2019, Available at: https://cst.org.uk/data/file/d/1/Web%20Engine%20of%20hate%20-%20The%20online%20networks%20behind%20the%20Labour%20Party%27s%20antisemitism%20crisis.1565192943.pdf, (hereafter, 'Engine Of Hate: The online networks behind the Labour party's antisemitism crisis')

75 Jonathan Cook, 'The Israel Lobby non-stop attacks on Corbyn will back fire', *Middle East Eye* , 6 September 2018. Available at: https://www.middleeasteye.net/opinion/israel-lobbys-non-stop-attacks-corbyn-will-backfire

76 Leo Panitch, 'Historical Record Shows Jeremy Corbyn is a defender of Jews', *The Star*, 4 December 2019. Available at: https://www.thestar.com/opinion/contribu-tors/2019/12/03/historical-record-shows-jeremy-corbyn-is-a-defender-of-jews.html

77 David Hirsh, 'The Livingstone formulation', *Engage*, 29 April 2016. Available at: https://engageonline.wordpress.com/2016/04/29/the-livingstone-formulation-david-hirsh-2/, (hereafter David Hirsh 'The Livingstone formulation')

78 Eldad Black, 'Almost 50% of Jews in UK say will leave if Labour's Corbyn wins general election', *Israel Hayom*, 4 November 2019. Available at: https://www.israel-hayom.com/2019/11/04/almost-50-of-jews-in-uk-say-will-leave-if-labours-corbyn-wins-general-elections/

79 Investigation into antisemitism in the Labour Party, Equalities and Human Rights Commission, October 2020. Available at: https://www.equalityhumanrights.com/sites/default/files/investigation-into-antisemitism-in-the-labour-party.pdf (hereafter, Investigation into antisemitism in the Labour Party, Equalities and Human Rights Commission)

80 Investigation into antisemitism in the Labour Party finds unlawful acts of discrimi-nation and harassment, Equalities and Human Rights Commission

81 Investigation into antisemitism in the Labour Party, Equalities and Human Rights Commission

82 Jeremy Corbyn, Facebook Post, 29 October 2020. Available at: https://www.facebook.com/JeremyCorbynMP/posts/my-statement-following-the-publica-tion-of-the-ehrc-reportantisemitism-is-absolut/10158939532253872/

83 Sara Lipton, 'The invention of the Jewish nose', *The New York Review of Books*, 14 November 2014. Available at: https://www.nybooks.com/daily/2014/11/14/invention-jewish-nose/.

84 Jorge Salavert Pinedo (tran.), '"To a man with a big nose": A new translation', study-lib.net (Study Lib). Available at: https://studylib.net/doc/8835321/to-a-man-with-a-big-nose%E2%80%9D--a-new-translation.

85 Izabella Tabarovsky, 'Understanding the Real Origin of that New York Times Cartoon', *The Tablet*, 6 June 2019. Available at: https://www.tabletmag.com/sections/arts-letters/articles/soviet-anti-semitic-cartoons

86 Cnaan Liphshiz, 'Belgian editor defends publication of column saying Jews have "ugly noses"', *The Times of Israel*, 7 August 2019. Available at: https://www.timesofisrael.com/belgian-editor-defends-publication-of-column-saying-jews-have-ugly-noses/

87 'Coronavirus and the plague of antisemitism of hate', *Community Security Trust*, 2020, Available at: https://cst.org.uk/data/file/d/9/Coronavirus%20and%20the%20plague%20of%20antisemitism.1586276450.pdf

88 Rita Rubin, 'A Nose Dive for Nose Jobs', *The Tablet*, 7 June 2012. Available at: https://www.tabletmag.com/sections/community/articles/a-nose-dive-for-nose-jobs

89 Emily Shire, 'The women's march might finally be ready to take Jewish women seriously', *Jewish Telegraphic Agency*, 25 September 2019. Available at: https://www.jta.org/2019/09/25/opinion/the-womens-march-might-finally-be-ready-to-take-jewish-women-seriously

90 Louis Farrakhan denies antisemitism – then refers to 'Satanic Jews', *The Guardian*, 11 May 2019. Available at: https://www.theguardian.com/us-news/2019/may/11/louis-farrakhan-denies-antisemitism-satanic-jews

91 Josefin Dolsten, 'Louis Farrakhan's 2018 tweet comparing Jews to termites is gone after twitter policy change', *Jewish Telegraphic Agency*, 9 July 2019. Available at: https://www.jta.org/quick-reads/louis-farrakhans-2018-tweet-comparing-jews-to-termites-is-gone-after-twitter-policy-change.

92 Charles Dunst, 'According to progressives, antisemitism isn't racism', *Jewish Ledger*, 15 August 2018. Available at: http://www.jewishledger.com/2018/08/according-progressives-antisemitism-isnt-racism/

93 'Madonna Instagram post of Louis Farrakhan video racks up 700,000 views, *Jewish News*, 21 July 2020. Available at: https://jewishnews.timesofisrael.com/madonna-instagram-post-of-louis-farrakhan-video-racks-up-700000-views/

94 George Orwell, 'Antisemitism in Britain', The Orwell Foundation. Available at: https://www.orwellfoundation.com/the-orwell-foundation/orwell/essays-and-other-works/antisemitism-in-britain/

95 Daniel Sugarman, 'Calls for Labour to expel candidate Salma Yaqoob, who shared article on "Rothschild Bankers"', *The Jewish Chronicle*, 24 October 2019. Available at: https://www.thejc.com/news/uk/calls-for-labour-to-expel-candidate-salma-yaqoob-who-shared-article-on-rothschild-bankers-1.490670

96 David Nirenberg, *Anti-Judaism: The Western Tradition* (New York: W. W. Norton & Company, 2014), (hereafter David Nirenberg, *Anti-Judaism: The Western Tradition)*

97 David Nirenberg, *Anti-Judaism: The Western Tradition*

98 David Nirenberg, *Anti-Judaism: The Western Tradition*

99 David Nirenberg, *Anti-Judaism: The Western Tradition*

100 David Nirenberg, *Anti-Judaism: The Western Tradition*

101 Michael Ezra, 'Karl Marx's radical antisemitism', *The Philosophers' Magazine*, 23 March 2015. Available at: https://www.philosophersmag.com/opinion/30-karl-marx-s-radical-antisemitism

102 'Money is the God of the Jews', German Propaganda Archive. Available at: https://research.calvin.edu/german-propaganda-archive/story15.htm.

103 David Nirenberg, *Anti-Judaism: The Western Tradition*

104 David Nirenberg, *Anti-Judaism: The Western Tradition*

105 Tyler Cowen, 'The socialist roots of modern anti-semitism', Independent Institute, 1 January 1997. Available at: https://www.independent.org/publications/article. asp?id=359.

106 David Nirenberg, *Anti-Judaism: The Western Tradition*

107 Rudy Malcolm, 'Progressives should not insist on anti-Zionism', *The John Hopkins News-Letter*, 25 April 2019. Available at: https://www.jhunewsletter.com/ article/2019/04/progressives-should-not-insist-on-anti-zionism

108 Hugh Jaeger, Twitter post, 31 July 2014. Available at: https://twitter.com/HughJaeger/ status/494778660566884353

109 David Nirenberg, *Anti-Judaism: The Western Tradition*

110 Peter Hayes, *Why? Explaining the Holocaust* (New York: W.W. Norton and Company, 2018).

111 'Maajid Nawaz speaks to David Collier on LBC 13-10-19', SoundCloud audio, 13 October 2019. Available at: https://soundcloud.com/user-970730897/maajid-nawaz-speaks-to-david-collier-on-lbc-13-10-19, (hereafter 'Maajid Nawaz speaks to David Collier on LBC 13-10-19')

112 Jeffrey Herf, Haj Amin al-Husseini, the Nazis and the Holocaust: The Origins, Nature and Aftereffects of Collaboration, *Jerusalem Center For Public Affairs*, 5 January 2016. Available at: https://jcpa.org/article/haj-amin-al-husseini-the-nazis-and-the-holocaust-the-origins-nature-and-aftereffects-of-collaboration/

113 Serge Schmemann, 'SOVIET STAKE IN THE P.L.O.', *New York Times*, 23 November 1983. Available at: https://www.nytimes.com/1983/11/23/world/soviet-stake-in-the-plo.html

114 Lee Harpin, 'Neo-Nazi meeting to discuss Princess Diana conspiracy theories cancelled on police advice', *The Jewish Chronicle*, 9 August 2017. Available at: https://www.thejc.com/news/uk/neo-nazi-meeting-to-discuss-princess-diana-conspiracy-theories-cancelled-1.442615

115 Ian Fantom, 'UK's Labour antisemitism split: Just what the doctor prescribed', *The Unz Review*, 21 March 2019. Available at: https://www.unz.com/article/uks-labour-antisemitism-split/

116 Rosa Doherty, 'Alison Chabloz branded "manifestly antisemitic" holocaust denier as she loses appeal against conviction', *The Jewish Chronicle*, 13 February 2019. Available at: https://www.thejc.com/news/uk/alison-chabloz-branded-manifestly-antisemit-ic-holocaust-denier-as-she-loses-appeal-against-convict-1.479999

117 Miko Peled, Twitter post, 19 August 2013. Available at: https://twitter.com/mikopeled/ status/369470418047860736

118 'Maajid Nawaz speaks to David Collier on LBC 13-10-19'

119 David Collier, '2018 and Antisemitism, a year in review', *Beyond The Great Divide*, 30 December 2018. Available at: http://david-collier.com/2018-antisemitism/

120 David Collier, AIPL Report Part One, *Beyond The Great Divide*, 6 March 2018. Available at: https://secureservercdn.net/198.71.188.149/3e8.04f.myftpupload.com/wp-content/uploads/2018/03/180305_livereport_part1_FINAL.pdf

121 David Collier, AIPL Report Part Two, *Beyond The Great Divide*, 6 March 2018. Available at: https://secureservercdn.net/198.71.188.149/3e8.04f.myftpupload.com/wp-content/uploads/2018/03/180305_livereport_part2_FINAL.pdf

122 'Nick Griffin declares his support for Jeremy Corbyn', *New Statesman,* 10 April 2018. Available at: https://www.newstatesman.com/politics/media/2018/04/nick-griffin-declares-his-support-jeremy-corbyn

123 James Tapsfield, 'With supporters like these… Holocaust denier David Irving says he is 'impressed' by Jeremy Corbyn', *Daily Mail,* 15 January 2017. Available at: https://www.dailymail.co.uk/news/article-4122370/With-supporters-like-Holocaust-denier-David-Irving-says-impressed-Jeremy-Corbyn.html

124 Henry Zeffman, 'Former KKK Wizard David Duke Praised Jeremy Corbyn Victory', *The Times,* 3 August 2018. Available at: https://www.thetimes.co.uk/article/former-kkk-wizard-praised-corbyn-victory-rztzv263g

125 Deborah Lipstadt, Twitter Post, 27 November 2019. Available at: https://twitter.com/deborahlipstadt/status/1199377794427506689

126 Avi Mayer, Twitter post, 10 June, 2019. Available at: https://twitter.com/AviMayer/status/1138098356096573440

127 Avi Mayer, Twitter post, 10 June 2019. Available at: https://twitter.com/AviMayer/status/1138098356096573440

128 Uri Bollag, 'German party runs for EU parliament under slogan "Israel is our misfortune"', *The Jerusalem Post,* 24 May 2019. Available at: https://www.jpost.com/Diaspora/German-party-runs-for-EU-parliament-with-Israel-is-our-misfortune-slogan-590510

129 Petra Marquardt-Bigman, 'Why neo-Nazis love the BDS movement so much', *Haaretz,* 16 June 2019. Available at: https://www.haaretz.com/world-news/.premium-why-neo-nazis-love-the-bds-movement-so-much-1.7372611

130 'German newspaper', United States Holocaust Memorial Museum. Available at: https://collections.ushmm.org/search/catalog/irn514440

131 'Who was Alfred Dreyfus', The National Library of Israel. Available at: https://web.nli.org.il/sites/nlis/en/education/pages/who-was-alfred-dreyfus.aspx

132 James Angelos, 'The new German anti-semitism', *The New York Times,* 21 May 2019. Available at: https://www.nytimes.com/2019/05/21/magazine/anti-semitism-germany.html

133 'Unorthodox: Deborah Feldman's escape from Brooklyn to Berlin'

134 'Cannot advise Jews to wear kippah everywhere in Germany: Official', NDTV.com, 26 May 2019. Available at: https://www.ndtv.com/world-news/german-official-felix-klein-says-cannot-advise-jews-to-wear-kippah-everywhere-in-the-country-2043078

135 Anshel Pfeffer, 'The New Dilemma for Jews in Ukraine', *Haaretz,* 26 February 2014. Available at: https://www.haaretz.com/jewish/.premium-ukraine-jews-new-dilemma-1.5326313

136 Jack Fischel, Putin's Hybrid War and the Jews: Antisemitism, Propaganda, and the Displacement of Ukrainian Jewry, *Jewish Book Council,* 26 April 2020. Available at: https://www.jewishbookcouncil.org/book/putins-hybrid-war-and-the-jews-antisemitism-propaganda-and-the-displacement-of-ukrainian-jewry

137 Cnaan Liphshiz, 'As Putin cracks down on democracy, Russian Jews increasingly moving to Israel', *The Times of Israel,* 22 September 2019. Available at: https://www.timesofisrael.com/as-putin-cracks-down-on-democracy-russian-jews-increasingly-moving-to-israel/

138 Graeme Hamilton, 'Ukraine's Jews caught in a propaganda war based on the 'political manipulation of anti-Semitism', *National Post,* 25 April 2014. Available at:

https://nationalpost.com/news/ukraines-jews-caught-in-a-propaganda-war-that-uses-the-political-manipulation-of-anti-semitism

139 Cody Nelson, 'Minnesota congresswoman ignites debate on Israel and anti-semitism', NPR, 7 March 2019. Available at: https://www.npr.org/2019/03/07/700901834/minnesota-congresswoman-ignites-debate-on-israel-and-anti-semitism

140 'Overview', BDS, Available at: https://bdsmovement.net/what-is-bds

141 'What is BDS?', Stand With Us. Available at: https://www.standwithus.com/fact sheets-bds

142 Bryant Harris, 'Ilhan Omar Seizes Spotlight to Push Pro-BDS Resolution', US News, 17 July 2019. Available at: https://www.usnews.com/news/politics/articles/2019-07-17/ilhan-omar-seizes-spotlight-to-push-pro-bds-resolution

143 David Hirsh, 'Why BDS is antisemitic', Engage, 1 June 2016. Available at: https://engageonline.wordpress.com/2016/06/01/why-bds-is-antisemitic-david-hirsh/

144 Lukas Mikelionis, 'Omar introduces resolution defending boycott of Israel, likens it to boycotts of Nazi Germany, Soviet Union', Fox News, 18 July 2019. Available at: https://www.foxnews.com/politics/omar-introduces-resolution-defending-boy-cotts-of-israel-likens-it-to-boycott-of-nazi-germany-soviet-union

145 Joshua Keating, 'J Street: There is no Democratic divide over Israel', Slate, 11 February 2019. Available at: https://slate.com/news-and-politics/2019/02/democrats-israel-ilhan-omar-j-street-ben-ami.html

146 Rahm Emanuel, 'I've Faced the Charge of Dual Loyalty', The Atlantic, 7 March 2019. Available at: https://www.theatlantic.com/ideas/archive/2019/03/ilhan-omars-dual-loyalty-charge-was-anti-semitic/584314/

147 Leah Greenberg, Twitter post, 5 March 2019. Available at: https://twitter.com/Leahgreenb/status/1102678444343783424

148 Symone D. Sanders, Twitter post, 5 March 2019. Available at: https://twitter.com/SymoneDSanders/status/1102765470602604547

149 Jonthan Salzman, 'Trump's Final "Argument for America" Ad is Rife with Anti-Semitic Tropes', Tablet, 8 November 2016. Available at: https://www.tabletmag.com/sections/news/articles/trumps-final-argument-for-america-ad-is-rife-with-anti-semitic-tropes

150 Julie Hirschfeld Davis, 'Trump accuses Jewish Democrats of "great disloyalty"', The New York Times, 21 August 2019. Available at: https://www.nytimes.com/2019/08/20/us/politics/trump-jewish-voters.html

151 Oma Seddiq, 'Textbook anti-Semitism': American Jews condemn Trump for repeatedly telling that that Israel is 'your country', Business Insider, 18 September 2020. Available at: https://www.businessinsider.com/american-jews-condemn-trump-for-saying-israel-is-your-country-2020-9

152 Rasha Ali, 'Ilhan Omar is me. Trump's "go back" tweet is painful reminder America won't accept us', USA Today, 30 July 2019. Available at: https://www.usatoday.com/story/opinion/voices/2019/07/30/donald-trump-racist-tweets-america-ilhan-omar-column/1808341001/

153 Knox Paulson, I Am The Winner: A Presidential Autobiography of Donald J. Trump (Place of publication not identified: LULU Press, 2019)

154 Isaac Stanley-Becker, 'Trump answers racism accusation with a charge of his own: Anti-Semitism', Washington Post, 16 July 2019. Available at: https://www.washington-post.com/nation/2019/07/16/trump-omar-racism-accusation-anti-semitism/

155 Isaac Stanley-Becker, 'Trump answers racism accusation with a charge of his own: Anti-Semitism', Washington Post, 16 July 2019. Available

at: https://www.washingtonpost.com/nation/2019/07/16/trump-omar-racism-accusation-anti-semitism/

156 Lizzie Dearden, 'Katie Hopkins leaves Mail Online days after video emerges of her anti-Muslim speech to far-right group', *The Independent*, 27 November 2017. Available at: https://www.independent.co.uk/news/media/press/katie-hopkins-muslims-far-right-speech-mailonline-racism-islamophobia-david-horowitz-freedom-center-a8078356.html

157 Cnaan Liphshiz, 'Some UK Jews embrace hard-right pundit Katie Hopkins amid her attacks on Muslims', *The Times of Israel*, 28 July 2019. Available at: https://www.timesofisrael.com/some-uk-jews-embrace-hard-right-pundit-katie-hopkins-amid-her-attacks-on-muslims/.

158 Jonathan Freedland, 'Beware of false friends like Rod Liddle and Katie Hopkins, their motive is hateful', *The Jewish Chronicle*, 8 August 2019. Available at: https://www.thejc.com/comment/opinion/beware-of-false-friends-like-katie-hopkins-their-motive-is-hateful-1.487280

159 Julia Manchester, 'Trump is most pro-Israel president since Truman, says political analyst', *The Hill*, 26 February 2019. Available at: https://thehill.com/hilltv/what-americas-thinking/431675-trump-is-most-pro-israel-president-since-truman-says-analyst.

160 Tzvi Fleischer, 'Hate's revival', AIJAC, 1 May 2007. Available at: https://aijac.org.au/australia-israel-review/hate-s-revival/

161 Albert Memmi, *Portrait of a Jew* (London: Eyre & Spottiswoode, 1963)

162 Debra Kaplan, 'Anti-Judaism and Luther's Jewish question', *Los Angeles Review of Books*, 10 December 2013. Available at: https://marginalia.lareviewofbooks.org/anti-judaism-and-luthers-jewish-question/

163 Eric Rentschler, 'The fascination of a fake: The Hitler diaries', *New German Critique*, no. 90 (2003): 177-92. doi:10.2307/3211115, (hereafter, Eric Rentschler, 'The fascination of a fake: The Hitler diaries.')

164 Allison C. Meier, 'An affordable radio brought Nazi propaganda home', *JStor Daily*, 30 August 2018. Available at: https://daily.jstor.org/an-affordable-radio-brought-nazi-propaganda-home/

165 C.N. Trueman, 'Radio in Nazi Germany', History Learning Site, 9 March 2015. Available at: https://www.historylearningsite.co.uk/nazi-germany/radio-in-nazi-germany/

166 Eric Rentschler, 'The fascination of a fake: The Hitler diaries'

167 'Suspect in Yom Kippur shooting against Halle synagogue goes on trial in Germany', World Jewish Congress, 23 July 2020. Available at: https://www.worldjewishcongress.org/en/news/suspect-in-yom-kippur-shooting-against-halle-synagogue-goes-on-trial-in-germany-7-4-2020?print=true

168 'Deadly attack exposes lapses in German security apparatus', *Der Spiegel*, 11 October 2019. Available at: https://www.spiegel.de/international/germany/far-right-terrorism-in-germany-shooting-exposes-lapses-in-security-apparatus-a-1291075.html

169 'Engine of hate: The online networks behind the Labour party's antisemitism crisis', Community Security Trust, 4 August 2019. Available at: https://cst.org.uk/news/blog/2019/08/04/engine-of-hate-the-online-networks-behind-the-labour-partys-antisemitism-crisis (hereafter 'Engine of hate: The online networks behind the Labour party's antisemitism crisis')

170 Aidan Milan, 'Why are people boycotting Rachel Riley?', *Metro*, 29 March 2019. Available at: https://metro.co.uk/2019/03/29/people-boycotting-countdowns-rachel-riley-9057808/.

171 'Engine of hate: The online networks behind the Labour party's antisemitism crisis'

172 James McAuley, 'France moves towards a law requiring Facebook to delete hate speech within 24 hours', *The Washington Post*, 9 July 2019. Available at: https://www.washingtonpost.com/world/europe/france-moves-toward-a-law-requring-facebook-to-delete-hate-speech-within-24-hours/2019/07/09/d43b24c2-a25d-11e9-a767-d7ab84aef3e9_story.html

173 Ben M Freeman, Twitter Post, 30 July 2019. Available at: https://twitter.com/BenMFreeman/status/1156148464407011328

174 Eric H. Cohen, 'Impact of the group of co-migrants on strategies of acculturation: Towards an expansion of the Berry model', *International Migration* 49, no. 4, July 4, 2011. Available at: https://doi.org/10.1111/j.1468-2435.2009.00589.x, (hereafter Eric H. Cohen, 'Impact of the group of co-migrants on strategies of acculturation: Towards an expansion of the Berry model')

175 Jean S. Phinney et al., 'Ethnic identity, immigration, and well-being: An interactional perspective', *Journal of Social Issues* 57, no. 3 (2001). Available at: https://doi.org/10.1111/0022-4537.00225

176 Rosamund Urwin, 'Luciana Berger: I never thought I'd be described on the news as "a Jewish MP"'

177 'Ancient Jewish history: Assimilation', Jewish Virtual Library. Available at: https://www.jewishvirtuallibrary.org/assimilation, (hereafter 'Ancient Jewish history: Assimilation')

178 Jaroslaw Piekalkiewicz, *A Holistic View of Saving Polish Jews During the Holocaust* (London: Hamilton Books, 2019)

179 'Ancient Jewish history: Assimilation'

180 Michael Shurkin, 'French Jewish History, 1650-1914', My Jewish Learning. Available at: https://www.myjewishlearning.com/article/french-jewish-history-1650-1914/

181 Irène Delage and Emmanuelle Papot, 'Napoleon I and the integration of the Jews in France: Some points of interest', napoleon.org. Available at: https://www.napoleon.org/en/history-of-the-two-empires/articles/napoleon-and-the-jews/

182 'Answers to Napoleon', The Assembly of Jewish Notables, University of Calgary. Available at: http://people.ucalgary.ca/~elsegal/363_Transp/Sanhedrin.html.

183 'The French Connection', Jewish Agency. Available at: http://archive.jewishagency.org/jewish-community/content/24142

184 Benjamin Herzberg, 'Happy like a Jew in France', *HuffPost*, 6 December 2017. Available at: https://www.huffpost.com/entry/happy-like-a-jew-in-franc_b_5619244

185 'Jews and the republican state', 1906, Dreyfus Rehabilitated. Available at: http://www.dreyfus.culture.fr/en/the-french-and-the-dreyfus-affair/jews-in-france/jews-and-the-republican-state.htm (hereafter 'Jews and the republican state')

186 'Jews and the republican state'

187 'The press', 1906, Dreyfus Rehabilitated. Available at: http://www.dreyfus.culture.fr/en/the-french-and-the-dreyfus-affair/the-formation-of-public-opinion/the-Press.htm

188 'Brochures and popular songs', 1906, Dreyfus Rehabilitated. Available at: http://www.dreyfus.culture.fr/en/the-french-and-the-dreyfus-affair/the-formation-of-public-opinion/brochures-and-popular-songs.htm

189 Matt Plen, 'Moses Mendelssohn', My Jewish Learning. Available at: https://www.myjewishlearning.com/article/moses-mendelssohn/

190 Louis Jacobs, 'Haskalah, the Jewish Enlightenment', My Jewish Learning. Available at: https://www.myjewishlearning.com/article/haskalah/

191 Marvin Perry and Frederick Schweitzer, *Anti-Semitism: Myth and Hate from Antiquity to the Present* (New York: Palgrave Macmillan, 2002), (hereafter Marvin Perry and Frederick Schweitzer, *Anti-Semitism: Myth and Hate from Antiquity to the Present*)

192 Frank Bajohr, *'Unser Hotel Ist Judenfrei': Bäder-Antisemitismus Im 19. Und 20. Jahrhundert* (Frankfurt am Main: Fischer-Taschenbuch-Verl., 2003)

193 Marvin Perry and Frederick Schweitzer, *Anti-Semitism: Myth and Hate from Antiquity to the Present*

194 Darlene Lancer, 'Are you overlooking or rationalizing abuse? that's denial!', *Psychology Today*, 1 December 2019. Available at: https://www.psychologytoday.com/us/blog/toxic-relationships/201912/are-you-overlooking-or-rationalizing-abuse-thats-denial

195 'Moses Seixas' letter from Congregation Yeshuat Israel', Touro Synagogue. Available at: https://www.tourosynagogue.org/history-learning/tsf-intro-menu/slom-scholarship/85-seixas-letter.

196 'George Washington and his letter to the Jews of Newport', Touro Synagogue. Available at: https://www.tourosynagogue.org/history-learning/gw-letter.

197 'US Constitution: First amendment', Constitution Annotated, Available at: https://constitution.congress.gov/constitution/amendment-1/.

198 Cynthia Weil, 'There are no cats in America', *An American Tail* (New York: MCA Records, 1986)

199 Jonathan Sarna and Jonathan Golden, 'The American Jewish experience in the twentieth century: Antisemitism and assimilation', National Humanities Center, Available at: http://nationalhumanitiescenter.org/tserve/twenty/tkeyinfo/jewishexpb.htm.

200 Jonathan Sarna, 'The redemption of Ulysses S. Grant', ReformJudaism.org. Available at: https://reformjudaism.org/redemption-ulysses-s-grant, (hereafter Jonathan Sarna, 'The redemption of Ulysses S. Grant')

201 Jonathan Sarna, 'The redemption of Ulysses S. Grant'

202 'History of the Reform movement', My Jewish Learning. Available at: https://www.myjewishlearning.com/article/reform-judaism/

203 James Parton, 'Our Israelitish brethren', *The Atlantic*, 1 October 1870. Available at: https://www.theatlantic.com/magazine/archive/1870/10/our-israelitish-brethren/306257/

204 'Reform Judaism: The Pittsburgh Platform', Jewish Virtual Library. Available at: https://www.jewishvirtuallibrary.org/the-pittsburgh-platform, (hereafter 'Reform Judaism: The Pittsburgh Platform')

205 'Reform Judaism: The Pittsburgh Platform'

206 Shmuel Almog, Jehuda Reinharz and Anita Shapira, *Zionism and Religion* (Hanover, NH: University Press of New England, 1998)

207 Michael Laitman, *The Jewish Choice: Unity or Anti-Semitism* (Toronto: Laitman Kabbalah Publishers, 2019)

208 Daniel Greene and Frank Newport, 'American public opinion and the Holocaust', Gallup, 23 April 2018. Available at: https://news.gallup.com/opinion/polling-matters/232949/american-public-opinion-holocaust.aspx

209 Matt Lebovic, 'Historian: New evidence shows FDR's bigotry derailed many Holocaust rescue plans', *The Times of Israel*, 4 November 2019. Available at: https://www.timesofisrael.com/historian-new-evidence-shows-fdrs-bigotry-derailed-many-holocaust-rescue-plans/

210 Matt Lebovic, 'How to explain the "timid" reaction of American Jewish leaders to Kristallnacht?', *The Times of Israel*, 10 November 2018. Available at: https://www.timesofisrael.com/how-to-explain-the-timid-reaction-of-american-jewish-leaders-to-kristallnacht/?utm_source=The+Weekend+Edition&utm_campaign=weekend-edition-2018-11-11&utm_medium=email

211 Anonymous, 'I married a Jew'

212 Julian E. Zelizer, 'Trump needs to demilitarize his rhetoric', *The Atlantic*, 29 October 2018. Available at: https://www.theatlantic.com/ideas/archive/2018/10/americas-long-history-anti-semitism/574234/

213 Jonathan Sarna, '1950s America: A "Golden Age" for Jews', My Jewish Learning. Available at: https://www.myjewishlearning.com/article/a-golden-age-for-jews/, (hereafter Jonathan Sarna, '1950s America: A "Golden Age" for Jews')

214 Jonathan Sarna, '1950s America: A "Golden Age" for Jews'

215 Frances Lee Ansley, *Stirring the Ashes: Race Class and the Future of Civil Rights Scholarship* , 74 Cornell L. Rev. 993, 1989. Available at: https://scholarship.law.cornell.edu/clr/vol74/iss6/1

216 Erik K. Ward, 'Skin in the game', Political Research Associates, 29 June 2017. Available at: https://www.politicalresearch.org/2017/06/29/skin-in-the-game-how-anti semitism-animates-white-nationalism, (hereafter Erik K. Ward, 'Skin in the game')

217 Erik K. Ward, 'Skin in the game'

218 'Critical race theory', The Bridge Project. Available at: https://cyber.harvard.edu/bridge/CriticalTheory/critical4.htm.

219 Richard Delgado and Jean Stefancic, *Critical Race Theory: An Introduction* (New York: New York University Press, 2001)

220 Eric K. Ward, 'The evolution of identity politics: An interview with Eric Ward', *Tikkun*, 4 April 2018. Available at: https://www.tikkun.org/the-evolution-of-identity-politics-an-interview-with-eric-ward, (hereafter Eric K. Ward, 'The evolution of identity politics: An interview with Eric Ward')

221 Eric K. Ward, 'The evolution of identity politics: An interview with Eric Ward'

222 'Shaare Tefila Congregation v. Cobb', Oyez. Available at: https://www.oyez.org/cases/1986/85-2156.

223 Eric K. Ward, 'Skin in the game'

224 Lux Alptraum, Twitter post, 1 May, 2020. Available at: https://twitter.com/LuxAlptraum/status/1256216311660773385

225 Michael Lerner, 'The white issue: "Jews are not white"'

226 Emma Green, 'Can Jews still assume they're white?', *The Atlantic*, 5 December 2016. Available at: https://www.theatlantic.com/politics/archive/2016/12/are-jews-white/509453/

227 Carly Regina, 'Not just "two old white men," this Democratic primary is now a serious fight between Joe Biden and Bernie Sanders', *Common Dreams*, 9 March 2020. Available at: https://www.commondreams.org/views/2020/03/09/not-just-two-old-white-men-democratic-primary-now-serious-fight-between-joe-biden

228 'Miss Davis hails Soviet's policies', *The New York Times*, 10 September 1972. Available

at: https://www.nytimes.com/1972/09/10/archives/miss-davis-hails-soviets-policies-but-the-comments-on-tour-arouse.html

229 Kristian Davis Bailey, 'Dream Defenders, Black Lives Matter & Ferguson reps take historic trip to Palestine', *Ebony*, 1 August 2016. Available at: https://www.ebony.com/news/dream-defenders-black-lives-matter-ferguson-reps-take-historic-trip-to-palestine/, (hereafter Kristian Davis Bailey, 'Dream Defenders, Black Lives Matter & Ferguson reps take historic trip to Palestine')

230 Kristian Davis Bailey, 'Dream Defenders, Black Lives Matter & Ferguson reps take historic trip to Palestine'

231 Palestinian BDS National Committee (BNC), 'Palestinians salute the movement for black lives emphasizing common struggle against racial oppression', BDS Movement, 19 September 2016. Available at: https://bdsmovement.net/news/palestinians-salute-movement-black-lives-emphasizing-common-struggle-against-racial-oppression

232 Osama Al-Sharif, 'Palestinians' unbreakable link with Black Lives Matter', *Arab News*, 16 June 2020. Available at: https://www.arabnews.com/node/1690701

233 'AJC survey of American Jews on antisemitism in America', AJC *Global Voice*. Available at: https://www.ajc.org/AntisemitismSurvey2019.

234 Anonymous, 'I married a Jew'

235 Benjamin Kerstein, 'Jewish student says she left City University of New York Law School after being targeted by antisemitic harassment for supporting Israel', *The Algemeiner*, 27 February 2020. Available at: https://www.algemeiner.com/2020/02/27/jewish-student-says-she-left-city-university-of-new-york-law-school-after-being-targeted-by-antisemitic-harassment-for-supporting-israel/.

236 Rachel Kaplan, Twitter Post, 24 September 2020. Available at: https://twitter.com/RachelMiniK/status/1309013393567879172

237 Jor-El Caraballo, 'Understanding the minority stress model', Talkspace, 26 December 2019. Available at: https://www.talkspace.com/blog/minority-stress-model/, (hereafter Jor-El Caraballo, 'Understanding the minority stress model')

238 Yo Jackson, *Encyclopedia of Multicultural Psychology* (Thousand Oaks, CA: Sage, 2006).

239 Donna K. Bivens, 'What is internalized racism?', Racial Equity Tools. Available at: https://www.racialequitytools.org/resourcefiles/What_is_Internalized_Racism.pdf, (hereafter Donna K. Bivens, 'What is internalized racism?')

240 Donna K. Bivens, 'What is internalized racism?'

241 Eli Kavon, 'Tiberius Julius Alexander: The Jew who destroyed Jerusalem', *The Jerusalem Post*, 2 December 2015. Available at: https://www.jpost.com/blogs/past-imperfect-confronting-jewish-history/tiberius-julius-alexander-the-jew-who-destroyed-jerusalem-436073

242 Flavius Josephus (trans. William Whiston), 'The antiquities of the Jews, 20.100', Lexundria. Available at: https://lexundria.com/j_aj/20.100/wst

243 Carlos Lévy, 'Philo of Alexandria,' *Stanford Encyclopedia of Philosophy*, 5 February 2018. Available at: https://plato.stanford.edu/entries/philo/

244 Martin Goodman, *Rome and Jerusalem: The Clash of Ancient Civilizations* (New York: Vintage Books, 2008, (hereafter Martin Goodman, *Rome and Jerusalem: The Clash of Ancient Civilizations*)

245 Marisa Elana James, 'The Jew who pulled down the walls: Tiberius Julius between Alexandria and Jerusalem', Academia, 19 January 2012. Available at: https://www.

academia.edu/2543723/The_Jew_who_Pulled_Down_the_Walls_Tiberius_Julius_between_Alexandria_and_Jerusalem

246 'Pogrom in Alexandria', Livius. Available at: https://www.livius.org/sources/content/pogrom-in-alexandria/, (hereafter 'Pogrom in Alexandria')

247 'Pogrom in Alexandria'

248 Flavius Josephus (trans. William Whiston), 'The Wars of the Jews, Book II, section 494'. Available at: http://www.perseus.tufts.edu/hopper/text?doc=J.+BJ+2.494

249 Aryeh Kasher, *The Jews in Hellenistic and Roman Egypt the Struggle for Equal Rights* (Tübingen: J.C.B. Mohr, 1985)

250 Martin Goodman, *Rome and Jerusalem: The Clash of Ancient Civilizations*

251 Thomas of Monmouth (trans. Augustus Jessopp and M. R. James), *The Life and Miracles of St. William of Norwich*, (Cambridge: Cambridge University Press, 2018), (hereafter, Thomas of Monmouth, *The Life and Miracles of St. William of Norwich*)

252 Thomas of Monmouth, *The Life and Miracles of St. William of Norwich*

253 Nora Levin, *The Jews in the Soviet Union since 1917* (New York: New York University Press, 1988)

254 Yehoshuna A. Gilboa, Yehoshuna, *A Language Silenced: The Suppression of Hebrew Literature and Culture in the Soviet Union* (Rutherford: Fairleigh Dickinson Univ. Press, 1982)

255 Richard Pipes, *Russia under the Bolshevik Regime: 1919-1924*, 4th ed. (London: Vintage, 1995)

256 Peter Beinart, 'Debunking the myth that anti-Zionism is antisemitic', *The Guardian*, 7 March 2019. Available at: https://www.theguardian.com/news/2019/mar/07/debunking-myth-that-anti-zionism-is-antisemitic

257 Daniel Sugarman, 'New Jewish group launched in Labour', *The Jewish Chronicle*, 25 August 2017. Available at: https://www.thejc.com/news/uk/new-jewish-group-launched-in-labour-1.443348, (hereafter Daniel Sugarman, 'New Jewish group launched in Labour')

258 Daniel Sugarman, 'New Jewish group launched in Labour'

259 JVLWatch, 'JVL: A vehicle to normalise antisemitism', 20 May 2018. Available at: https://jvlwatch.wordpress.com/2018/05/19/jvl-a-vehicle-to-normalise-antisemitism/amp/?__twitter_impression=true

260 Jewish Voice for Labour, 'Jeremy Corbyn's Labour a crucial ally in the fight against antisemitism', 20 February 2019. Available at: https://www.jewishvoiceforlabour.org.uk/statement/jeremy-corbyns-labour-a-crucial-ally-in-the-fight-against-antisemitism/

261 'What is JVL? The "Jewish Voice" that backs Corbyn on Labour antisemitism', *The Jewish Chronicle*, 9 April 2018. Available at: https://www.thejc.com/news/features/what-is-jewish-voice-for-labour-jvl-1.462012.

262 Rushaa Louise Hamid, 'New polling of British Jews shows tensions remain strong between Labour and the British Jewish community', Survation, 25 March 2019. Available at: https://www.survation.com/new-polling-of-british-jews-shows-tensions-remain-strong-between-labour-and-the-british-jewish-community/

263 Euan Phillips, Email, 'BBC Complaints – Case Number CAS-5607285-4YK3G4', 24 April 2020

264 Euan Phillips, Twitter post, 12 July 2019. Available at: https://twitter.com/EuanPhilipps/status/1149375638496829440

265 Jessica Elgot, 'Labour expels Jackie Walker for leaked antisemitic remarks', *The*

Guardian, 27 March 2019. Available at: https://www.theguardian.com/politics/2019/mar/27/labour-expels-jackie-walker-for-leaked-antisemitism-comments

266 David Hirsh, 'Excerpt from *Contemporary Left Antisemitism* relating to Jackie Walker', *Engage*, 28 March 2019. Available at: https://engageonline.wordpress.com/2019/03/28/exerpt-relating-to-jackie-walker-from-contemporary-left-antisemitism-david-hirsh/

267 Marcus Dysch, 'Labour suspends Momentum supporter who claimed Jews caused "an African Holocaust"', *The Jewish Chronicle*, 4 May 2106. Available at: https://www.thejc.com/news/uk/labour-suspends-momentum-supporter-who-claimed-jews-caused-an-african-holocaust-1.56449

268 Batya Ungar-Sargson, 'Is Jewish control over the slave trade a Nation of Islam lie or scholarly truth?', *Tablet*, 5 August 2013. Available at: https://www.tabletmag.com/sections/arts-letters/articles/slave-trade-black-muslim, (hereafter Batya Ungar-Sargson, 'Is Jewish control over the slave trade a Nation of Islam lie or scholarly truth?')

269 Batya Ungar-Sargson, 'Is Jewish control over the slave trade a Nation of Islam lie or scholarly truth?'

270 Keith Kahn-Harris, *Strange Hate: Antisemitism, Racism and the Limits of Diversity* (London: Repeater Books, 2019)

271 Dave Rich, Twitter post, 8 October 2018. Available at: https://twitter.com/daverich1/status/1049261581186596864

272 Dave Rich, Twitter post, 8 October, 2018. Available at: https://twitter.com/daverich1/status/1049261585292845058/photo/1

273 Paul Shindman, 'Israel and the dysfunctional UN Human Rights Council', Honest Reporting, 21 January 2020. Available at: https://honestreporting.com/israel-dysfunctional-un-human-rights-council/

274 'The UN and Israel: Key statistics from UN Watch', UN Watch, 23 August 2016. Available at: https://unwatch.org/un-israel-key-statistics/, (hereafter 'The UN and Israel: Key statistics from UN Watch')

275 'The UN and Israel: Key statistics from UN Watch'

276 Thomas of Monmouth, *The Life and Miracles of St. William of Norwich*

277 Judy Maltz, 'Vast numbers of progressive California Jews are disengaging from Israel, survey finds', *Haaretz*, 14 February 2018. Available at: https://www.haaretz.com/us-news/.premium-vast-numbers-of-california-jews-disengaging-from-israel-survey-finds-1.5821675

278 Yaakov Astor, 'Me, myself and I: Ethics of the Fathers 1:14', *Aish*, 5 June 2004. Available at: https://www.aish.com/sp/pg/48893292.html

279 Matanya Harrow, 'Strength is Israel's only real path to peace', *Israel Hayom*, 21 July 2019. Available at: https://www.israelhayom.com/opinions/strength-is-israels-only-real-path-to-peace/.

280 'Our Principles', IfNotNowMovement. Available at: https://www.ifnotnowmovement.org/our-principles.

281 Nathan Goldman, 'A new generation of Jewish activists is transforming Judaism itself', *The Nation*, 26 September 2019. Available at: https://www.thenation.com/article/archive/bds-anti-zionist-activism-atalia-omer-interview/

282 Lizzie Horn, 'Tikkun Olam Today', *Protocols*, 2019. Available at: https://prtcls.com/article/tikkun-olam-today/

283 Josh Yuter, 'Tikkun Olam', Yutopia: The Online Home of Rabbi Josh Yuter, 18 September 2018. Available at: https://joshyuter.com/2018/09/18/special-features/sacred-slogans/tikkun-olam/

284 'Leviticus 18:25,' www.sefaria.org. Available at: https://www.sefaria.org/Leviticus. 18.25?lang=bi.

285 'A Portrait of Jewish Americans', Pew Research Center, 1 October 2013. Available at: https://www.pewforum.org/2013/10/01/jewish-american-beliefs-attitudes-culture-survey/

286 IfNotNow, Twitter post, 25 April, 2016. Available at: https://twitter.com/IfNot NowOrg/status/724422487119896577

287 'Neveen Ayesh', Canary Mission. Available at: https://canarymission.org/individual/ Neveen_Ayesh

288 'Neveen Ayesh', Canary Mission. Available at: https://canarymission.org/individual/ Neveen_Ayesh

289 'Taher Herzallah', Canary Mission. Available at: https://canarymission.org/ individual/Taher_Herzallah

290 'Taher Herzallah', Canary Mission. Available at: https://canarymission.org/ individual/Taher_Herzallah

291 Chaim Redman, Twitter post, 15 May 2019. Available at: https://twitter.com/ The_Bear_Jew18/status/1128683640685199360

292 IfNowNow, Twitter post, 5 April 2018. Available at: https://twitter.com/IfNotNow Org/status/981663896179179520

293 Yonah Jeremy Bob, 'Report: 80% of Palestinians killed in Gaza border crisis were "terrorists"', *The Jerusalem Post*, 11 April 2018. Available at: https://www.jpost.com/ Arab-Israeli-Conflict/Report-80-percent-of-Palestinians-killed-in-Gaza-border-cri-sis-were-terrorists-549511, (hereafter Yonah Jeremy Bob, 'Report: 80% of Palestinians killed in Gaza border crisis were "terrorists"')

294 Abraham Riesman, 'The Jewish revolt', *New York*. Available at: https://nymag.com/ intelligencer/2018/07/ifnotnow-birthright-ramah-bds-israel.html

295 Jeremy Sharon, 'IfNotNow includes Palestinian terrorist in list of "heartbreaking" deaths', *The Jerusalem Post*, 5 May 2019. Available at: https://www.jpost.com/israel-news/ ifnotnow-includes-palestinian-terrorist-in-list-of-heartbreaking-deaths-588822

296 IfNotNow, Twitter post, 25 September, 2019. Available at https://twitter.com/ IfNotNowOrg/status/1176888087479238656

297 David Hirsh 'The Livingstone formulation'

298 Shoshanna Keats Jaskoll, 'How IfNotNow lost its way', *The Forward*, 14 August 2019. Available at: https://forward.com/opinion/429562/ifnotnow-just-lied-about-bernie-sanders-of-course-they-did-its-their/, (hereafter Shoshanna Keats Jaskoll, 'How IfNotNow lost its way')

299 Shoshanna Keats Jaskoll, 'How IfNotNow lost its way'

300 IfNotNow, Twitter post, 14 August 2019. Available at: https://twitter.com/IfNot NowOrg/status/1161356353966944257

301 Michael Laitman, 'Jewish self-hatred is the leaven we must clear out', *The Jerusa-lem Post*, 30 March 2017. Available at: https://www.jpost.com/opinion/jewish-self-hatred-is-the-leaven-we-must-clear-out-485515

302 Patricia Cohen, 'Essay linking liberal Jews and anti-semitism sparks a furor', *The New York Times*, 31 January 2007. Available at: https://www.nytimes.com/2007/01/31/arts/31jews.html

303 David P. Goldman, 'The vicissitudes of Jewish exceptionalism', *The American Interest*, 12 February 2013. Available at: https://www.the-american-interest.com/2013/02/12/ the-vicissitudes-of-jewish-exceptionalism/

304 Rachel Riley, Twitter post, 4 September 2018. Available at: https://twitter.com/RachelRileyRR/status/1036949171360735232

305 Günther Jikeli, 'Antisemitism in Muslim communities and Muslim countries: Debates and studies of a complex issue', *Revue d'histoire moderne et contemporaine*, vol. no 62-2/3, no. 2, 2015

306 Batya Ungar-Sargon and Jodi Rudoren, 'Meet The Forward's new columnists', *The Forward*, 23 December 2019. Available at: https://forward.com/opinion/437132/meet-the-forwards-new-columnists/.

307 Steven Kaplan, 'Beta Israel', in Merid W. Aregay et al. (eds.), *Encyclopaedia Aethiopica: A–C* (Wiesbaden: Harrassowitz Verlag, 2003)

308 Mordechai Abir, *Ethiopia and the Red Sea: The Rise and Decline of the Solomonic dynasty and Muslim-European Rivalry in the Region* (New York: Routledge, 1980)

309 'Australia sees 30% spike in anti-semitic incidents in 2019', *Israel Hayom*, 28 November 2019. Available at: https://www.israelhayom.com/2019/11/28/australia-sees-30-spike-in-anti-semitic-incidents-in-2019/

310 Gareth Narunsky, 'Covid-19 antisemitism reaches Australia', *The Australian Jewish News*, 30 April 2020. Available at: https://ajn.timesofisrael.com/covid-19-antisemitism-reaches-australia/

311 'Transgender people and suicide', Centre for Suicide Prevention. Available at: https://www.suicideinfo.ca/resource/transgender-people-suicide/.

312 Julie Nathan, 'Antipodean Resistance: The Rise and Goals of Australia's New Nazis', *ABC Religion and Ethics*, 20 April 2018. Available at: https://www.abc.net.au/religion/antipodean-resistance-the-rise-and-goals-of-australias-new-nazis/10094794

313 'Activist Sarsour says Israel built on idea of Jewish supremacy', *The Times of Israel*, 4 December 2019. Available at: https://www.timesofisrael.com/activist-sarsour-says-israel-built-on-idea-of-jewish-supremacy/

314 Susie Linfield, *The Lions' Den: Zionism and the Left from Hannah Arendt to Noam Chomsky* (New Haven, CT: Yale University Press, 2019), (hereafter Susie Linfield, *The Lions' Den: Zionism and the Left from Hannah Arendt to Noam Chomsky*)

315 Lao Tzu, 'Learning English – Moving Words', BBC, Available at: https://www.bbc.co.uk/worldservice/learningenglish/movingwords/shortlist/laotzu.shtml

316 Mordecai M. Kaplan, *Judaism as a Civilization: Toward a Reconstruction of American Jewish Life* (Philadelphia: The Jewish Publication Society, 2010), (hereafter Mordecai M. Kaplan, *Judaism as a Civilization: Toward a Reconstruction of American Jewish Life*)

317 Mordecai M. Kaplan, *Judaism as a Civilization: Toward a Reconstruction of American Jewish Life*

318 Mordecai M. Kaplan, *Judaism as a Civilization: Toward a Reconstruction of American Jewish Life*

319 'Shevuot 39a,' Sefaria. Available at: https://www.sefaria.org/Shevuot.39a?lang=bi.

320 Susie Linfield, 'Albert Memmi: Zionism as national liberation', *Fathom*, June 2019: Available at: https://fathomjournal.org/albert-memmi-zionism-as-national-liberation/, (hereafter Susie Linfield, 'Albert Memmi: Zionism as national liberation')

321 Susie Linfield, 'Albert Memmi: Zionism as national liberation'

322 Susie Linfield, 'Albert Memmi: Zionism as national liberation'

323 Susie Linfield, *The Lions' Den: Zionism and the Left from Hannah Arendt to Noam Chomsky*

324 Jonathan Sacks, 'Antisemitism, or any hate, become dangerous when three things happen', Speech in the House of Lords, 13 September 2018. Available at: https://rabbisacks.org/antisemitism-hate-become-dangerous-three-things-happen-rabbi-sacks-speaks-house-lords/.

325 '30 British Jewish victims of coronavirus buried in three-day span', *The Times of Israel*, 6 April 2020. Available at: https://www.timesofisrael.com/30-british-jewish-victims-of-coronavirus-buried-in-three-day-span/

326 Daniel J. Elazar, 'Jewish religious, ethnic, and national identities: Convergences and conflicts', Jerusalem Centre for Public Affairs. Available at: https://www.jcpa.org/dje/articles2/jewreleth.htm

327 Walt Hunter, 'The story behind the poem on the Statue of Liberty', *The Atlantic*, 16 January 2018. Available at: https://www.theatlantic.com/entertainment/archive/2018/01/the-story-behind-the-poem-on-the-statue-of-liberty/550553/

328 'Hedy Lamarr', Jewish Women's Archive. Available at: https://jwa.org/people/lamarr-hedy

329 'Actress Hedy Lamarr patents the basis for WiFi', Jewish Women's Archive. Available at: https://jwa.org/thisweek/aug/11/1942/actress-hedy-lamarr-patents-basis-for-wifi

330 Michael Fox, 'To Hedy Lamarr, the hidden Jew, beauty was only skin deep', *Jewish Journal*, 8 March 2018. Available at: https://jewishjournal.org/2018/03/08/to-hedy-lamarr-the-hidden-jew-beauty-was-only-skin-deep/, (hereafter Michael Fox, 'To Hedy Lamarr, the hidden Jew, beauty was only skin deep')

331 Michael Fox, 'To Hedy Lamarr, the hidden Jew, beauty was only skin deep'

332 Rob Gloster, 'The essential Jewishness of Harvey Milk', *Jewish News of Northern California*, 14 June 2018. Available at: https://www.jweekly.com/2018/06/14/the-essential-jewishness-of-harvey-milk/, (hereafter Rob Gloster, 'The essential Jewishness of Harvey Milk')

333 Rob Gloster, 'The essential Jewishness of Harvey Milk'

334 'Freedom to Marry', The Roadmap to Victory. Available at: http://www.freedomtomarry.org/pages/roadmap-to-victory

335 Little Big Mouth, Twitter post, 16 June 2019. Available at: https://twitter.com/1littleBIGMOUTH/status/1139937314409537537

336 Abba Zaga, *Letter Beta Israel to Israel-Israel from the mid-nineteenth century: From the Hebrew version Firkobitz*. Available at: http://www.ybz.org.il/_Uploads/dbs AttachedFiles/Article_110.8.pdf

337 Donald E. Wagner and Walter T. Davis (eds). *Zionism and the Quest for Justice in the Holy Land* (Cambridge: The Lutterworth Press, 2014)

338 Ashager Araro, Twitter post, 26 June 2019. Available at: https://twitter.com/ashagerararo/status/1143588304220229633

INDEX